WHAT SOCIAL SECURITY WILL PAY

RATES OF RETURN BY CONGRESSIONAL DISTRICT

By

Gareth G. Davis and Philippe J. Lacoude

The Heritage Foundation
214 Massachusetts Avenue, N.E.
Washington, D.C. 20002
1-202-546-4400
www.heritage.org

Copyright © 2000 by The Heritage Foundation

ISBN 0-89195-086-9

TABLE OF CONTENTS

ACKNOWLEDGMENTS

The authors deeply appreciate the support of James Hamilton, Social Security Project Manager at The Heritage Foundation, who first proposed this study in 1998. We also thank Stuart M. Butler, Vice President of Domestic and Economic Policy Studies, and Ralph Rector, Project Manager of the Center for Data Analysis, who ensured we had both the time and resources to pursue this project. We appreciate the contributions of William W. Beach, Director of the Center for Data Analysis, not only for his direct participation with several sections, but also as one of the original developers of the rates of return project at The Heritage Foundation and author of some of the first studies in this area. His involvement with this project was indispensable. We thank our co-workers at Heritage for their valuable assistance with this project, including Isabel Isidro, Research Assistant in the Center for Data Analysis; Rea Hederman, Policy Analyst in the Center for Data Analysis; David John, Senior Policy Analyst for Social Security; and Jennifer Larkin, Director of Congressional Relations for the U.S. House of Representatives. We are grateful for the research assistance of the CDA's 1999 interns: Jonathan Huntley, Nicholas Racculia, Meredith Walkley, and Jason Hollrah. Finally, we want to thank Ann Klucsarits, Director of Publishing Services; Richard Odermatt, Senior Editor; Janice Smith, Managing Editor; Daryl Malloy, Copyeditor; Michelle Smith, Senior Design and Layout Specialist; and Thomas J. Timmons, Manager of Graphic Design Services, for their assistance.

TABLES AND ILLUSTRATIONS

Tables

INTRODUCTION

Nearly everyone is concerned about how much money they will have for retirement. Today's workers know that they must save and invest more than their parents did to maintain the same standard of living after retirement. They also sense that the role Social Security will play in providing them with sufficient retirement income will be significantly smaller than the role it plays for today's retirees.

No doubt, sentiments such as these fuel much of the current debate over how to reform Social Security. But is this widespread sense of Social Security's dwindling status as a provider of retirement income rooted in financial reality? Are the millions of today's workers who believe they will have no other income after retirement than what Social Security will provide justified in suspecting that Social Security's rate of return is dismally low? Sadly, the evidence presented in this study of rates of return at the congressional district level as well as in the companion studies published by The Heritage Foundation over the past two years seem to validate these concerns.

Social Security's rates of return have reached a critically low level. For example, a married couple, both born in 1965, who have two children, and who both earn an annual income equal to the national average for their respective gender (the prototypical couple used in this study), can expect a rate of return from Social Security of only 1.29 percent.[1] The news is no less disappointing for wage earners in states and congressional districts that we found to offer the "best" rates of return. For example, if our prototypical couple lived in North Dakota, which has the highest rate of return in the nation, they could expect to receive a return of only 2.39 percent, after adjusting for inflation. Moreover, this couple working in North Dakota will receive $230,288 (in 2000 dollars) less than if both had invested the equivalent of their payroll retirement (OASI) taxes in a conservative investment portfolio made up of 50 percent long-term U.S. Treasury bonds and 50 percent large company stocks.

Features of This Study. This study continues the series of analyses on Social Security's rates of return published by Heritage's Center for Data Analysis (CDA). The study also breaks new analytical ground: It is the first to calculate life expectancies by congressional district. The predictions of

---

1. Our estimates of Social Security's rate of return relate only to the retirement, or Old-Age Insurance, portion of current Social Security payroll tax deductions. Disability Insurance (DI) benefits and taxes and Survivors Insurance (SI) benefits are not a part of these rate of return calculations and are assumed to continue unaffected by any reform of Social Security's retirement program. See the Appendix for a discussion of the factors that are employed in constructing the rates of return.

mortality are based on one of the most detailed studies of the effects of socioeconomic characteristics on life expectancy ever undertaken. Further, the estimate of lifetime earnings presented are derived from detailed earnings data for workers from every congressional district.

Findings. The conclusions reached by this study confirm those of previous Heritage CDA studies on Social Security's rate of return:

- *First,* inflation-adjusted returns after a lifetime of payroll tax payments are falling for each successive birth cohort;

- *Second,* the returns are currently low and getting worse for the very Americans the program is supposed to help the most;

- *Third,* without fundamental reform, the present system will widen the income gap between workers who are fully dependent on Social Security for retirement income and those who are better able to create supplemental retirement savings on their own.

In addition, this study found dismal returns for working Americans of specific demographic groups. Some of these findings include:

- In its current form, the Social Security system performs poorly for workers in virtually every congressional district in the United States. Even in congressional districts that suffer the least losses, the average married couple born in 1965 will lose at least $200,000 under the current system compared with an amount they could expect to receive if they had placed their OASI payroll tax dollars in secure private investments.

- Congressional districts with the largest dollar losses under the current system tend to be highly populated and heavily urbanized with relatively high earnings.

- The lowest rate of return is found in Michigan's 15th Congressional District, which includes part of Detroit. At -0.01 percent, this return indicates that average income, two-earner couples born in 1965 will not live long enough to earn back the payroll taxes they paid into the retirement portion of Social Security.

- Dollar losses are high for Americans living in congressional districts with the highest percentage of manufacturing workers.

- The 15 congressional districts with the highest percentage of foreign-born workers have rates of return below 1.6 percent. Eight of these districts have large Hispanic populations.

- The five congressional districts with the highest percentage of non-Hispanic black workers have rates of return below 0.6 percent. Two of these districts (New York's 11th District and Michigan's 15th District) have rates of return below 0.2 percent.

UNDERSTANDING SOCIAL SECURITY'S RATE OF RETURN

The public debate over reforming Social Security is rooted in the perception of Social Security's retirement rate of return—what will Social Security pay at retirement—not some arcane concern over social insurance trust fund accounting.

The fact is millions of today's workers will have no other retirement income than what they will receive from Social Security. The reason: Many low- and moderate-income families cannot save for their own retirement because payroll taxes and other basic, everyday costs are so high. For those with the greatest stake in the performance of Social Security's Old-Age and Survivors Insurance program (OASI), it matters a great deal whether the income returns from Social Security are keeping up with the modest 4 percent return they could obtain by placing their payroll taxes in long-term savings accounts.

If Social Security's rate of return on the taxes workers pay for retirement security is significantly lower than that of alternative retirement savings vehicles, such as inflation-adjusted savings bonds, then workers are, in effect, forfeiting hundreds of thousands of dollars in retirement income. This foregone income hurts most low- and moderate-income families who have no pension or savings program other than Social Security—ironically, the very Americans the program was created to help. Given the threat of a lower financial status after retirement, rates of return and control over savings intended to produce sufficient retirement income should indeed matter to millions of American workers and their families.

Unfortunately, the current debate over the future of the Social Security system has focused on the financial solvency of the system rather than on improving the system's rate of return. Concern only with the future balances of Social Security's trust funds ignores the key problem: In its current form, Social Security is reducing the lifetime wealth of the great majority of its participants. In theory, it may be possible to ensure the program's financial viability by either cutting benefits or raising payroll taxes. But while such solutions may balance the trust funds, they also reduce Social

Security's rate of return below its current dismal level, hurting ordinary Americans.

An honest dialogue on Social Security requires knowledge not only about how the system is funded, but also about the rates of return that working Americans and their families can expect to receive from the current system. To advance that dialogue, Heritage analysts in the Center for Data Analysis (CDA) examined the rates of return for American workers, ranging from the population as a whole to various demographic groups arranged by income level, family structure, race and ethnicity, age, geographic area, and gender. Heritage's findings have been published in CDA *Reports* since January 1998 (see sidebar).[1] This book builds on the work of those previous studies by analyzing rates of return by congressional districts.

Defining Rate of Return. Rate of return is one of the most commonly used statistics for measuring payouts from investments. Social

---

**Previous Heritage CDA
Social Security Rate of Return Studies**

"Social Security's Rate of Return," by William W. Beach and Gareth G. Davis, *Report* No. CDA98-01, January 15, 1998.

"Social Security's Rate of Return for Hispanic Americans," by William W. Beach and Gareth G. Davis, *Report* No. CDA98-02, March 27, 1998.

"A State-by-State Analysis of the Returns from Social Security," by William W. Beach, Gareth G. Davis, and Sarah Youssef, *Report* No. CDA98-05, July 30, 1998.

"Social Security's Rates of Return for Union Households," by William W. Beach and Gareth G. Davis, *Report* No. CDA98-06, September 7, 1998.

Security's rate of return is equivalent to the interest rate that workers earn on their payroll retirement tax dollars. This can be compared to the 7 percent and 2.8 percent rates of return that the Social Security Administration projects stocks and long-term U.S. Treasury bonds will earn, respectively, over the next 75 years.[2]

Therefore, a Treasury bond's projected, inflation-adjusted rate of return of 2.8 percent can be translated into a dollar value: For example, by investing $1,000 today in Treasury bonds, an investor will receive $1,028 next year. By continuing to reinvest this money, the investor will accumulate $1,057 after two years (1.028 × 1.028 × $1,000), or $1,318 after 10 years.

In short, Social Security's rates of return matter because of the direct relationship between the return workers earn on their payroll tax dollars and wealth they have accumulated at retirement. If the rate of return is equal to zero (after being adjusted for inflation) a worker will get $1 of retirement benefits at age 65 for every $1 he paid in taxes at age 20. However, if the inflation-adjusted rate of return is equal to 1.0 percent, he will get $1.56 at age 65 for each $1 he paid at age 20. Moreover, if the inflation-adjusted rate of return were equal to 4 percent, this same worker would receive almost $6.00 at age 65 for each $1 paid in Social Security payroll taxes at age 20. These numbers help illustrate why Albert Einstein called compound interest the most powerful force in the universe.

---

1. These *Reports* are available in print and on the Heritage Website at *http://www.heritage.org/library/bytype.html*.

2. Social Security Administration, *Report of the 1994–1996 Advisory Council on Social Security* (Baltimore: Social Security Administration, 1997).

These figures also stress the importance of accumulating assets early in life: One dollar invested in large company stocks at the rate of 7 percent is worth about $15 some 40 years later—$2.00 invested in the very same stocks would only be worth $7.74 after 20 years. *The time span of an investment is almost as important as its amount.* At a time when the average American family can barely save because of historically high taxes, the creation of some form of personal retirement accounts is crucial to helping them maintain their standard of living during retirement.

A two-income married couple born in 1965 who each earns a wage equal to the national average for their respective gender and who have two minor children (the prototypical couple used in this study) will earn 1.29 percent, or $148,824, from their "investment" in Social Security.[3] Raising this low rate of return by as little as 1.06 percentage points (or to 2.35 percent, the level of U.S. Treasury bonds) would give them an extra $83,319 at retirement.

We chose a married couple, both born in 1965, with minor children as the major cohort to analyze in this study because, in 1999, the median age of the U.S. population of the United States was 35.2 years. In other words, close to half of all Americans alive today were born before 1964 and half were born after 1964. Of the four age groups for which the U.S. Bureau of the Census has collected data for analysis (those born in 1945, 1955, 1965, and 1975), Americans born in 1965 were the closest to the median age; hence, more likely to be representative of the general population.[4]

It is important to note that in this study, we are not comparing Social Security to any specific privatization or partial privatization plan (each of which differs significantly in its rate of return implications for different workers as well as in the amount of payroll tax it allows workers to invest). Rather, we are comparing Social Security with a hypothetical private system so that we can benchmark the performance of the current system in a meaningful way. In effect, the results of this study show how workers fare under the current Social Security system in comparison with the returns they would have received had Congress created a Social Security system based on privately owned accounts in 1935.

The Burden on American Workers. Defenders of the current Social Security system argue that rates of return from Social Security payroll taxes are irrelevant: The system was merely intended to provide basic retirement income and stopgap benefits for the spouses of deceased workers. Such an argument would be valid if Social Security taxes were a minor inconvenience. But Social Security taxes are burdensomely high.[5] The Social Security program began in 1937 with a 1.0 percent payroll tax rate. By 1972, workers were taxed for the Social Security Old-Age and Survivors Insurance (OASI) portion alone at 8.1 percent on the first $21,500 (in 1997 dollars) of earnings. By 1999, workers were paying 10.7 percent on the first $72,600 of their employment income.[6]

---

3. In a given year, the spouses each earn the average prevailing wage for their age group and gender. In 1999, the husband earned $41,000 and the wife earned $23,800.

4. Heritage calculation. See U.S. Bureau of the Census, *Statistical Abstract of the United States 1995*, September 1995, Table No. 13, p. 14.

5. See a forthcoming CDA *Report* by D. Mark Wilson, Research Fellow at The Heritage Foundation, entitled "Who Pays the Payroll Tax?"

6. Social Security Administration, *Social Security Bulletin: Annual Statistical Supplement for 1997*, December 1997, p. 34. This tax rate does not include additional taxes paid into the Disability Insurance Trust Fund or the Health Insurance Trust Fund.

RATES OF RETURN FOR SOCIAL SECURITY'S PAYROLL TAXES

Rate of return represents the annual rate of increase in the value of an investment and usually is expressed in percentage terms.

The methodology we used to conduct our analysis can be summarized by the following key points:

- All calculations were adjusted for inflation. Dollar amounts are expressed in terms of 2000 dollars.

- All estimates were made on the basis of the intermediate assumptions in the *1998 Annual Report of the Trustees of the Federal Old-Age and Survivors and Disability Insurance Trust Funds*.

- All rate of return estimates assume that Social Security will pay benefits based on the current law. Revenues to pay these benefits will be generated by increases in the payroll tax used to support Social Security's retirement program.

- In every case, life expectancy was adjusted for gender and age. It was also adjusted by congressional district. For example, life expectancy for 25-year-olds ranges from 72.4 for males to 84.9 for females. All life-expectancy projections include projected future increases in longevity and are based on data from the Social Security Administration and the Centers for Disease Control and Prevention.

- The actuarial value of pre-retirement Survivors Insurance (SI) benefits and taxes were calculated and fully included in Social Security's rate of return. However, both Disability Insurance (DI) benefits and taxes were not included in our rate of return calculations and were assumed to continue unaffected by any reform of Social Security's retirement program.

- In calculating the rates of return and the value of retirement accumulations generated under a system that allows personal accounts, it is assumed that workers with personal accounts are required to purchase life insurance equal to the value of the Survivors Insurance coverage provided by Social Security OASI taxes.

- It is assumed that workers place their OASI payroll taxes (net of the amount required to purchase life insurance equivalent to pre-retirement Survivors Insurance) into a personally owned investment account. Also, it is assumed that workers invest in a portfolio composed of 50 percent large company stocks and 50 percent long-term U.S. Treasury Bonds, and do not withdraw money from these account until they reach retirement age . For the years after 1998, investments in these accounts are assumed to earn an annual post-inflation return of 4.2 percent after adjusting for administrative costs.[1]

---

1. Additional information on our methodology can be found in Chapter 3 and the Appendix.

According to data from the U.S. Bureau of the Census, the average American family now spends a higher proportion of income on Social Security taxes than it does on food.[7]

These high payroll taxes mean that workers—especially those at lower income levels—have few dollars left over to invest in personal savings. More families are forced to rely on Social Security as their primary, if not sole, source of income after retirement and their primary means for which to save for retirement. As such, whether workers are receiving an adequate return from the large amount of taxes they are forced to pay into the system should be the key criterion on which the Social Security system is judged.

---

7. Data on average family consumption expenditures from U.S. Department of Labor, Bureau of Labor Statistics, *Consumer Expenditure Survey for 1997* (Washington, DC: U.S. Government Printing Office, June 1998). See Table 4, "Size of consumer unit: Average annual expenditures and characteristics, Consumer Expenditure Survey, 1997," at *ftp://ftp.bls.gov/pub/special.requests/ce/standard/1997*. "Taxes" include employee and employer share of FICA taxes.

CALCULATING RETURNS BY DISTRICT

This Center for Data Analysis book is the first study by any research organization, either inside or outside of government, to calculate rates of return from Social Security by congressional district. Accomplishing this task required several innovations:

- **The first calculations of life expectancy by congressional district.** To calculate Social Security's rate of return, Heritage economists estimated life expectancies in every U.S. congressional district for men and women born in 1945, 1955, 1965, and 1975. Although the federal government has generated life expectancy estimates at the national and state levels, official estimates of life expectancies for local areas generally have not been available (except in a few isolated instances).[8] Indeed, it is only within the past two years that nationwide estimates of life expectancy by county have been published.[9]

- **Predictions of mortality based on a detailed analysis of socioeconomic characteristics.** To estimate life expectancies in every congressional district, Heritage economists developed one of the most detailed models of mortality ever created.[10] This model uses advanced econometric techniques to link mortality data from the U.S. Centers for Disease Control and Prevention with socioeconomic data from the U.S. Bureau of the Census. Over 140 socioeconomic variables (including income, race, and poverty rates) were used to estimate life expectancy for every congressional district in the United States. Comparable cross-sectional studies of geographic differences in life expectancy are typically limited to examining 10 or fewer socioeconomic variables.[11]

  Estimating life expectancies for the nation's 435 congressional districts and the District of Columbia alone required constructing a database containing over 500,000 values. Because the mortality relationships developed in this model are based on data from the 1990 Decennial Census, the Heritage mortality model is capable of estimating life expectancy for almost any geographic entity—including ZIP Codes, specific towns and municipalities, and individual census tracts, which may contain only a few thousand people.

---

8. David A. Swanson, "A State-Based Regression Model for Estimating Substate Life Expectancy," *Demography*, Vol. 26, No. 1 (February 1989), pp. 161–170.

9. See C. J. L. Murray, C. M. Michaud, M. T. McKenna, J. S. Marks, *U.S. Patterns of Mortality by County and Race: 1965–1994*, Harvard Center for Population and Development Studies, 1998.

10. Similar studies using econometric estimates based on socioeconomic data date back to the late 1960s. See, for example, D. Peter Mazur, "Expectancy of Life at Birth in 36 Nationalities of the Soviet Union 1958–1960," *Population Studies*, Vol. 23, No. 2 (July 1969), pp. 225–246. For a more recent example, see Swanson, "A State-Based Regression Model." In general, earlier studies used socioeconomic data at a higher geographical level to estimate life expectancies at a subgeographical level (e.g., state-by-state data have been used to estimate unavailable county-by-county data). In addition, they are typically limited to a small number of variables. Heritage researchers used available county-by-county death rates to estimate previously unavailable congressional district-by-congressional district information. Basing the computation of a small set of values (436 congressional districts) on a large set of observations (3,146 counties) leads to results that are more robust than estimating county-level information based on state-level data. The primary reason for this is that smaller geographic areas tend to show a greater variety than larger ones. In general, a large and diverse data set leads to better econometric fits than smaller sets that are less diverse. In addition, Heritage researchers were also able to evaluate a sizeable number of variables for potential inclusion in the final model. See the Appendix for further details of our methodology.

11. See Paul E. Zopf, *Mortality Patterns and Trends in the United States* (Westport, Conn.: Greenwood Press, 1992).

- **Estimates of lifetime earnings for workers in every congressional district.** The calculation of Social Security's rate of return requires not only life expectancy information, but also earnings information. This CDA study uses an earnings profile for the average male and female worker in each congressional district. The income of every worker is adjusted for their age, gender, and congressional district using data drawn from the U.S. Bureau of the Census' 1990 Decennial Census Public Use Micro Sample (PUMS). The Public Use Micro Sample is a random sample based on the 1990 Decennial Census and contains data on the earnings of over 2.5 million Americans. This is the first time that a unique earnings profile of such detail has been created for the average worker in every congressional district.

WHY SOCIAL SECURITY RATES OF RETURN VARY

A beneficiary's rate of return from Social Security will vary depending on age, marital status, life expectancy, work history, and income.

Age

Returns for older workers tend to be higher than they are for younger workers. This difference stems largely from the increase in payroll tax rates brought about by the steady rise in the ratio of retirees to workers:

- In 1950, with 16.5 workers per beneficiary, the OASI payroll tax rate was 3 percent.

- In 1998, with 3.4 workers per beneficiary, the OASI tax rate was 10.6 percent.

- By 2048, the Social Security Administration estimates there will be only 2.0 workers per retiree; payroll tax rates must be hiked by 41 percent by 2048 if benefits promised in current law are to be paid.[12]

Because of a long-term increase in the share of the population made up of retirees (thanks to the nation's increasing life expectancies and declining birth rates), only a system that uses a worker's own savings to fund retirement, as opposed to one that relies on the taxes of younger workers, can allow future generations of workers to escape continually declining rates of return.

Marital Status

Social Security's rates of return tend to be especially low for single and childless workers. Even though they face the same payroll tax rates, single workers do not receive the spousal benefits Social Security pays to the husbands and the wives of retired workers. Social Security also provides survivors' benefits to both the children of deceased workers under the age of 18 and the spouse caring for the minors.

Life Expectancy

Life expectancy differentials can lead to large differences in returns from Social Security. Workers in high-risk occupations are more likely to die before reaching retirement age. Even if they do reach retirement age, such workers are likely to draw benefits for a shorter period of time than workers in occupations with lower mortality rates. Life expectancy differs widely across groups on

---

12. See the *1998 Annual Report of the Board of Trustees of the Federal Old-Age and Survivors and Disability Insurance Trust Funds,* Table II.F13 and Table II.F19. The ratio of workers to beneficiaries includes Disability Insurance recipients.

the basis of such characteristics as ethnicity, gender, income, occupation, and marital status. Generally, African-Americans have lower life expectancies than other racial groups; single persons face higher mortality rates than married persons; individuals with lower incomes have higher death rates; and men have shorter life expectancies than women.[13]

Income and Work History

The Social Security benefits that workers, their spouses, or their survivors will receive are paid on the basis of the worker's earnings record. Generally, a worker's retirement benefits are calculated using the 35 years of highest earnings. This can mean that workers with an intermittent work record can receive a higher rate of return. For example, if a worker works for only 35 years from the period between ages 20 and 65, his or her Old-Age benefits will be the same as those for a worker with identical annual wage rates who worked the entire 45 years from age 20 to 65. The worker who worked only 35 years receives a higher rate of return from Social Security and the same benefits as the worker who paid taxes for 10 more years. Higher-income workers also tend to receive lower returns from Social Security because under the progressive formulae used by the Social Security Administration to compute benefits, upper-income workers receive a lower benefit relative to their wages than lower-income workers.

As the discussion thus far demonstrates, the rate of return compares the amount of money a family pays into Social Security with the amount of money it will receive in benefits in retirement. Knowing Social Security's rates of return will allow families to compare Social Security benefits to other investment vehicles.[14] If the rate of return from Social Security is lower than what the family would receive from another investment, then allowing workers to place their Social Security payroll tax dollars into alternative, private investments would allow their money to grow more quickly (and provide them with a higher retirement income in the future).

Rates of return from Social Security can be compared with the projected return (after deducting for administrative costs) on a portfolio consisting 50 percent long-term Treasury bonds and 50 percent large company stocks. According to the Social Security Administration's projections, such a portfolio is likely to yield 4.2 percent after inflation.[15]

Despite its status as a universal social insurance program, Social Security affects different types of people in significantly different ways. Variations in income and life expectancy mean different groups are affected in ways that are surprisingly different, which, undoubtedly, was not the original intention of the founders of Social Security.

Social Security has two features that determine how different groups will fare:

- First, under the formula used to calculate retirement or survivors' benefits, the annual benefit paid to the low-income worker will be a higher proportion of his or her wages than the benefit paid to the high-income worker. Assuming a similar life expectancy, the low-income worker should expect to receive a higher rate of return than would a high-income worker.

---

13. For a survey of the overall pattern in death rates, see Zopf, *Mortality Patterns and Trends*.

14. Estimates in this *Report* relate only to the retirement, or Old-Age Insurance, portion of current Social Security payroll taxes. As noted above, Disability Insurance benefits and taxes are not included in these rate of return calculations and are assumed to continue unaffected by any reform of Social Security's Old-Age and Survivors Insurance program. See the Appendix for a discussion of factors employed in constructing rates of return.

15. See Chapter 3 for details of calculations.

- Second, because Social Security is similar to a life annuity program, benefits are paid only as long as a worker or his or her survivors are alive. This means, all things being equal, that a worker with a longer life expectancy can expect to receive a greater number of benefit payments (and consequently a higher rate of return) than a similarly situated worker with a shorter life expectancy.

However, it is important to note that the relationship between income level and life expectancy can cancel out the positive effect the progressive formula has on low-income workers' rates of return, compared to high-income workers, because low-income workers typically have shorter life expectancies than high-income workers.

Social Security is by far the largest government program most Americans participate in during their lifetimes. And for many Americans, Social Security will be their primary means of support after retirement. Thus, the program should be judged by the impact it has on every American's ability to build wealth. In this context, we present calculations in the next chapter that show exactly how the Social Security program treats average families in each of the congressional districts in the United States.

SOCIAL SECURITY RATES OF RETURN BY CONGRESSIONAL DISTRICT

The data presented in this chapter clearly demonstrate a regional pattern to Social Security's rates of return. The map on the back of the foldout shows the rate of return for each congressional district that results from a two-earner married couple, born in 1965, who have two children and earning wages equal to the national average for their respective gender (the prototype used in this study).[1]

The study found that congressional districts with the lowest rates of return are located in the South (an area with comparatively low life expectancies) and in metropolitan areas in the Northeast, Midwest, and West (where relatively high earnings and lower life expectancies are common). Many areas in the West, especially the rural Upper Midwest and the rural Mountain regions, tend to have higher rates of return. These regional differences in returns reflect the higher life expectancies that prevail in these areas.

Our analysis also found that congressional districts with the largest dollar losses under the current Social Security system tend to be densely populated with relatively high earnings. Some of the highest dollar losses occur in relatively affluent suburban areas. The areas with the lowest dollar losses tend to be rural with low average earnings combined with relatively high life expectancies. There is a geographic concentration of states with relatively low absolute-dollar losses from Social Security in the upper Midwest and along the Southern border of the United States. And there is a concentration of districts that have large absolute-dollar losses in the highly urbanized Eastern, Midwestern, and Western states.

Map 2.1 shows the multiple influences of ethnicity, income, and other factors on the rates of return for prototypical couples living in the Los Angeles, California, area. Two areas face particu-

---

1. Income values were calculated for men and women in each age group using average earnings data for each congressional district.

■ Map 2.1 ▬▬▬▬▬▬▬▬▬▬▬▬▬▬▬▬▬▬▬▬▬▬▬▬▬▬▬▬▬▬▬▬▬

Los Angeles Metropolitan Area Congressional Districts

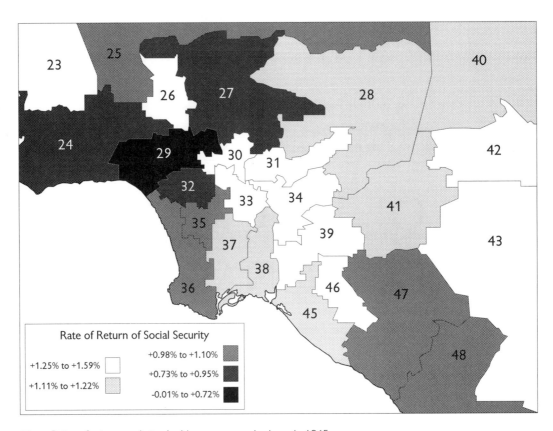

Note: Rates of return apply to double-earner couples born in 1965.

larly low rates of return. One is affluent West Los Angeles, where relatively high-income workers are penalized by a benefit formula that pays them little in return for the OASI taxes they pay. The other is the heavily African-American, South Central area, where lower life expectancies mean that many workers die before collecting significant amounts of retirement benefits. The areas faring best under Social Security are the heavily Hispanic East Los Angeles and western San Bernardino Valley areas, where relatively high life expectancies and low earnings are characteristic. Falling in between these two extremes are moderate-income suburban areas in Orange County and in the eastern and northern areas of Los Angeles, where both life expectancies and incomes lie in the mid-range.

It should be noted that compared with the rates of return available on personal investments, even workers in the Los Angeles congressional district with the highest rate of return (1.59 percent in the 33rd District) fare badly under Social Security.[2]

The pattern for Los Angeles is typical of urban areas, as seen in map on the front of the foldout, which shows rates of return for congressional districts in the 12 largest metropolitan areas. Typically, both highly affluent and low-income, African-American districts fare worst; Hispanic areas

───────────────

2. For example, using a mixed portfolio of bonds and equities, the returns would be over 4 percent per year.

■ Table 2.1 ■■■■■

Congressional District Ranking by Social Security Rate of Return for Double-Earner Couples Born in 1965

Ranking	Congressional District	Representative	Dollar Loss Under Social Security	Social Security Rate of Return
1	North Dakota (At-large)	Earl Pomeroy (D)	$230,288	2.39%
2	South Dakota (At-large)	John R. Thune (R)	238,972	2.33%
3	Montana (At-large)	Rick Hill (R)	265,016	2.25%
4	Utah 3	Christopher Cannon (R)	264,150	2.24%
5	Minnesota 7	Collin C. Peterson (D)	254,244	2.21%
6	Nebraska 3	Bill Barrett (R)	269,581	2.17%
7	Iowa 5	Tom Latham (R)	283,944	2.14%
8	Iowa 3	Leonard L. Boswell (D)	283,727	2.11%
9	Kansas 1	Jerry Moran (R)	290,373	2.09%
10	Minnesota 2	David Minge (D)	321,462	2.06%
427	Georgia 5	John Lewis (D)	680,228	0.36%
428	Louisiana 2	William J. Jefferson (D)	554,199	0.33%
429	New York 15	Charles B. Rangel (D)	574,063	0.25%
430	New York 11	Major R. Owens (D)	647,241	0.19%
431	New York 8	Jerrold L. Nadler (D)	1,094,797	0.18%
432	District of Columbia	Eleanor Holmes Norton (D)	786,850	0.16%
433	Illinois 7	Danny K. Davis (D)	728,526	0.13%
434	New York 10	Edolphus Towns (D)	692,773	0.10%
435	New York 14	Carolyn B. Maloney (D)	1,369,748	0.07%
436	Michigan 15	Carolyn C. Kilpatrick (D)	598,572	-0.01%

with low incomes have the highest returns; and middle- and upper-middle income suburbs have returns that lie in the mid-range.

It is widely accepted that the United States is a sparsely populated country. This is particularly true when it is compared with Japan or European countries such as Belgium, where population density, or inhabitants per square mile, is 12 times higher than it is in the United States.[3] The U.S. population does, however, follow European and Japanese patterns in that it is highly concentrated in urban and suburban areas. Almost one-fourth of the population lives on less than half a percent of the total U.S. geographical area. The 115 congressional districts represented on the front of the foldout map cover a mere 1.02 percent of the territory. And the least densely populated 25 percent of all congressional districts cover 83 percent of the country's land area.

The congressional districts represented on the front of the foldout map have rates of return ranging from 0.01 percent to 1.59 percent for two-earner couples born in 1965. By contrast, if we take the 115 most rural congressional districts, the rates of return for these same households range from 1.59 percent to 2.39 percent. These differentials reflect the fact that rural areas typically have lower incomes and higher life expectancies than urban congressional districts.

---

3. See *OECD in Figures* (Paris: OECD, July 1999), p. 6.

THE BEST AND WORST CONGRESSIONAL DISTRICTS

Table 2.1 lists Social Security's rate of return in the 10 congressional districts that showed the highest returns as well as in the 10 districts with the lowest returns. The lowest return is found in Michigan's 15th District, which covers part of Detroit. At -0.01 percent, this rate indicates that our couple born in 1965 will not live long enough to earn back all of the payroll taxes they would have contributed to the current system. These workers could have earned $598,572 more than Social Security would pay them in benefits had they been permitted to invest their payroll tax dollars in a portfolio of U.S. Treasury bonds and blue-chip equities.

On the other hand, North Dakota's At-Large Congressional District has the highest rate of return. Our two-earner couple from this district will earn a rate of return of 2.39 percent, over a full percent above the national average of 1.29 percent. Even so, this working couple in North Dakota would still have been able to save $230,288 more for retirement had they been permitted to invest in a secure bond-and-equity portfolio.

Table 2.2 shows that districts with the lowest rates of return for two-income couples born in 1965 are concentrated in affluent as well as low-income districts with an African-American majority. These results reflect the low life expectancies prevailing in the eight low-income black districts and the punitive effects of Social Security's progressive benefit formula on high earners (New York's 14th and 8th Districts).

Districts with higher rates of return (see Table 2.1) are concentrated in the rural West and Midwest. These areas have very high life expectancies and low earnings compared with the rest of the

■ Table 2.2 ■

Congressional District Ranking by Losses Under Social Security for Double-Earner Couples Born in 1965

Ranking	Congressional District	Representative	Dollar Loss Under Social Security	Social Security Rate of Return
1	New York 14	Carolyn B. Maloney (D)	$1,369,748	0.07%
2	California 29	Henry A. Waxman (D)	1,156,765	0.51%
3	New York 8	Jerrold L. Nadler (D)	1,094,797	0.18%
4	Connecticut 4	Christopher Shays (R)	1,003,567	0.82%
5	Illinois 10	John Edward Porter (R)	988,303	0.71%
6	New York 18	Nita M. Lowey (D)	977,038	0.61%
7	New York 5	Gary L. Ackerman (D)	961,996	0.72%
8	Maryland 8	Constance A. Morella (R)	944,813	0.85%
9	New Jersey 11	Rodney P. Frelinghuysen (R)	927,584	0.91%
10	California 24	Brad Sherman (D)	924,372	0.95%
427	California 33	Lucille Roybal-Allard (D)	303,417	1.59%
428	Kansas 1	Jerry Moran (R)	290,373	2.09%
429	Iowa 5	Tom Latham (R)	283,944	2.14%
430	Iowa 3	Leonard L. Boswell (D)	283,727	2.11%
431	Nebraska 3	Bill Barrett (R)	269,581	2.17%
432	Montana (At-large)	Rick Hill (R)	265,016	2.25%
433	Utah 3	Christopher Cannon (R)	264,150	2.24%
434	Minnesota 7	Collin C. Peterson (D)	254,244	2.21%
435	South Dakota (At-large)	John R. Thune (R)	238,972	2.33%
436	North Dakota (At-large)	Earl Pomeroy (D)	230,288	2.39%

Note: Dollar figures and rates of return apply to double-earner couples born in 1965.

Districts with higher rates of return (see Table 2.1) are concentrated in the rural West and Midwest. These areas have very high life expectancies and low earnings compared with the rest of the nation. Workers in these districts will be able to collect benefits for a longer period than workers with shorter life expectancies. They also benefit from Social Security's progressive benefit formula. However, all of the workers in this group fare badly when compared with the 4 percent return available from a conservative portfolio of investments.

Table 2.2 also shows the amount families lose under Social Security if they were not able to invest their payroll taxes in a personal account. The pattern for congressional districts with relatively small dollar losses is similar to those with relatively high rates of return. States with low dollar losses tend to be located in rural areas in the Upper Midwest and the West. The one exception is California's 33rd District, which is located in East Los Angeles. But even in the district with the lowest dollar loss (North Dakota), our prototypical two-income couple born in 1965 would lose over $230,000 in retirement income because they are not able to invest tax dollars in a personal retirement account.

Congressional districts with large dollar losses under the current system are concentrated in affluent urban and suburban areas. These dollar losses reflect the high payroll taxes paid by upper-income workers relative to the benefits they receive. Six of these districts, as Table 2.2 shows, are concentrated in the greater New York area.

It should be noted that the dollar accumulations reported here are for illustrative purposes only and do not reflect actual outcomes that would result if Social Security were privatized. The dollar amounts show our two-income couple's wealth at retirement had they been able to place all of their past, current, and future OASI taxes (the net of the amount needed to purchase life insurance coverage equivalent to pre-retirement Survivors Insurance) into a personal account. These dollar amounts also represent the full opportunity cost of setting up the current pay-as-you-go Social Security system. In practice, however, almost all the proposed reforms that establish personal retirement accounts would allow workers to invest only a portion of their payroll taxes. The rest would be retained to pay benefits to existing retirees and to help fund a basic safety net of retirement income for those who could not accumulate enough in their personal accounts.

OTHER SOCIOECONOMIC FACTORS AFFECTING RATES OF RETURN

Manufacturing

Table 2.3 shows the returns from Social Security faced by the two-earner couple born in 1965 in the 10 congressional districts with the largest proportion of workers employed in manufacturing. These districts are located primarily in the South and outside of major metropolitan areas, except for California's 33rd District (located in an inner-city section of Los Angeles), Illinois' 4th District (based in the Hispanic-majority areas of Chicago's West Side), and Ohio's 5th District (located in northwestern Ohio).

Dollar losses for the two-earner couple range from $303,417 in California's heavily Hispanic 33rd District up to $491,226 in North Carolina's 6th District. Rates of return range from a 1.12 percent low in South Carolina's 5th District up to 1.59 percent in California's 33rd District. While these manufacturing districts in general fare slightly better than the national average of 1.29 percent, workers and their families in each state still face dollar losses under the current system equal to hundreds of thousands of dollars.

■ Table 2.3 ▬▬▬▬▬▬▬▬▬▬▬▬▬▬▬▬▬▬▬▬▬▬▬▬

Congressional District Ranking by Percentage of Workers Employed in Manufacturing

% of Workers Employed in Manufacturing	Congressional District	Representative	Dollar Loss Under Social Security	Social Security Rate of Return
38.6%	North Carolina 10	Cass Ballenger (R)	$453,440	1.45%
35.7%	California 33	Lucille Roybal-Allard (D)	303,417	1.59%
35.6%	South Carolina 5	John M. Spratt, Jr. (D)	442,697	1.12%
35.1%	Mississippi 1	Roger F. Wicker (R)	393,505	1.31%
34.5%	Tennessee 4	Van Hilleary (R)	359,675	1.56%
34.3%	South Carolina 3	Lindsey O. Graham (R)	443,638	1.25%
33.5%	Illinois 4	Luis V. Gutierrez (D)	383,956	1.36%
33.4%	North Carolina 8	Robin Hayes (R)	429,659	1.33%
33.3%	Ohio 5	Paul E. Gillmor (R)	454,205	1.48%
32.9%	North Carolina 6	Howard Coble (R)	491,226	1.38%

Note: Dollar figures and rates of return apply to double-earner couples born in 1965.

■ Table 2.4 ▬▬▬▬▬▬▬▬▬▬▬▬▬▬▬▬▬▬▬▬▬▬▬▬

Congressional District Ranking by Percentage of People Living in Poverty

% of Individuals in Poverty	Congressional District	Representative	Dollar Loss Under Social Security	Social Security Rate of Return
41.8%	New York 16	Jose E. Serrano (D)	$481,459	0.50%
37.7%	Mississippi 2	Bennie G. Thompson (D)	422,973	0.69%
37.5%	Texas 15	Ruben Hinojosa (D)	305,633	1.72%
36.6%	Michigan 15	Carolyn C. Kilpatrick (D)	598,572	-0.01%
33.0%	New York 15	Charles B. Rangel (D)	574,063	0.25%
32.7%	Kentucky 5	Harold Rogers (R)	410,743	1.21%
31.2%	Alabama 7	Earl F. Hilliard (D)	412,517	0.82%
31.0%	Louisiana 2	William J. Jefferson (D)	554,199	0.33%
30.4%	New York 12	Nydia M. Velazquez (D)	424,401	1.11%
29.7%	Texas 27	Solomon P. Ortiz (D)	384,513	1.55%
29.5%	Illinois 7	Danny K. Davis (D)	728,526	0.13%
29.5%	Texas 23	Henry Bonilla (R)	420,744	1.47%
28.3%	New York 10	Edolphus Towns (D)	692,773	0.10%
28.2%	Texas 28	Ciro D. Rodriguez (D)	314,104	1.69%
28.0%	California 33	Lucille Roybal-Allard (D)	303,417	1.59%

Note: Dollar figures and rates of return apply to double-earner couples born in 1965.

Families in Poverty

One of the expressed goals of Social Security is to help lower-income workers achieve financial security during retirement. Indeed, the benefit formula of the current system is structured so as to pay low-income workers an annual benefit that is a larger proportion of their lifetime wages than that paid to higher income workers. In this context, the return for low-income workers is particularly important.

Table 2.4 shows Social Security returns for the 15 congressional districts having the highest proportion of persons living in poverty. These districts cover a diverse range of areas, from the

■ Table 2.5 ■■

Congressional District Ranking by Percentage of Households with a Child Under the Age of 18

% of Households With a Child Under 18	Congressional District		Representative	Dollar Loss Under Social Security	Social Security Rate of Return
49.1%	Utah	3	Christopher Cannon (R)	$264,150	2.24%
48.9%	California	33	Lucille Roybal-Allard (D)	$303,417	1.59%
48.5%	California	20	Calvin M. Dooley (D)	$333,813	1.48%
47.7%	Texas	15	Ruben Hinojosa (D)	$305,633	1.72%
47.0%	Utah	1	James V. Hansen (R)	$331,147	2.05%
46.9%	Texas	16	Silvestre Reyes (D)	$376,728	1.51%
46.8%	Texas	23	Henry Bonilla (R)	$420,744	1.47%
46.7%	California	37	Juanita Millender-McDonald (D)	$474,993	1.12%
46.3%	California	42	George E. Brown, Jr. (D)	$540,795	1.32%
46.0%	California	41	Gary G. Miller (R)	$685,766	1.16%
45.4%	Illinois	4	Luis V. Gutierrez (D)	$383,956	1.36%
44.7%	Minnesota	6	William P. Luther (D)	$513,345	1.67%
44.4%	Texas	28	Ciro D. Rodriguez (D)	$314,104	1.69%
44.3%	Alaska		Don Young (R)	$585,812	1.47%
44.2%	Texas	27	Solomon P. Ortiz (D)	$384,513	1.55%

Note: Dollar figures and rates of return apply to double-earner couples born in 1965. Rankings are for the 104th Congress.

overwhelmingly white Appalachia area to the mostly black or Hispanic inner-city. Relative to the national average, the returns from these districts vary substantially.

A number of patterns among this diverse group of districts stand out. The most significant is that two-earner couples endure substantial dollar losses under Social Security in each of these areas. The difference between OASI benefits, in terms of year 2000 dollars, and the amount they could accumulate in a personal account ranges from an average of $303,417 in California's mostly Hispanic 33rd District to $728,526 in Illinois' primarily African-American 7th District.

In general, congressional districts with large proportions of their population living in poverty fare slightly better in the West than in other parts of the country. Poorer districts with large numbers of Hispanic residents generally fare better than other districts, the one exception being the very low returns in the three New York City districts with a large proportion of Puerto Ricans (New York's 16th, 15th, and 12th Districts).

Families with Children

The performance of the Social Security system for married couples with children is of particular importance. These families must depend on the Social Security system to provide benefits to the surviving spouse or children should a working parent die. Also, parents often have a particular interest in accumulating wealth that can be passed on to their children. Unfortunately under the current system, unless their child is under 18 years of age when a worker and his or her spouse die, their investment in the current Social Security system dies with them.

Table 2.5 ranks the 15 congressional districts with the highest percentage of households composed of families with at least one child under the age of 18. Most of these districts are located in Hispanic neighborhoods in central Los Angeles, in farming California and along the Texas border. The remaining districts are scattered around the U.S. in mostly white rural religious areas.

■ Table 2.6 ▬▬▬▬▬▬▬▬▬▬▬▬▬▬▬▬▬▬▬▬▬▬▬▬▬▬▬▬▬▬▬▬▬▬

Congressional District Ranking by Percentage of Foreign-Born Population

% Foreign-Born	Congressional District	Representative	Dollar Loss Under Social Security	Social Security Rate of Return
58.5%	California 30	Xavier Becerra (D)	$392,155	1.44%
56.9%	Florida 18	Ileana Ros-Lehtinen (R)	552,354	1.27%
56.0%	California 33	Lucille Roybal-Allard (D)	303,417	1.59%
55.8%	Florida 21	Lincoln Diaz-Balart (R)	485,727	1.47%
45.2%	California 31	Matthew G. Martinez (D)	417,329	1.55%
42.8%	New York 12	Nydia M. Velazquez (D)	424,401	1.11%
42.8%	California 46	Loretta Sanchez (D)	422,312	1.56%
42.2%	California 26	Howard L. Berman (D)	484,942	1.39%
39.4%	New York 11	Major R. Owens (D)	647,241	0.19%
36.0%	New York 7	Joseph Crowley (D)	631,986	0.83%
33.7%	California 8	Nancy Pelosi (D)	700,208	0.83%
32.8%	California 35	Maxine Waters (D)	488,383	1.01%
32.5%	Illinois 4	Luis V. Gutierrez (D)	383,956	1.36%
32.5%	New Jersey 13	Robert Menendez (D)	563,918	0.98%
32.5%	California 37	Juanita Millender-McDonald (D)	474,993	1.12%

Note: Dollar figures and rates of return apply to double-earner couples born in 1965.

Relatively rural areas tend to have average incomes. They are moderately hurt by the progressive Social Security benefit formula. Family and marital stability are associated with factors that increase life expectancy (such as lower crime rates and less risk-taking behavior). As a result, the moderate incomes of such areas are also likely to be matched by higher life expectancies.

The net result of higher life expectancies and moderate incomes is that while 13 of these 15 congressional districts have rates of return above the national average, they are also likely to face severe dollar losses under the current system compared with an alternative system consisting of personal accounts. Two of the congressional districts with the largest absolute dollar losses under Social Security ($685,766 and $540,795, respectively, in year 2000 dollars) are California's 41st and 42nd Districts. They tend to be suburban areas populated by Los Angeles workers.

Foreign-Born Workers

Table 2.6 shows the returns faced by workers in the 15 congressional districts with the largest proportion of foreign-born residents. These districts are concentrated in New York, California, and Florida.

These congressional districts are very diverse, ranging from New York's 7th District with a large concentration of European immigrants to Florida's heavily Cuban-American 18th and 21st Districts, to New York's 11th District with its large concentration of African and Afro-Caribbean residents, to California's 30th District, which is heavily Mexican-American. In addition, most of the districts listed are also heavily Hispanic.

While this diversity is reflected in the returns faced by the average worker in each of these congressional districts, our prototypical two-earner couple faces dollar losses ranging from $303,417 (California's 33rd District) to $700,208 (California's 8th District, which contains a large Asian population). Rates of return varied from 0.19 percent in New York's 11th District (Brooklyn) to 1.59 percent for California's 33rd District.

Inflation-Adjusted Rate of Return from Social Security (OASI) for Double-Earner Couple Born in 1965

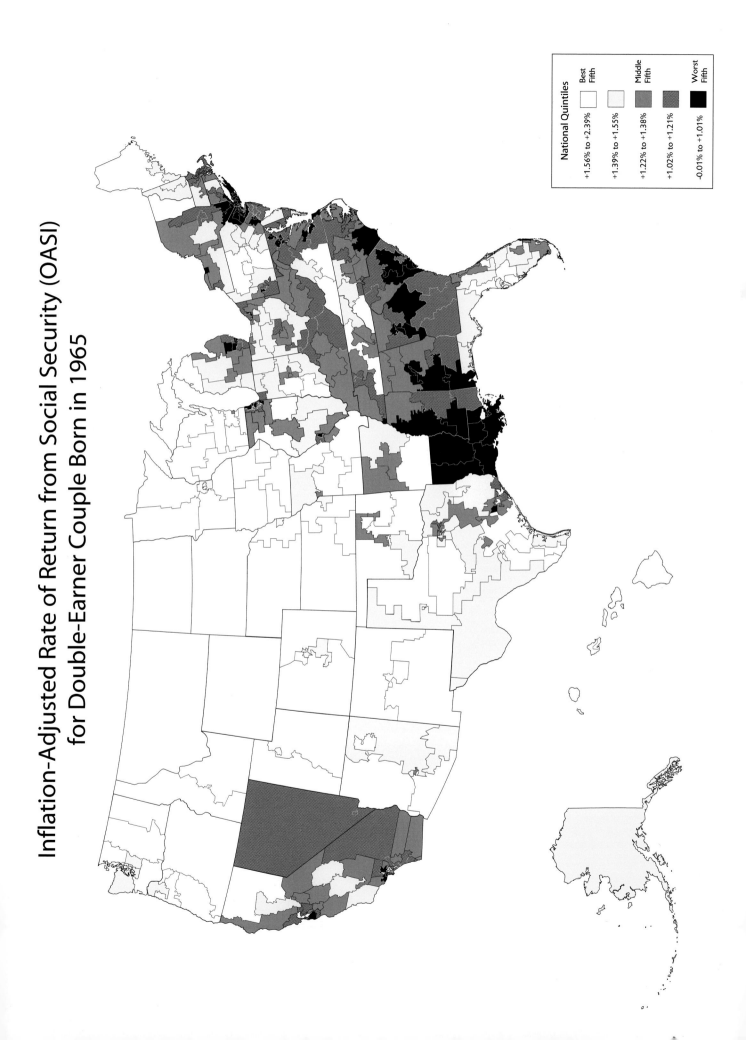

National Quintiles

Best Fifth	+1.56% to +2.39%
	+1.39% to +1.55%
Middle Fifth	+1.22% to +1.38%
	+1.02% to +1.21%
Worst Fifth	-0.01% to +1.01%

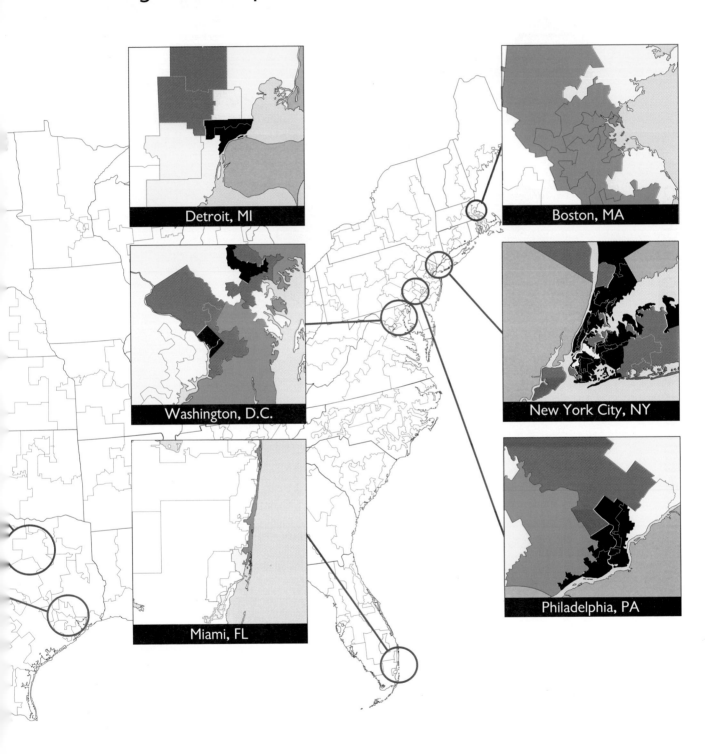

Detroit, MI

Boston, MA

Washington, D.C.

New York City, NY

Miami, FL

Philadelphia, PA

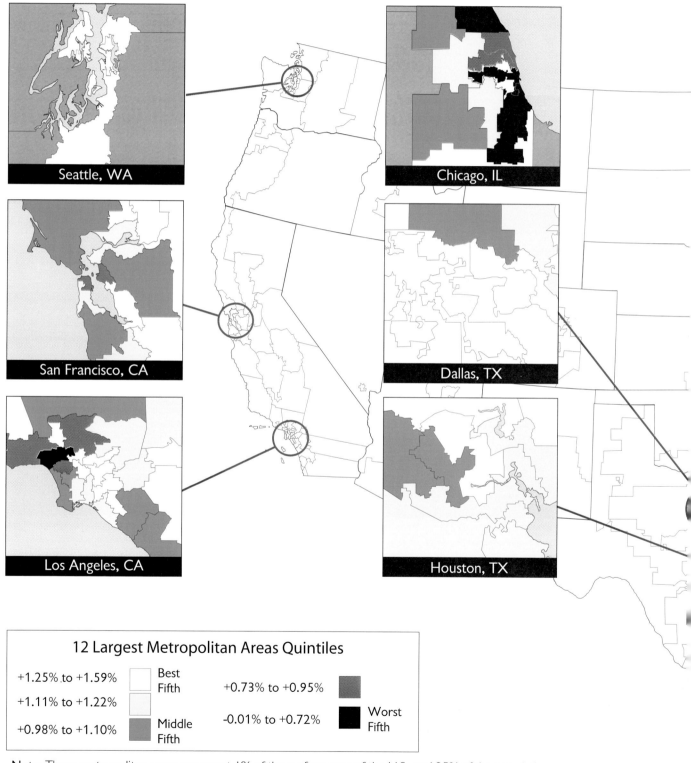

Inflation-Adjusted Rate of Retur[n]
for Double-Earner Couple Born in 1965 [...]

Seattle, WA

Chicago, IL

San Francisco, CA

Dallas, TX

Los Angeles, CA

Houston, TX

12 Largest Metropolitan Areas Quintiles

+1.25% to +1.59%	Best Fifth
+1.11% to +1.22%	
+0.98% to +1.10%	Middle Fifth

| +0.73% to +0.95% | |
| -0.01% to +0.72% | Worst Fifth |

Note: These metropolitan areas represent 1% of the surface area of the U.S., and 25% of the population.

■ Table 2.7 ■■

Congressional District Ranking by Percentage of
Non-Hispanic Black Population

% Non-Hispanic Black	Congressional District	Representative	Dollar Loss Under Social Security	Social Security Rate of Return
70.8%	Maryland 7	Elijah Cummings (D)	$551,113	0.56%
69.9%	Michigan 15	Carolyn C. Kilpatrick (D)	598,572	-0.01%
69.7%	New York 11	Major R. Owens (D)	647,241	0.19%
69.3%	Illinois 1	Bobby L. Rush (D)	592,699	0.46%
68.9%	Michigan 14	John Conyers, Jr. (D)	613,970	0.44%
68.1%	Illinois 2	Jesse L. Jackson, Jr. (D)	578,054	0.65%
67.3%	Alabama 7	Earl F. Hilliard (D)	412,517	0.82%
65.3%	District of Columbia	Eleanor Holmes Norton (D)	786,850	0.16%
65.3%	Illinois 7	Danny K. Davis (D)	728,526	0.13%
64.1%	Virginia 3	Robert C. Scott (D)	426,816	1.01%
62.9%	Mississippi 2	Bennie G. Thompson (D)	422,973	0.69%
62.1%	South Carolina 6	James E. Clyburn (D)	397,460	0.89%
62.0%	Pennsylvania 2	Chaka Fattah (D)	586,062	0.58%
61.7%	Georgia 5	John Lewis (D)	680,228	0.36%
60.4%	Louisiana 2	William J. Jefferson (D)	554,199	0.33%
59.2%	Tennessee 9	Harold E. Ford, Jr. (D)	513,216	0.79%
59.0%	New Jersey 10	Donald M. Payne (D)	597,678	0.61%
58.3%	Ohio 11	Stephanie Tubbs Jones (D)	595,884	0.61%
57.8%	Maryland 4	Albert R. Wynn (D)	676,559	0.79%
57.2%	New York 10	Edolphus Towns (D)	692,773	0.10%

Note: Dollar figures and rates of return apply to double-earner couples born in 1965.

In sum, private investments outperform Social Security in every district.

Ethnic Minorities

Table 2.7 shows the returns faced by typical residents of the 20 congressional districts that have the largest proportion of non-Hispanic blacks. This set of districts ranges from poor inner-city districts in the Northeast and Midwest (such as Michigan's 15th District) to affluent suburban districts (such as Maryland's 4th District, where fewer than 7 percent of residents live below the poverty line) and largely rural Southern districts (such as South Carolina's 6th District).

Strikingly, returns in all of these districts lie below a 1.29 percent return, the national average. Returns for a two-earner couple born in 1965 range from -0.01 percent in Michigan's 15th District (located in inner-city Detroit) to 1.01 percent in Virginia's 3rd District. Dollar losses range from $786,850 in the District of Columbia to $412,517 in Alabama's 7th District. The reason for the large difference is that African-American life expectancies tend to fall below the national average.[4]

While losses under Social Security are relatively large for all of the congressional districts listed in Table 2.7, inner-city districts fare especially badly. The five congressional districts with the low-

---

4. Several researchers have examined possible reasons for these differences. See Paul Menchik, "Economic Status as a Determinant of Mortality among Black and White Older Men: Does Poverty Kill?" *Population Studies*, Vol. 47, No. 3 (November 1993), pp. 427–436. See also Lloyd Potter, "Socio-Economic Determinants of White and Black Males' Life Expectancy Differentials–1980," *Demography*, Vol. 28, No. 2 (May 1991), pp. 303–321.

■ Table 2.8 ■

Congressional District Ranking by Percentage of Hispanic Population

% Hispanic	Congressional District	Representative	Dollar Loss Under Social Security	Social Security Rate of Return
83.2%	California 33	Lucille Roybal-Allard (D)	$303,417	1.59%
74.5%	Texas 15	Ruben Hinojosa (D)	305,633	1.72%
70.3%	Texas 16	Silvestre Reyes (D)	376,728	1.51%
69.5%	Florida 21	Lincoln Diaz-Balart (R)	485,727	1.47%
66.7%	Florida 18	Ileana Ros-Lehtinen (R)	552,354	1.27%
65.9%	Texas 27	Solomon P. Ortiz (D)	384,513	1.55%
64.0%	Illinois 4	Luis V. Gutierrez (D)	383,956	1.36%
62.4%	Texas 23	Henry Bonilla (R)	420,744	1.47%
61.7%	California 34	Grace F. Napolitano (D)	491,152	1.46%
60.5%	California 30	Xavier Becerra (D)	392,155	1.44%
60.4%	Texas 20	Charles A. Gonzalez (D)	343,545	1.60%
60.2%	Texas 28	Ciro D. Rodriguez (D)	314,104	1.69%
59.0%	New York 16	Jose E. Serrano (D)	481,459	0.50%
58.2%	California 31	Matthew G. Martinez (D)	417,329	1.55%
57.3%	New York 12	Nydia M. Velazquez (D)	424,401	1.11%

Note: Dollar figures and rates of return apply to double-earner couples born in 1965.

est rates of return are located in Detroit, Brooklyn, the District of Columbia, and the West Side of Chicago. Poverty and crime are major causes of the high mortality in these areas.

Table 2.8 shows rate of return information for the 15 congressional districts with the highest proportion of Hispanics. These districts are concentrated in California, Florida, Illinois, New York, and Texas.

These Hispanic districts can be divided into two groups. A majority of New York's Hispanic districts (with a large concentration of Puerto Ricans) face very low rates of return relative to the national average. The second group (with a large population of Mexican- or Cuban-Americans, located mainly in California, Florida, and Texas) tend to have rates of return that exceed the national average. However, these returns are all well below the 4.2 percent that is available from private investments.

Dollar losses for the two-earner couple born in 1965 range from $303,417, for California's heavily Mexican-American 33rd District, to $552,354, for Florida's mostly Cuban-American 18th District.

Generally, Hispanic-Americans, except those who are of Puerto Rican ancestry, tend to have greater life expectancies than the other Americans within the general population. Hispanics also, with the exception of Cuban-Americans, tend to have lower incomes than the rest of the population.

Congressional District Rankings

Table 2.9 summarizes the rates of return for the 435 congressional districts and the District of Columbia for our prototypical two-earner couple born in 1965.

The table illustrates the range of results within each state. For a two-earner household with an income and life expectancy equal to the state average, the rate of return ranges from 0.77 percent to 2.59 percent. The same comparison within the 52 congressional districts of California would lead to rates of return ranging from 0.51 percent to 1.59 percent if the analysis is conducted at the congressional district level. The smaller the geographical unit, the richer the analysis becomes. The aggregation of geographical units—without totally masking the conclusions of this chapter—tends to blur the general understanding of the impact of the Social Security program.

As we shall see in the methodological appendix, the Heritage model developed for this study could easily be extended to study rates of return for counties, ZIP codes, or even Census tracts. Without altering our findings, an analysis of the rates of return at the Census tracts level would reveal even greater contrasts.

KEY FINDINGS

As these tables illustrate, the current Social Security system is a very bad deal for many American workers. Our analysis of congressional district rates of return finds:

- **In its current form, the Social Security system is performing poorly for workers in virtually every congressional district in the United States.** Even in those districts that suffer the lowest losses, our two-earner couple with children loses at least $200,000 under the current system, compared with the amount they would have at retirement if they had been able to place their payroll taxes in a secure portfolio of investments.

- **Congressional districts with the largest dollar losses under the current Social Security system tend to be highly populated, heavily urbanized, and affluent.** Some of the highest dollar losses occur in relatively affluent suburban areas. The areas with the lowest dollar losses tend to be comparatively rural and have low average earnings and relatively high life expectancies.

- **The lowest rate of return is found in Michigan's 15th Congressional District, which covers part of inner-city Detroit.** At -0.01 percent, this return indicates that two-earner couples born in 1965 and earning the average wage in their state will not live long enough to earn back all of the payroll taxes they paid into Social Security. These workers could have earned $598,572 more from their payroll taxes (OASI) had they been permitted to invest in a portfolio composed equally of U.S. Treasury bonds and retirement grade equities.

- **Dollar losses under the current system are high for Americans living in congressional districts that have the highest percentages of manufacturing workers.** Dollar losses for two-earner married couples in the 10 districts with the highest proportion of manufacturing workers range from $303,417 in California's heavily Hispanic 33rd District to $491,226 in North Carolina's 6th District. Social Security rates of return range from a low of 1.12 percent in South Carolina's 5th District to 1.59 percent in California's 33rd District.

- **The 15 congressional districts that have the highest percentage of foreign-born workers have Social Security inflation-adjusted rates of return below 1.6 percent.** Eight of these districts are located in California and have large Hispanic populations.

- **The five congressional districts with the highest percentage of non-Hispanic black workers have Social Security rates of return below 0.6 percent.** Two of these districts (New York's 11th and Michigan's 15th) have rates of return below 0.2 percent. For the top 15 congressional districts with the highest proportion of black workers, only Virginia's 3rd District has a rate of return above 1.0 percent.

Congressional District Rankings by Social Security (OASI)
Rate of Return for Double-Earner Couples Born in 1965

District	Representative	Annual Rate of Return From Social Security	Ranking From Highest Return to Lowest Return
Alabama			
1	Sonny Callahan (R)	1.01%	351 / 436
2	Terry Everett (R)	1.12	313 / 436
3	Bob Riley (R)	1.26	238 / 436
4	Robert Aderholt (R)	1.38	172 / 436
5	Robert E. Cramer, Jr. (D)	1.09	322 / 436
6	Spencer Bachus (R)	0.98	366 / 436
7	Earl F. Hilliard (D)	0.82	397 / 436
Alaska			
At-large	Don Young (R)	1.47	133 / 436
Arizona			
1	Matt Salmon (R)	1.55	90 / 436
2	Ed Pastor (D)	1.70	43 / 436
3	Bob Stump (R)	1.68	53 / 436
4	John B. Shadegg (R)	1.33	198 / 436
5	Jim Kolbe (R)	1.55	92 / 436
6	J. D. Hayworth (R)	1.45	148 / 436
Arkansas			
1	Marion Berry (D)	1.47	135 / 436
2	Vic Snyder (D)	1.29	223 / 436
3	Asa Hutchinson (R)	1.68	50 / 436
4	Jay Dickey (R)	1.38	174 / 436
California			
1	Mike Thompson (D)	1.35	192 / 436
2	Wally Herger (R)	1.56	85 / 436
3	Doug Ose (R)	1.49	122 / 436
4	John T. Doolittle (R)	1.26	242 / 436
5	Robert T. Matsui (D)	1.24	248 / 436
6	Lynn C. Woolsey (D)	1.08	328 / 436
7	George Miller (D)	1.17	286 / 436
8	Nancy Pelosi (D)	0.83	393 / 436
9	Barbara Lee (D)	0.87	385 / 436
10	Ellen O. Tauscher (D)	1.09	319 / 436
11	Richard W. Pombo (R)	1.32	207 / 436
12	Tom Lantos (D)	1.13	306 / 436
13	Fortney Stark (D)	1.26	243 / 436
14	Anna G. Eshoo (D)	1.00	358 / 436
15	Tom Campbell (R)	1.16	292 / 436
16	Zoe Lofgren (D)	1.28	224 / 436
17	Sam Farr (D)	1.29	219 / 436
18	Gary Condit (D)	1.35	195 / 436
19	George P. Radanovich (R)	1.40	168 / 436
20	Calvin M. Dooley (D)	1.48	124 / 436

■ Table 2.9 ■

Congressional District Rankings by Social Security (OASI) Rate of Return for Double-Earner Couples Born in 1965

District	Representative	Annual Rate of Return From Social Security	Ranking From Highest Return to Lowest Return
California			
21	William M. Thomas (R)	1.33%	199 / 436
22	Lois Capps (D)	1.42	163 / 436
23	Elton Gallegly (R)	1.32	206 / 436
24	Brad Sherman (D)	0.95	370 / 436
25	Howard P. McKeon (R)	1.09	321 / 436
26	Howard L. Berman (D)	1.39	171 / 436
27	James E. Rogan (R)	0.93	371 / 436
28	David Dreier (R)	1.22	256 / 436
29	Henry A. Waxman (D)	0.51	423 / 436
30	Xavier Becerra (D)	1.44	155 / 436
31	Matthew G. Martinez (D)	1.55	89 / 436
32	Julian C. Dixon (D)	0.80	399 / 436
33	Lucille Roybal-Allard (D)	1.59	78 / 436
34	Grace F. Napolitano (D)	1.46	139 / 436
35	Maxine Waters (D)	1.01	350 / 436
36	Steven T. Kuykendall (R)	0.98	367 / 436
37	Juanita Millender-McDonald (D)	1.12	310 / 436
38	Steve Horn (R)	1.15	297 / 436
39	Edward R. Royce (R)	1.30	214 / 436
40	Jerry Lewis (R)	1.21	261 / 436
41	Gary G. Miller (R)	1.16	291 / 436
42	Joe Baca (D)	1.32	202 / 436
43	Ken Calvert (R)	1.27	233 / 436
44	Mary Bono (R)	1.31	212 / 436
45	Dana Rohrabacher (R)	1.18	279 / 436
46	Loretta Sanchez (D)	1.56	86 / 436
47	Christopher Cox (R)	1.04	341 / 436
48	Ron Packard (R)	1.05	337 / 436
49	Brian P. Bilbray (R)	1.08	327 / 436
50	Bob Filner (D)	1.38	173 / 436
51	Randy Cunningham (R)	1.17	287 / 436
52	Duncan L. Hunter (R)	1.38	177 / 436
Colorado			
1	Diana DeGette (D)	1.49	123 / 436
2	Mark Udall (D)	1.72	40 / 436
3	Scott McInnis (R)	1.94	21 / 436
4	Bob Schaffer (R)	1.96	19 / 436
5	Joel Hefley (R)	1.44	151 / 436
6	Thomas G. Tancredo (R)	1.52	110 / 436
Connecticut			
1	John B. Larson (D)	1.17	288 / 436
2	Sam Gejdenson (D)	1.41	165 / 436
3	Rosa L. DeLauro (D)	1.27	228 / 436
4	Christopher Shays (R)	0.82	398 / 436

Congressional District Rankings by Social Security (OASI) Rate of Return for Double-Earner Couples Born in 1965

District	Representative	Annual Rate of Return From Social Security	Ranking From Highest Return to Lowest Return
Connecticut			
5	James H. Maloney (D)	1.15%	293 / 436
6	Nancy L. Johnson (R)	1.27	232 / 436
Delaware			
At-large	Michael N. Castle (R)	1.43	156 / 436
District of Columbia			
	Eleanor Holmes Norton (D)	0.16	432 / 436
Florida			
1	Joe Scarborough (R)	1.50	120 / 436
2	F. Allen Boyd, Jr. (D)	1.54	102 / 436
3	Corrine Brown (D)	1.37	182 / 436
4	Tillie K. Fowler (R)	1.27	236 / 436
5	Karen L. Thurman (D)	1.62	67 / 436
6	Cliff Stearns (R)	1.54	103 / 436
7	John L. Mica (R)	1.56	83 / 436
8	Bill McCollum (R)	1.50	117 / 436
9	Michael Bilirakis (R)	1.48	130 / 436
10	C. W. Bill Young (R)	1.52	107 / 436
11	Jim Davis (D)	1.48	126 / 436
12	Charles T. Canady (R)	1.57	80 / 436
13	Dan Miller (R)	1.63	66 / 436
14	Porter J. Goss (R)	1.53	106 / 436
15	David Weldon (R)	1.52	111 / 436
16	Mark Foley (R)	1.43	161 / 436
17	Carrie P. Meek (D)	1.19	270 / 436
18	Ileana Ros-Lehtinen (R)	1.27	230 / 436
19	Robert Wexler (D)	1.28	225 / 436
20	Peter Deutsch (D)	1.28	226 / 436
21	Lincoln Diaz-Balart (R)	1.47	134 / 436
22	E. Clay Shaw, Jr. (R)	1.01	355 / 436
23	Alcee L. Hastings (D)	1.29	222 / 436
Georgia			
1	Jack Kingston (R)	1.03	347 / 436
2	Sanford D. Bishop, Jr. (D)	1.20	267 / 436
3	Michael Collins (R)	0.93	373 / 436
4	Cynthia McKinney (D)	0.77	403 / 436
5	John Lewis (D)	0.36	427 / 436
6	Johnny Isakson (R)	0.74	407 / 436
7	Bob Barr (R)	1.13	307 / 436
8	Saxby Chambliss (R)	1.09	320 / 436
9	Nathan Deal (R)	1.32	204 / 436
10	Charles W. Norwood, Jr. (R)	0.98	364 / 436
11	John Linder (R)	1.07	332 / 436

■ Table 2.9 ■

Congressional District Rankings by Social Security (OASI)
Rate of Return for Double-Earner Couples Born in 1965

District	Representative	Annual Rate of Return From Social Security	Ranking From Highest Return to Lowest Return
Hawaii			
1	Neil Abercrombie (D)	1.61%	68 / 436
2	Patsy T. Mink (D)	1.82	33 / 436
Idaho			
1	Helen P. Chenoweth (R)	2.02	18 / 436
2	Michael K. Simpson (R)	2.02	16 / 436
Illinois			
1	Bobby L. Rush (D)	0.46	425 / 436
2	Jesse L. Jackson, Jr. (D)	0.65	415 / 436
3	William O. Lipinski (D)	1.18	275 / 436
4	Luis V. Gutierrez (D)	1.36	187 / 436
5	Rod R. Blagojevich (D)	0.88	383 / 436
6	Henry J. Hyde (R)	1.14	301 / 436
7	Danny K. Davis (D)	0.13	433 / 436
8	Philip M. Crane (R)	1.08	329 / 436
9	Janice D. Schakowsky (D)	0.89	381 / 436
10	John Edward Porter (R)	0.71	411 / 436
11	Jerry Weller (R)	1.25	246 / 436
12	Jerry F. Costello (D)	1.27	237 / 436
13	Judy Biggert (R)	1.03	345 / 436
14	J. Dennis Hastert (R)	1.27	229 / 436
15	Thomas W. Ewing (R)	1.60	71 / 436
16	Donald A. Manzullo (R)	1.29	220 / 436
17	Lane Evans (D)	1.59	76 / 436
18	Ray LaHood (R)	1.36	189 / 436
19	David D. Phelps (D)	1.53	104 / 436
20	John Shimkus (R)	1.46	145 / 436
Indiana			
1	Peter J. Visclosky (D)	1.15	295 / 436
2	David M. McIntosh (R)	1.54	101 / 436
3	Timothy J. Roemer (D)	1.45	146 / 436
4	Mark E. Souder (R)	1.48	128 / 436
5	Stephen E. Buyer (R)	1.55	97 / 436
6	Dan Burton (R)	1.24	247 / 436
7	Edward A. Pease (R)	1.66	58 / 436
8	John N. Hostettler (R)	1.65	61 / 436
9	Baron P. Hill (D)	1.59	74 / 436
10	Julia Carson (R)	1.22	257 / 436
Iowa			
1	James A. Leach (R)	1.83	32 / 436
2	Jim Nussle (R)	2.04	13 / 436
3	Leonard L. Boswell (D)	2.11	8 / 436
4	Greg Ganske (R)	1.82	34 / 436
5	Tom Latham (R)	2.14	7 / 436

Congressional District Rankings by Social Security (OASI)
Rate of Return for Double-Earner Couples Born in 1965

District	Representative	Annual Rate of Return From Social Security	Ranking From Highest Return to Lowest Return
Kansas			
1	Jerry Moran (R)	2.09%	9 / 436
2	Jim Ryun (R)	1.81	36 / 436
3	Dennis Moore (D)	1.47	136 / 436
4	Todd Tiahrt (R)	1.66	57 / 436
Kentucky			
1	Edward Whitfield (R)	1.38	175 / 436
2	Ron Lewis (R)	1.38	178 / 436
3	Anne M. Northup (R)	1.03	344 / 436
4	Ken Lucas (D)	1.21	264 / 436
5	Harold Rogers (R)	1.21	266 / 436
6	Ernest L. Fletcher (R)	1.36	186 / 436
Louisiana			
1	David Vitter (R)	0.75	405 / 436
2	William J. Jefferson (D)	0.33	428 / 436
3	W. J. Tauzin (R)	0.83	395 / 436
4	Jim McCrery (R)	0.75	404 / 436
5	John Cooksey (R)	0.95	369 / 436
6	Richard H. Baker (R)	0.72	408 / 436
7	Christopher John (D)	0.87	386 / 436
Maine			
1	Thomas H. Allen (D)	1.55	94 / 436
2	John Elias Baldacci (D)	1.74	39 / 436
Maryland			
1	Wayne T. Gilchrest (R)	1.13	304 / 436
2	Robert L. Ehrlich, Jr. (R)	1.09	323 / 436
3	Benjamin L. Cardin (D)	0.93	372 / 436
4	Albert R. Wynn (D)	0.79	401 / 436
5	Steny H. Hoyer (D)	1.07	333 / 436
6	Roscoe G. Bartlett (R)	1.17	282 / 436
7	Elijah Cummings (D)	0.56	422 / 436
8	Constance A. Morella (R)	0.85	390 / 436
Massachusetts			
1	John W. Olver (D)	1.51	112 / 436
2	Richard E. Neal (D)	1.37	184 / 436
3	James P. McGovern (D)	1.31	209 / 436
4	Barney Frank (D)	1.06	334 / 436
5	Martin T. Meehan (D)	1.04	339 / 436
6	John F. Tierney (D)	1.17	289 / 436
7	Edward J. Markey (D)	1.10	317 / 436
8	Michael E. Capuano (D)	1.03	343 / 436
9	John Joseph Moakley (D)	1.04	340 / 436
10	William D. Delahunt (D)	1.21	263 / 436

Congressional District Rankings by Social Security (OASI) Rate of Return for Double-Earner Couples Born in 1965

District	Representative	Annual Rate of Return From Social Security	Ranking From Highest Return to Lowest Return
Michigan			
1	Bart T. Stupak (D)	1.60%	70 / 436
2	Peter Hoekstra (R)	1.46	144 / 436
3	Vernon J. Ehlers (R)	1.30	213 / 436
4	Dave Camp (R)	1.52	109 / 436
5	James A. Barcia (D)	1.26	239 / 436
6	Fred S. Upton (R)	1.42	164 / 436
7	Nick Smith (R)	1.31	208 / 436
8	Debbie Stabenow (D)	1.29	217 / 436
9	Dale E. Kildee (D)	0.92	374 / 436
10	David E. Bonior (D)	1.17	285 / 436
11	Joseph Knollenberg (R)	0.86	388 / 436
12	Sander M. Levin (D)	1.12	312 / 436
13	Lynn N. Rivers (D)	1.19	272 / 436
14	John Conyers, Jr. (D)	0.44	426 / 436
15	Carolyn C. Kilpatrick (D)	-0.01	436 / 436
16	John D. Dingell (D)	1.15	294 / 436
Minnesota			
1	Gil Gutknecht (R)	2.02	17 / 436
2	David Minge (D)	2.06	10 / 436
3	Jim Ramstad (R)	1.46	140 / 436
4	Bruce F. Vento (D)	1.59	79 / 436
5	Martin Olav Sabo (D)	1.52	108 / 436
6	William P. Luther (D)	1.67	54 / 436
7	Collin C. Peterson (D)	2.21	5 / 436
8	James L. Oberstar (D)	1.92	22 / 436
Mississippi			
1	Roger F. Wicker (R)	1.31	210 / 436
2	Bennie G. Thompson (D)	0.69	414 / 436
3	Charles Pickering, Jr. (R)	1.03	342 / 436
4	Ronnie Shows (D)	0.89	382 / 436
5	Gene Taylor (D)	1.08	326 / 436
Missouri			
1	William Clay (D)	0.91	375 / 436
2	James M. Talent (R)	1.08	325 / 436
3	Richard A. Gephardt (D)	1.36	190 / 436
4	Ike Skelton (D)	1.65	60 / 436
5	Karen McCarthy (D)	1.23	254 / 436
6	Pat Danner (D)	1.55	95 / 436
7	Roy Blunt (R)	1.82	35 / 436
8	Jo Ann Emerson (R)	1.70	45 / 436
9	Kenny C. Hulshof (R)	1.69	47 / 436
Montana			
At-large	Rick Hill (R)	2.25	3 / 436

■ Table 2.9 ■

Congressional District Rankings by Social Security (OASI) Rate of Return for Double-Earner Couples Born in 1965

District	Representative	Annual Rate of Return From Social Security	Ranking From Highest Return to Lowest Return
Nebraska			
1	Doug Bereuter (R)	2.06%	11 / 436
2	Lee Terry (R)	1.55	98 / 436
3	Bill Barrett (R)	2.17	6 / 436
Nevada			
1	Shelley Berkley (D)	1.14	298 / 436
2	James A. Gibbons (R)	1.21	265 / 436
New Hampshire			
1	John E. Sununu (R)	1.48	127 / 436
2	Charles F. Bass (R)	1.50	116 / 436
New Jersey			
1	Robert E. Andrews (D)	1.10	316 / 436
2	Frank A. LoBiondo (R)	1.12	309 / 436
3	Jim Saxton (R)	1.03	346 / 436
4	Christopher H. Smith (R)	1.05	338 / 436
5	Marge Roukema (R)	0.91	376 / 436
6	Frank Pallone, Jr. (D)	1.06	335 / 436
7	Bob Franks (R)	0.87	387 / 436
8	William Pascrell, Jr. (D)	0.85	391 / 436
9	Steven R. Rothman (D)	0.87	384 / 436
10	Donald M. Payne (D)	0.61	419 / 436
11	Rodney P. Frelinghuysen (R)	0.91	377 / 436
12	Rush D. Holt (D)	0.90	378 / 436
13	Robert Menendez (D)	0.98	363 / 436
New Mexico			
1	Heather Wilson (R)	1.66	59 / 436
2	Joe Skeen (R)	1.86	27 / 436
3	Tom Udall (D)	1.64	62 / 436
New York			
1	Michael P. Forbes (D)	1.01	352 / 436
2	Rick A. Lazio (R)	0.99	362 / 436
3	Peter T. King (R)	0.85	389 / 436
4	Carolyn McCarthy (D)	0.84	392 / 436
5	Gary L. Ackerman (D)	0.72	410 / 436
6	Gregory M. Meeks (D)	0.61	418 / 436
7 *	Joseph Crowley (D)	0.83	396 / 436
8	Jerrold L. Nadler (D)	0.18	431 / 436
9 *	Anthony D. Weiner (D)	0.70	412 / 436
10 *	Edolphus Towns (D)	0.10	434 / 436
11 *	Major R. Owens (D)	0.19	430 / 436
12 *	Nydia M. Velazquez (D)	1.11	315 / 436
13	Vito Fossella (R)	0.74	406 / 436
14 *	Carolyn B. Maloney (D)	0.07	435 / 436

■ Table 2.9 ■

Congressional District Rankings by Social Security (OASI) Rate of Return for Double-Earner Couples Born in 1965

District	Representative	Annual Rate of Return From Social Security	Ranking From Highest Return to Lowest Return
New York			
15	Charles B. Rangel (D)	0.25%	429 / 436
16	Jose E. Serrano (D)	0.50	424 / 436
17	Eliot L. Engel (D)	0.58	421 / 436
18	Nita M. Lowey (D)	0.61	417 / 436
19	Sue W. Kelly (R)	0.72	409 / 436
20	Benjamin A. Gilman (R)	0.83	394 / 436
21	Michael R. McNulty (D)	1.19	268 / 436
22	John E. Sweeney (R)	1.21	262 / 436
23	Sherwood L. Boehlert (R)	1.44	152 / 436
24	John M. McHugh (R)	1.35	196 / 436
25	James T. Walsh (R)	1.27	235 / 436
26	Maurice D. Hinchey (D)	1.31	211 / 436
27	Thomas M. Reynolds (R)	1.22	255 / 436
28	Louise McIntosh Slaughter (D)	0.99	361 / 436
29	John J. LaFalce (D)	1.27	231 / 436
30	Jack Quinn (R)	1.18	277 / 436
31	Amo Houghton, Jr. (R)	1.46	137 / 436
North Carolina			
1 *	Eva M. Clayton (D)	1.18	280 / 436
2 *	Bob Etheridge (D)	1.32	205 / 436
3 *	Walter B. Jones, Jr. (R)	1.36	188 / 436
4 *	David E. Price (D)	1.17	283 / 436
5 *	Richard M. Burr (R)	1.43	157 / 436
6 *	Howard Coble (R)	1.38	180 / 436
7 *	Mike McIntyre (D)	1.01	356 / 436
8 *	Robin Hayes (R)	1.33	200 / 436
9 *	Sue Myrick (R)	1.15	296 / 436
10 *	Cass Ballenger (R)	1.45	150 / 436
11 *	Charles H. Taylor (R)	1.57	81 / 436
12 *	Melvin Watt (D)	1.24	250 / 436
North Dakota			
At-large	Earl Pomeroy (D)	2.39%	1 / 436
Ohio			
1	Steven J. Chabot (R)	1.17	284 / 436
2	Rob Portman (R)	1.12	311 / 436
3	Tony P. Hall (D)	1.14	299 / 436
4	Michael G. Oxley (R)	1.45	149 / 436
5	Paul E. Gillmor (R)	1.48	125 / 436
6	Ted Strickland (D)	1.46	138 / 436
7	David L. Hobson (R)	1.38	176 / 436
8	John A. Boehner (R)	1.46	141 / 436
9	Marcy Kaptur (D)	1.23	253 / 436
10	Dennis J. Kucinich (D)	1.18	276 / 436
11	Stephanie Tubbs Jones (D)	0.61	416 / 436

Congressional District Rankings by Social Security (OASI)
Rate of Return for Double-Earner Couples Born in 1965

District	Representative	Annual Rate of Return From Social Security	Ranking From Highest Return to Lowest Return
Ohio			
12	John R. Kasich (R)	1.13%	302 / 436
13	Sherrod Brown (D)	1.28	227 / 436
14	Thomas C. Sawyer (D)	1.27	234 / 436
15	Deborah Pryce (R)	1.36	191 / 436
16	Ralph Regula (R)	1.43	159 / 436
17	James A. Traficant, Jr. (D)	1.29	221 / 436
18	Robert W. Ney (R)	1.53	105 / 436
19	Steven C. LaTourette (R)	1.19	271 / 436
Oklahoma			
1	Steve Largent (R)	1.26	241 / 436
2	Tom A. Coburn (R)	1.60	73 / 436
3	Wes Watkins (R)	1.64	63 / 436
4	J.C. Watts, Jr. (R)	1.44	154 / 436
5	Ernest J. Istook, Jr. (R)	1.32	203 / 436
6	Frank D. Lucas (R)	1.59	77 / 436
Oregon			
1	David Wu (D)	1.46	142 / 436
2	Greg Walden (R)	1.87	26 / 436
3	Earl Blumenauer (D)	1.66	56 / 436
4	Peter A. DeFazio (D)	1.85	28 / 436
5	Darlene Hooley (D)	1.75	38 / 436
Pennsylvania			
1	Robert A. Brady (D)	0.70	413 / 436
2	Chaka Fattah (D)	0.58	420 / 436
3	Robert A. Borski (D)	1.13	305 / 436
4	Ron Klink (D)	1.35	193 / 436
5	John E. Peterson (R)	1.69	48 / 436
6	Tim Holden (D)	1.43	160 / 436
7	Curt Weldon (R)	1.00	359 / 436
8	James C. Greenwood (R)	1.11	314 / 436
9	Bud Shuster (R)	1.56	84 / 436
10	Don Sherwood (R)	1.51	113 / 436
11	Paul E. Kanjorski (D)	1.50	119 / 436
12	John P. Murtha (D)	1.51	115 / 436
13	Joseph M. Hoeffel III (D)	0.90	379 / 436
14	William J. Coyne (D)	0.98	365 / 436
15	Patrick J. Toomey (R)	1.33	197 / 436
16	Joseph R. Pitts (R)	1.24	249 / 436
17	George W. Gekas (R)	1.39	169 / 436
18	Michael F. Doyle (D)	1.14	300 / 436
19	William F. Goodling (R)	1.48	129 / 436
20	Frank Mascara (D)	1.17	281 / 436
21	Philip S. English (R)	1.50	121 / 436

■ Table 2.9

Congressional District Rankings by Social Security (OASI) Rate of Return for Double-Earner Couples Born in 1965

District	Representative	Annual Rate of Return From Social Security	Ranking From Highest Return to Lowest Return
Rhode Island			
1	Patrick J. Kennedy (D)	1.35%	194 / 436
2	Robert Weygand (D)	1.38	179 / 436
South Carolina			
1	Marshall Sanford (R)	1.02	349 / 436
2	Floyd Spence (R)	1.01	353 / 436
3	Lindsey O. Graham (R)	1.25	245 / 436
4	Jim DeMint (R)	1.13	303 / 436
5	John M. Spratt, Jr. (D)	1.12	308 / 436
6	James E. Clyburn (D)	0.89	380 / 436
South Dakota			
At-large	John R. Thune (R)	2.33	2 / 436
Tennessee			
1	William L. Jenkins (R)	1.48	131 / 436
2	John J. Duncan, Jr. (R)	1.29	215 / 436
3	Zachary P. Wamp (R)	1.22	259 / 436
4	Van Hilleary (R)	1.56	82 / 436
5	Bob Clement (D)	1.05	336 / 436
6	Bart Gordon (D)	1.33	201 / 436
7	Ed Bryant (R)	1.07	330 / 436
8	John S. Tanner (D)	1.37	183 / 436
9	Harold E. Ford, Jr. (D)	0.79	400 / 436
Texas			
1	Max Sandlin (D)	1.55	96 / 436
2	Jim Turner (D)	1.42	162 / 436
3	Sam Johnson (R)	1.18	273 / 436
4	Ralph M. Hall (D)	1.50	118 / 436
5	Pete Sessions (R)	1.37	185 / 436
6	Joe L. Barton (R)	1.25	244 / 436
7	Bill Archer (R)	1.00	360 / 436
8	Kevin Brady (R)	1.26	240 / 436
9	Nicholas V. Lampson (D)	1.18	278 / 436
10	Lloyd Doggett (D)	1.37	181 / 436
11	Chet Edwards (D)	1.41	167 / 436
12	Kay Granger (R)	1.46	143 / 436
13	William M. Thornberry (R)	1.71	42 / 436
14	Ron Paul (R)	1.63	65 / 436
15	Ruben Hinojosa (D)	1.72	41 / 436
16	Silvestre Reyes (D)	1.51	114 / 436
17	Charles W. Stenholm (D)	1.68	51 / 436
18	Sheila Jackson-Lee (D)	1.09	318 / 436
19	Larry Combest (R)	1.55	88 / 436
20	Charles A. Gonzalez (D)	1.60	72 / 436
21	Lamar S. Smith (R)	1.39	170 / 436

Congressional District Rankings by Social Security (OASI)
Rate of Return for Double-Earner Couples Born in 1965

District	Representative	Annual Rate of Return From Social Security	Ranking From Highest Return to Lowest Return
Texas			
22	Tom DeLay (R)	1.22%	258 / 436
23	Henry Bonilla (R)	1.47	132 / 436
24	Martin Frost (D)	1.45	147 / 436
25	Kenneth E. Bentsen, Jr. (D)	1.16	290 / 436
26	Richard K. Armey (R)	1.02	348 / 436
27	Solomon P. Ortiz (D)	1.55	93 / 436
28	Ciro D. Rodriguez (D)	1.69	46 / 436
29	Gene Green (D)	1.56	87 / 436
30	Eddie Bernice Johnson (D)	1.22	260 / 436
Utah			
1	James V. Hansen (R)	2.05	12 / 436
2	Merrill Cook (R)	1.87	25 / 436
3	Christopher Cannon (R)	2.24	4 / 436
Vermont			
At-large	Bernard Sanders (I)	1.92	23 / 436
Virginia			
1 *	Herbert H. Bateman (R)	1.23	252 / 436
2 *	Owen B. Pickett (D)	.96	368 / 436
3 *	Robert C. Scott (D)	1.01	354 / 436
4 *	Norman Sisisky (D)	1.19	269 / 436
5	Virgil H. Goode, Jr. (D)	1.59	75 / 436
6	Robert W. Goodlatte (R)	1.55	91 / 436
7 *	Thomas J. Bliley, Jr. (R)	1.18	274 / 436
8	James P. Moran (D)	.78	402 / 436
9	Rick Boucher (D)	1.68	52 / 436
10	Frank R. Wolf (R)	1.08	324 / 436
11	Thomas M. Davis III (R)	1.01	357 / 436
Washington			
1	Jay Inslee (D)	1.44	153 / 436
2	Jack Metcalf (R)	1.63	64 / 436
3	Brian Baird (D)	1.68	49 / 436
4	Richard Hastings (R)	1.83	31 / 436
5	George R. Nethercutt, Jr. (R)	1.84	30 / 436
6	Norman D. Dicks (D)	1.54	100 / 436
7	Jim McDermott (D)	1.41	166 / 436
8	Jennifer Dunn (R)	1.43	158 / 436
9	Adam Smith (D)	1.54	99 / 436
West Virginia			
1	Alan B. Mollohan (D)	1.29	216 / 436
2	Robert E. Wise, Jr. (D)	1.24	251 / 436
3	Nick J. Rahall II (D)	1.07	331 / 436

■ Table 2.9 ■

Congressional District Rankings by Social Security (OASI)
Rate of Return for Double-Earner Couples Born in 1965

District	Representative	Annual Rate of Return From Social Security	Ranking From Highest Return to Lowest Return
Wisconsin			
1	Paul Ryan (R)	1.70%	44 / 436
2	Tammy Baldwin (D)	1.85	29 / 436
3	Ron Kind (D)	2.04	15 / 436
4	Gerald D. Kleczka (D)	1.67	55 / 436
5	Thomas M. Barrett (D)	1.29	218 / 436
6	Thomas E. Petri (R)	1.89	24 / 436
7	David R. Obey (D)	1.95	20 / 436
8	Mark Green (R)	1.80	37 / 436
9	F. James Sensenbrenner, Jr. (R)	1.61	69 / 436
Wyoming			
At-large	Barbara Cubin (R)	2.04	14 / 436

Note: Rates of return exclude both Disability Insurance benefits and taxes, but include all Old-Age and Survivors Insurance (OASI) benefits and taxes (including pre-retirement Survivors Insurance). All values include both the portion of the OASI tax paid directly by workers and the portion paid by the employer on a worker's behalf. All rates of return are net of inflation. Calculations are based on life expectancies and average earnings for each district. Districts marked * have been redistricted between the 105th and 106th Congresses.

SUMMARY OF FINDINGS

For each congressional district, the following charts and maps show the annual real rate of return from Social Security (OASI) for a two-income married couple with two children. Computations assume that both spouses were born in 1965 and earn wages equal to the average for their respective gender in their congressional district. For the purposes of comparison, the ranking of the rate of return is shown in each table, and every map has shading that indicates the return received in each district. Information is also provided on the dollar difference between the value of the benefits that such a couple can actually expect to receive from the current system and the amount that this couple could have accumulated in a personal account, had they been allowed to invest their payroll taxes.[1]

The calculations reported on here were made on the basis of projections provided by the Social Security Administration's own *1998 Report of the Board of Trustees of the Federal Old-Age and Survivors Insurance and Disability Insurance Trust Funds*. Additional data were drawn from the U.S. Bureau of the Census 1990 Decennial Census *STF3A* tape and from the Centers for Disease Control's *Compressed Mortality File*.

---

1. The personal retirement account would consist of equal parts long-term U.S. Treasury bonds and large company stocks.

ALABAMA

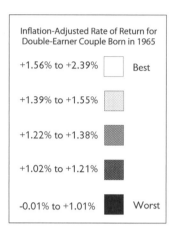

Inflation-Adjusted Rate of Return for
Double-Earner Couple Born in 1965

+1.56% to +2.39% Best

+1.39% to +1.55%

+1.22% to +1.38%

+1.02% to +1.21%

-0.01% to +1.01% Worst

Lifetime Dollar Losses Under Social Security (OASI) Compared with Personal Retirement Accounts for Double-Earner Couples Born in 1965

District	Member of Congress	Loss Under Social Security (3)-(2)	Ranking from Lowest Loss to Highest Loss	Social Security Taxes Paid (1)	Social Security Benefits (2)	Personal Retirement Accounts (3)
Senate						
	Richard C. Shelby (R)					
	Jeff Sessions (R)					
Statewide		$ 480,176	30	$ 310,675	$ 413,076	$ 893,253
House of Representatives						
1	Sonny Callahan (R)	485,701	200 / 436	308,576	401,654	887,355
2	Terry Everett (R)	465,876	172	303,603	407,179	873,055
3	Bob Riley (R)	406,556	95	274,280	382,177	788,733
4	Robert Aderholt (R)	402,070	89	280,895	405,685	807,756
5	Robert E. Cramer, Jr. (D)	536,027	265	348,018	464,751	1,000,778
6	Spencer Bachus (R)	640,405	351	406,595	528,820	1,169,225
7	Earl F. Hilliard (D)	412,517	106	250,949	309,123	721,640

Note: Column (1) shows the total amount of Old-Age and Survivors Insurance (OASI) taxes paid during the individual's working life. Column (2) shows the total value of Old-Age and Survivors Insurance benefits collected by the worker and his or her spouse following retirement. Column (3) shows the amount accumulated in a Personal Retirement Account had the worker been able to place his or her OASI taxes in a Personal Retirement Account. The accumulation in this personal account has been reduced by the cost of purchasing life insurance coverage equivalent to the pre-retirement Survivors Insurance portion of Social Security. All amounts exclude both Disability Insurance benefits and taxes. All values include both the portion of the OASI tax paid directly by workers and the portion paid by the employer on a worker's behalf. The losses from not participating in a Personal Retirement Account (columns (3)-(2)) are for illustrative purposes only and do not reflect any specific plan for reforming Social Security. All amounts are expressed in inflation-adjusted dollars for the year 2000. Calculations are based on life expectancies and average earnings for each district. Because of non-linearity in the benefit function, amounts for each district may not sum to the state average.

Inflation-Adjusted Rate of Return from Social Security (OASI) by Birth Year

District	Member of Congress	Single Males			Single Females			Double-Earner Couples		
		1955	1965	1975	1955	1965	1975	1955	1965	1975
Senate										
	Richard C. Shelby (R)									
	Jeff Sessions (R)									
Statewide		0.35%	-0.12%	-0.65%	2.40%	2.22%	2.02%	1.40%	1.09%	0.73%
House of Representatives										
1	Sonny Callahan (R)	0.29	-0.20	-0.76	2.34	2.15	1.96	1.34	1.01	0.64
2	Terry Everett (R)	0.38	-0.17	-0.79	2.47	2.29	2.10	1.45	1.12	0.73
3	Bob Riley (R)	0.61	0.13	-0.42	2.52	2.33	2.14	1.59	1.26	0.90
4	Robert Aderholt (R)	0.75	0.37	-0.07	2.53	2.36	2.17	1.66	1.38	1.07
5	Robert E. Cramer, Jr. (D)	0.32	-0.05	-0.48	2.34	2.17	1.99	1.35	1.09	0.78
6	Spencer Bachus (R)	0.09	-0.23	-0.60	2.29	2.12	1.93	1.22	0.98	0.69
7	Earl F. Hilliard (D)	0.06	-0.75	-1.64	2.43	2.20	1.98	1.29	0.82	0.33

Note: Rates of return exclude both Disability Insurance benefits and taxes, but include all Old-Age and Survivors Insurance (OASI) benefits and taxes (including pre-retirement Survivors Insurance). All values include both the portion of the OASI tax paid directly by workers and the portion paid by the employer on a worker's behalf. All rates of return are net of inflation. Calculations are based on life expectancies and average earnings for each district. Because of non-linearity in the benefit function, amounts for each district may not sum to the state average.

ALASKA

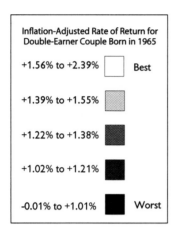

Inflation-Adjusted Rate of Return for
Double-Earner Couple Born in 1965

+1.56% to +2.39% [ ] Best

+1.39% to +1.55% [ ]

+1.22% to +1.38% [ ]

+1.02% to +1.21% [ ]

-0.01% to +1.01% [ ] Worst

Lifetime Dollar Losses Under Social Security (OASI) Compared with Personal Retirement Accounts for Double-Earner Couples Born in 1965

District	Member of Congress	Loss Under Social Security (3)-(2)	Ranking from Lowest Loss to Highest Loss	Social Security Taxes Paid (1)	Social Security Benefits (2)	Personal Retirement Accounts (3)
Senate						
	Ted Stevens (R)					
	Frank H. Murkowski (R)					
Statewide		$ 585,812	43	$ 430,401	$ 651,870	$ 1,237,682
House of Representatives						
At large	Don Young (R)	585,812	313 / 436	430,401	651,870	1,237,682

Note: Column (1) shows the total amount of Old-Age and Survivors Insurance (OASI) taxes paid during the individual's working life. Column (2) shows the total value of Old-Age and Survivors Insurance benefits collected by the worker and his or her spouse following retirement. Column (3) shows the amount accumulated in a Personal Retirement Account had the worker been able to place his or her OASI taxes in a Personal Retirement Account. The accumulation in this personal account has been reduced by the cost of purchasing life insurance coverage equivalent to the pre-retirement Survivors Insurance portion of Social Security. All amounts exclude both Disability Insurance benefits and taxes. All values include both the portion of the OASI tax paid directly by workers and the portion paid by the employer on a worker's behalf. The losses from not participating in a Personal Retirement Account (columns (3)-(2)) are for illustrative purposes only and do not reflect any specific plan for reforming Social Security. All amounts are expressed in inflation-adjusted dollars for the year 2000. Calculations are based on life expectancies and average earnings for each district.

Inflation-Adjusted Rate of Return from Social Security (OASI) by Birth Year

District	Member of Congress	Single Males			Single Females			Double-Earner Couples		
		1955	1965	1975	1955	1965	1975	1955	1965	1975
Senate										
	Ted Stevens (R)									
	Frank H. Murkowski (R)									
Statewide		0.95 %	0.70 %	0.32 %	2.45 %	2.27 %	2.07 %	1.70 %	1.47 %	1.17 %
House of Representatives										
At large	Don Young (R)	0.95	0.70	0.32	2.45	2.27	2.07	1.70	1.47	1.17

Note: Rates of return exclude both Disability Insurance benefits and taxes, but include all Old-Age and Survivors Insurance (OASI) benefits and taxes (including pre-retirement Survivors Insurance). All values include both the portion of the OASI tax paid directly by workers and the portion paid by the employer on a worker's behalf. All rates of return are net of inflation. Calculations are based on life expectancies and average earnings for each district.

ARIZONA

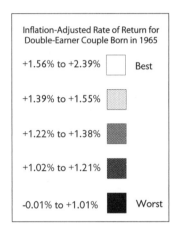

Inflation-Adjusted Rate of Return for
Double-Earner Couple Born in 1965

+1.56% to +2.39%	☐	Best
+1.39% to +1.55%		
+1.22% to +1.38%		
+1.02% to +1.21%		
-0.01% to +1.01%		Worst

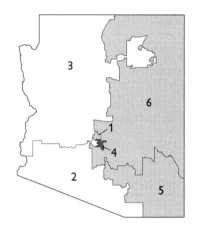

Lifetime Dollar Losses Under Social Security (OASI) Compared with Personal Retirement Accounts for Double-Earner Couples Born in 1965

District	Member of Congress	Loss Under Social Security (3)-(2)	Ranking from Lowest Loss to Highest Loss	Social Security Taxes Paid (1)	Social Security Benefits (2)	Personal Retirement Accounts (3)
Senate						
	John McCain (R)					
	Jon L. Kyl (R)					
Statewide		$ 455,853	23	$ 336,946	$ 512,935	$ 968,788
House of Representatives						
1	Matt Salmon (R)	489,930	209 / 436	367,614	567,197	1,057,128
2	Ed Pastor (D)	321,837	18	249,359	395,231	717,068
3	Bob Stump (R)	410,396	102	320,020	509,869	920,265
4	John B. Shadegg (R)	618,513	335	433,859	629,113	1,247,626
5	Jim Kolbe (R)	441,940	142	329,680	506,103	948,043
6	J. D. Hayworth (R)	444,815	147	319,465	473,854	918,669

Note: Column (1) shows the total amount of Old-Age and Survivors Insurance (OASI) taxes paid during the individual's working life. Column (2) shows the total value of Old-Age and Survivors Insurance benefits collected by the worker and his or her spouse following retirement. Column (3) shows the amount accumulated in a Personal Retirement Account had the worker been able to place his or her OASI taxes in a Personal Retirement Account. The accumulation in this personal account has been reduced by the cost of purchasing life insurance coverage equivalent to the pre-retirement Survivors Insurance portion of Social Security. All amounts exclude both Disability Insurance benefits and taxes. All values include both the portion of the OASI tax paid directly by workers and the portion paid by the employer on a worker's behalf. The losses from not participating in a Personal Retirement Account (columns (3)-(2)) are for illustrative purposes only and do not reflect any specific plan for reforming Social Security. All amounts are expressed in inflation-adjusted dollars for the year 2000. Calculations are based on life expectancies and average earnings for each district. Because of non-linearity in the benefit function, amounts for each district may not sum to the state average.

Inflation-Adjusted Rate of Return from Social Security (OASI) by Birth Year

District	Member of Congress	Single Males			Single Females			Double-Earner Couples		
		1955	1965	1975	1955	1965	1975	1955	1965	1975
Senate										
	John McCain (R)									
	Jon L. Kyl (R)									
Statewide		0.91 %	0.59 %	0.17 %	2.60 %	2.45 %	2.28 %	1.76 %	1.53 %	1.23 %
House of Representatives										
1	Matt Salmon (R)	0.91	0.67	0.34	2.58	2.43	2.27	1.75	1.55	1.30
2	Ed Pastor (D)	1.18	0.73	0.15	2.80	2.64	2.47	2.00	1.70	1.34
3	Bob Stump (R)	1.07	0.78	0.41	2.69	2.55	2.39	1.89	1.68	1.40
4	John B. Shadegg (R)	0.60	0.36	0.04	2.44	2.29	2.13	1.53	1.33	1.08
5	Jim Kolbe (R)	0.94	0.56	0.10	2.66	2.51	2.35	1.81	1.55	1.24
6	J. D. Hayworth (R)	0.87	0.49	0.03	2.55	2.39	2.21	1.72	1.45	1.13

Note: Rates of return exclude both Disability Insurance benefits and taxes, but include all Old-Age and Survivors Insurance (OASI) benefits and taxes (including pre-retirement Survivors Insurance). All values include both the portion of the OASI tax paid directly by workers and the portion paid by the employer on a worker's behalf. All rates of return are net of inflation. Calculations are based on life expectancies and average earnings for each district. Because of non-linearity in the benefit function, amounts for each district may not sum to the state average.

ARKANSAS

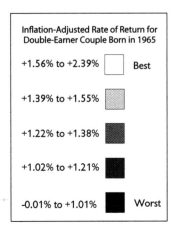

Inflation-Adjusted Rate of Return for
Double-Earner Couple Born in 1965

+1.56% to +2.39%   Best

+1.39% to +1.55%

+1.22% to +1.38%

+1.02% to +1.21%

-0.01% to +1.01%   Worst

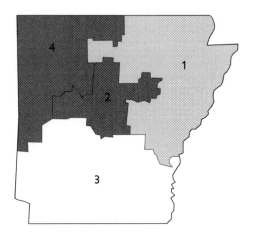

Lifetime Dollar Losses Under Social Security (OASI) Compared with Personal Retirement Accounts for Double-Earner Couples Born in 1965

District	Member of Congress	Loss Under Social Security (3)-(2)	Ranking from Lowest Loss to Highest Loss	Social Security Taxes Paid (1)	Social Security Benefits (2)	Personal Retirement Accounts (3)
Senate						
	Blanche L. Lincoln (D)					
	Tim Hutchinson (R)					
Statewide		$ 388,238	11	$ 278,402	$ 412,223	$ 800,460
House of Representatives						
1	Marion Berry (D)	356,482	43 / 436	255,166	377,284	733,767
2	Vic Snyder (D)	462,619	169	316,239	446,774	909,393
3	Asa Hutchinson (R)	353,578	40	272,941	431,306	784,884
4	Jay Dickey (R)	384,586	62	268,333	387,046	771,632

Note: Column (1) shows the total amount of Old-Age and Survivors Insurance (OASI) taxes paid during the individual's working life. Column (2) shows the total value of Old-Age and Survivors Insurance benefits collected by the worker and his or her spouse following retirement. Column (3) shows the amount accumulated in a Personal Retirement Account had the worker been able to place his or her OASI taxes in a Personal Retirement Account. The accumulation in this personal account has been reduced by the cost of purchasing life insurance coverage equivalent to the pre-retirement Survivors Insurance portion of Social Security. All amounts exclude both Disability Insurance benefits and taxes. All values include both the portion of the OASI tax paid directly by workers and the portion paid by the employer on a worker's behalf. The losses from not participating in a Personal Retirement Account (columns (3)-(2)) are for illustrative purposes only and do not reflect any specific plan for reforming Social Security. All amounts are expressed in inflation-adjusted dollars for the year 2000. Calculations are based on life expectancies and average earnings for each district. Because of non-linearity in the benefit function, amounts for each district may not sum to the state average.

Inflation-Adjusted Rate of Return from Social Security (OASI) by Birth Year

District	Member of Congress	Single Males			Single Females			Double-Earner Couples		
		1955	1965	1975	1955	1965	1975	1955	1965	1975
Senate										
	Blanche L. Lincoln (D)									
	Tim Hutchinson (R)									
Statewide		0.83 %	0.44 %	-0.01 %	2.62 %	2.46 %	2.27 %	1.74 %	1.47 %	1.15 %
House of Representatives										
1	Marion Berry (D)	0.85	0.41	-0.08	2.65	2.48	2.30	1.77	1.47	1.14
2	Vic Snyder (D)	0.55	0.16	-0.30	2.52	2.36	2.17	1.56	1.29	0.97
3	Asa Hutchinson (R)	1.07	0.78	0.43	2.71	2.56	2.39	1.90	1.68	1.41
4	Jay Dickey (R)	0.72	0.26	-0.28	2.61	2.44	2.25	1.69	1.38	1.03

Note: Rates of return exclude both Disability Insurance benefits and taxes, but include all Old-Age and Survivors Insurance (OASI) benefits and taxes (including pre-retirement Survivors Insurance). All values include both the portion of the OASI tax paid directly by workers and the portion paid by the employer on a worker's behalf. All rates of return are net of inflation. Calculations are based on life expectancies and average earnings for each district. Because of non-linearity in the benefit function, amounts for each district may not sum to the state average.

CALIFORNIA

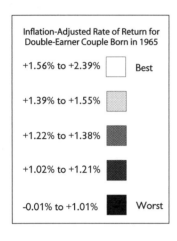

Inflation-Adjusted Rate of Return for
Double-Earner Couple Born in 1965

+1.56% to +2.39%   Best

+1.39% to +1.55%

+1.22% to +1.38%

+1.02% to +1.21%

-0.01% to +1.01%   Worst

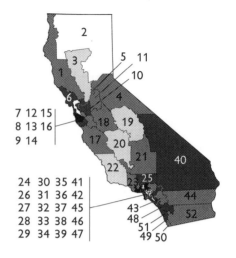

Lifetime Dollar Losses Under Social Security (OASI) Compared with Personal Retirement Accounts for Double-Earner Couples Born in 1965

District	Member of Congress	Loss Under Social Security (3)-(2)	Ranking from Lowest Loss to Highest Loss	Social Security Taxes Paid (1)	Social Security Benefits (2)	Personal Retirement Accounts (3)
Senate						
	Dianne Feinstein (D)					
	Barbara Boxer (D)					
Statewide		$ 624,692	46	$ 415,664	$ 570,424	$ 1,195,116
House of Representatives						
1	Mike Thompson (D)	510,999	236 / 436	357,512	517,081	1,028,080
2	Wally Herger (R)	420,916	117	313,184	479,692	900,608
3	Doug Ose (R)	474,441	184	347,138	523,805	998,247
4	John T. Doolittle (R)	601,692	323	411,565	581,826	1,183,518
5	Robert T. Matsui (D)	559,662	289	379,804	532,522	1,092,184
6	Lynn C. Woolsey (D)	753,217	397	491,983	662,273	1,415,489
7	George Miller (D)	622,082	337	414,789	570,705	1,192,787
8	Nancy Pelosi (D)	700,208	381	430,231	536,984	1,237,192
9	Barbara Lee (D)	650,918	357	402,876	507,612	1,158,529
10	Ellen O. Tauscher (D)	859,182	417	552,685	751,539	1,610,721
11	Richard W. Pombo (R)	526,737	255	364,579	521,664	1,048,401
12	Tom Lantos (D)	728,541	390	483,175	661,082	1,389,623
13	Fortney Stark (D)	650,079	355	445,456	630,895	1,280,975
14	Anna G. Eshoo (D)	877,030	418	551,193	728,608	1,605,638
15	Tom Campbell (R)	798,905	409	528,868	731,629	1,530,533
16	Zoe Lofgren (D)	579,778	308	398,950	567,463	1,147,240
17	Sam Farr (D)	508,702	231	349,511	496,369	1,005,071
18	Gary Condit (D)	486,472	204	338,681	487,456	973,928
19	George P. Radanovich (R)	516,907	245	367,313	539,356	1,056,263
20	Calvin M. Dooley (D)	333,813	26	239,224	354,112	687,925
21	William M. Thomas (R)	526,993	256	366,702	527,514	1,054,507
22	Lois Capps (D)	508,738	232	363,822	537,487	1,046,225
23	Elton Gallegly (R)	611,441	329	426,270	614,364	1,225,804
24	Brad Sherman (D)	924,372	427	568,902	742,796	1,667,168
25	Howard P. McKeon (R)	758,621	398	497,233	672,394	1,431,015
26	Howard L. Berman (D)	484,942	199	342,268	499,299	984,241

Lifetime Dollar Losses Under Social Security Compared with Personal Retirement Accounts for Double-Earner Couples Born in 1965

District	Member of Congress	Loss Under Social Security (3)-(2)	Ranking from Lowest Loss to Highest Loss	Social Security Taxes Paid (1)	Social Security Benefits (2)	Personal Retirement Accounts (3)
27	James E. Rogan (R)	$ 807,869	410	$ 508,143	$ 656,265	$ 1,464,134
28	David Dreier (R)	692,901	377	471,283	662,342	1,355,243
29	Henry A. Waxman (D)	1,156,765	435	625,817	720,280	1,877,046
30	Xavier Becerra (D)	392,155	73	278,700	409,289	801,444
31	Matthew G. Martinez (D)	417,329	114	309,724	473,327	890,656
32	Julian C. Dixon (D)	639,097	347	389,343	480,518	1,119,615
33	Lucille Roybal-Allard (D)	303,417	10	224,782	342,978	646,395
34	Grace F. Napolitano (D)	491,152	213	355,793	531,983	1,023,135
35	Maxine Waters (D)	488,383	206	310,601	404,796	893,179
36	Steven T. Kuykendall (R)	896,694	422	558,071	732,753	1,629,447
37	Juanita Millender-McDonald (D)	474,993	187	310,115	416,790	891,783
38	Steve Horn (R)	628,692	341	417,020	570,512	1,199,203
39	Edward R. Royce (R)	658,206	361	458,179	659,357	1,317,563
40	Jerry Lewis (R)	561,333	291	377,940	525,488	1,086,821
41	Gary G. Miller (R)	685,766	375	457,680	630,361	1,316,126
42	Joe Baca (D)	540,795	270	375,625	539,369	1,080,165
43	Ken Calvert (R)	591,154	316	405,238	574,168	1,165,322
44	Mary Bono (R)	545,964	272	377,743	540,291	1,086,255
45	Dana Rohrabacher (R)	732,383	392	491,514	681,725	1,414,108
46	Loretta Sanchez (D)	422,312	119	314,233	481,313	903,624
47	Christopher Cox (R)	884,587	419	559,220	748,862	1,633,449
48	Ron Packard (R)	719,755	387	466,666	622,214	1,341,969
49	Brian P. Bilbray (R)	583,275	310	379,313	507,496	1,090,771
50	Bob Filner (D)	422,980	121	296,631	430,026	853,006
51	Randy Cunningham (R)	732,372	391	490,744	679,464	1,411,836
52	Duncan L. Hunter (R)	522,244	251	369,069	539,070	1,061,314

Note: Column (1) shows the total amount of Old-Age and Survivors Insurance (OASI) taxes paid during the individual's working life. Column (2) shows the total value of Old-Age and Survivors Insurance benefits collected by the worker and his or her spouse following retirement. Column (3) shows the amount accumulated in a Personal Retirement Account had the worker been able to place his or her OASI taxes in a Personal Retirement Account. The accumulation in this personal account has been reduced by the cost of purchasing life insurance coverage equivalent to the pre-retirement Survivors Insurance portion of Social Security. All amounts exclude both Disability Insurance benefits and taxes. All values include both the portion of the OASI tax paid directly by workers and the portion paid by the employer on a worker's behalf. The losses from not participating in a Personal Retirement Account (columns (3)-(2)) are for illustrative purposes only and do not reflect any specific plan for reforming Social Security. All amounts are expressed in inflation-adjusted dollars for the year 2000. Calculations are based on life expectancies and average earnings for each district. Because of non-linearity in the benefit function, amounts for each district may not sum to the state average.

Inflation-Adjusted Rate of Return from Social Security (OASI) by Birth Year

District	Member of Congress	Single Males			Single Females			Double-Earner Couples		
		1955	1965	1975	1955	1965	1975	1955	1965	1975
Senate										
	Dianne Feinstein (D)									
	Barbara Boxer (D)									
Statewide		0.49%	0.08%	-0.38%	2.36%	2.21%	2.03%	1.43%	1.16%	0.84%
House of Representatives										
1	Mike Thompson (D)	0.72	0.29	-0.20	2.51	2.37	2.20	1.63	1.35	1.03
2	Wally Herger (R)	1.01	0.65	0.24	2.59	2.45	2.29	1.80	1.56	1.27
3	Doug Ose (R)	0.91	0.61	0.23	2.51	2.37	2.21	1.72	1.49	1.22
4	John T. Doolittle (R)	0.57	0.20	-0.23	2.41	2.28	2.12	1.50	1.26	0.96
5	Robert T. Matsui (D)	0.60	0.22	-0.21	2.40	2.24	2.06	1.51	1.24	0.94
6	Lynn C. Woolsey (D)	0.34	-0.06	-0.47	2.32	2.17	2.00	1.35	1.08	0.79
7	George Miller (D)	0.45	0.11	-0.30	2.35	2.20	2.02	1.41	1.17	0.87
8	Nancy Pelosi (D)	0.17	-0.55	-1.18	2.29	2.09	1.90	1.26	0.83	0.45
9	Barbara Lee (D)	0.15	-0.50	-1.12	2.31	2.12	1.93	1.26	0.87	0.49
10	Ellen O. Tauscher (D)	0.33	0.14	-0.12	2.11	1.99	1.82	1.25	1.09	0.87
11	Richard W. Pombo (R)	0.70	0.35	-0.07	2.41	2.26	2.09	1.56	1.32	1.01
12	Tom Lantos (D)	0.38	0.07	-0.29	2.33	2.17	2.00	1.37	1.13	0.86
13	Fortney Stark (D)	0.54	0.32	-0.01	2.34	2.19	2.02	1.44	1.26	1.00
14	Anna G. Eshoo (D)	0.26	-0.06	-0.40	2.13	1.98	1.81	1.23	1.00	0.74
15	Tom Campbell (R)	0.41	0.18	-0.09	2.24	2.10	1.94	1.34	1.16	0.93
16	Zoe Lofgren (D)	0.64	0.33	-0.08	2.38	2.23	2.06	1.51	1.28	0.99
17	Sam Farr (D)	0.69	0.16	-0.45	2.51	2.36	2.20	1.62	1.29	0.93
18	Gary Condit (D)	0.83	0.44	-0.03	2.40	2.25	2.09	1.61	1.35	1.03
19	George P. Radanovich (R)	0.79	0.49	0.10	2.45	2.30	2.13	1.62	1.40	1.11
20	Calvin M. Dooley (D)	1.02	0.46	-0.27	2.63	2.48	2.30	1.83	1.48	1.06
21	William M. Thomas (R)	0.71	0.35	-0.09	2.43	2.29	2.13	1.58	1.33	1.03
22	Lois Capps (D)	0.80	0.41	-0.05	2.54	2.39	2.23	1.68	1.42	1.11
23	Elton Gallegly (R)	0.64	0.35	-0.02	2.40	2.27	2.11	1.53	1.32	1.04
24	Brad Sherman (D)	0.24	-0.08	-0.40	2.03	1.88	1.71	1.18	0.95	0.70
25	Howard P. McKeon (R)	0.33	0.02	-0.35	2.26	2.13	1.97	1.31	1.09	0.82
26	Howard L. Berman (D)	0.88	0.38	-0.15	2.53	2.36	2.18	1.71	1.39	1.04
27	James E. Rogan (R)	0.17	-0.30	-0.76	2.26	2.09	1.91	1.24	0.93	0.62
28	David Dreier (R)	0.46	0.25	-0.07	2.32	2.19	2.02	1.40	1.22	0.97
29	Henry A. Waxman (D)	-0.08	-0.72	-1.21	1.67	1.46	1.26	0.89	0.51	0.20
30	Xavier Becerra (D)	1.03	0.31	-0.43	2.68	2.49	2.30	1.87	1.44	1.00
31	Matthew G. Martinez (D)	1.03	0.65	0.15	2.60	2.44	2.26	1.82	1.55	1.21
32	Julian C. Dixon (D)	0.10	-0.61	-1.29	2.28	2.08	1.88	1.22	0.80	0.39
33	Lucille Roybal-Allard (D)	1.17	0.38	-0.49	2.86	2.70	2.52	2.03	1.59	1.12
34	Grace F. Napolitano (D)	0.86	0.57	0.14	2.49	2.34	2.17	1.68	1.46	1.15
35	Maxine Waters (D)	0.41	-0.30	-1.04	2.41	2.21	2.01	1.43	1.01	0.58
36	Steven T. Kuykendall (R)	0.24	-0.05	-0.39	2.07	1.92	1.75	1.19	0.98	0.72
37	Juanita Millender-McDonald (D)	0.55	-0.04	-0.71	2.40	2.22	2.03	1.49	1.12	0.71
38	Steve Horn (R)	0.47	0.00	-0.52	2.40	2.24	2.06	1.45	1.15	0.81
39	Edward R. Royce (R)	0.59	0.38	0.06	2.35	2.23	2.06	1.47	1.30	1.05
40	Jerry Lewis (R)	0.54	0.10	-0.42	2.41	2.27	2.11	1.49	1.21	0.88
41	Gary G. Miller (R)	0.43	0.13	-0.28	2.30	2.17	2.00	1.38	1.16	0.87
42	Joe Baca (D)	0.69	0.41	0.03	2.37	2.23	2.07	1.54	1.32	1.04
43	Ken Calvert (R)	0.59	0.28	-0.12	2.38	2.24	2.08	1.49	1.27	0.98
44	Mary Bono (R)	0.66	0.29	-0.16	2.44	2.30	2.13	1.56	1.31	1.00
45	Dana Rohrabacher (R)	0.44	0.16	-0.18	2.31	2.17	2.01	1.39	1.18	0.91
46	Loretta Sanchez (D)	1.07	0.61	0.10	2.62	2.48	2.31	1.85	1.56	1.22
47	Christopher Cox (R)	0.28	0.02	-0.28	2.11	1.97	1.81	1.23	1.04	0.80
48	Ron Packard (R)	0.29	-0.20	-0.74	2.34	2.21	2.05	1.34	1.05	0.71
49	Brian P. Bilbray (R)	0.45	-0.34	-1.12	2.51	2.34	2.16	1.51	1.08	0.66
50	Bob Filner (D)	0.84	0.23	-0.49	2.61	2.46	2.28	1.74	1.38	0.97
51	Randy Cunningham (R)	0.41	0.11	-0.24	2.33	2.20	2.04	1.38	1.17	0.91
52	Duncan L. Hunter (R)	0.75	0.41	0.00	2.47	2.33	2.17	1.62	1.38	1.09

Note: Rates of return exclude both Disability Insurance benefits and taxes, but include all Old-Age and Survivors Insurance (OASI) benefits and taxes (including pre-retirement Survivors Insurance). All values include both the portion of the OASI tax paid directly by workers and the portion paid by the employer on a worker's behalf. All rates of return are net of inflation. Calculations are based on life expectancies and average earnings for each district. Because of non-linearity in the benefit function, amounts for each district may not sum to the state average.

COLORADO

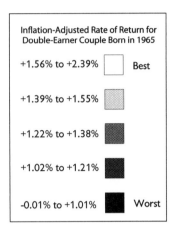

Inflation-Adjusted Rate of Return for
Double-Earner Couple Born in 1965

+1.56% to +2.39%   Best

+1.39% to +1.55%

+1.22% to +1.38%

+1.02% to +1.21%

-0.01% to +1.01%   Worst

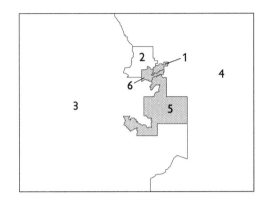

Lifetime Dollar Losses Under Social Security (OASI) Compared with Personal Retirement Accounts for Double-Earner Couples Born in 1965

District	Member of Congress	Loss Under Social Security (3)-(2)	Ranking from Lowest Loss to Highest Loss	Social Security Taxes Paid (1)	Social Security Benefits (2)	Personal Retirement Accounts (3)
Senate						
	Ben Nighthorse Campbell (R)					
	Wayne Allard (R)					
Statewide		$ 452,104	22	$ 353,019	$ 562,897	$ 1,015,001
House of Representatives						
1	Diana DeGette (D)	472,236	179 / 436	344,828	519,369	991,605
2	Mark Udall (D)	461,964	167	370,581	603,696	1,065,660
3	Scott McInnis (R)	340,432	30	296,780	513,004	853,436
4	Bob Schaffer (R)	349,002	36	308,009	536,723	885,725
5	Joel Hefley (R)	513,187	238	371,016	553,726	1,066,913
6	Thomas G. Tancredo (R)	569,345	300	425,138	653,201	1,222,547

Note: Column (1) shows the total amount of Old-Age and Survivors Insurance (OASI) taxes paid during the individual's working life. Column (2) shows the total value of Old-Age and Survivors Insurance benefits collected by the worker and his or her spouse following retirement. Column (3) shows the amount accumulated in a Personal Retirement Account had the worker been able to place his or her OASI taxes in a Personal Retirement Account. The accumulation in this personal account has been reduced by the cost of purchasing life insurance coverage equivalent to the pre-retirement Survivors Insurance portion of Social Security. All amounts exclude both Disability Insurance benefits and taxes. All values include both the portion of the OASI tax paid directly by workers and the portion paid by the employer on a worker's behalf. The losses from not participating in a Personal Retirement Account (columns (3)-(2)) are for illustrative purposes only and do not reflect any specific plan for reforming Social Security. All amounts are expressed in inflation-adjusted dollars for the year 2000. Calculations are based on life expectancies and average earnings for each district. Because of non-linearity in the benefit function, amounts for each district may not sum to the state average.

Inflation-Adjusted Rate of Return from Social Security (OASI) by Birth Year

District	Member of Congress	Single Males			Single Females			Double-Earner Couples		
		1955	1965	1975	1955	1965	1975	1955	1965	1975
Senate										
	Ben Nighthorse Campbell (R)									
	Wayne Allard (R)									
Statewide		1.07 %	0.85 %	0.52 %	2.62 %	2.48 %	2.32 %	1.84 %	1.66 %	1.41 %
House of Representatives										
1	Diana DeGette (D)	0.89	0.54	0.12	2.58	2.41	2.24	1.75	1.49	1.18
2	Mark Udall (D)	1.12	0.98	0.72	2.60	2.47	2.32	1.86	1.72	1.50
3	Scott McInnis (R)	1.44	1.25	0.95	2.77	2.64	2.48	2.11	1.94	1.70
4	Bob Schaffer (R)	1.43	1.28	1.01	2.76	2.64	2.49	2.10	1.96	1.73
5	Joel Hefley (R)	0.79	0.42	-0.04	2.56	2.43	2.27	1.68	1.44	1.14
6	Thomas G. Tancredo (R)	0.84	0.67	0.40	2.50	2.37	2.21	1.67	1.52	1.29

Note: Rates of return exclude both Disability Insurance benefits and taxes, but include all Old-Age and Survivors Insurance (OASI) benefits and taxes (including pre-retirement Survivors Insurance). All values include both the portion of the OASI tax paid directly by workers and the portion paid by the employer on a worker's behalf. All rates of return are net of inflation. Calculations are based on life expectancies and average earnings for each district. Because of non-linearity in the benefit function, amounts for each district may not sum to the state average.

CONNECTICUT

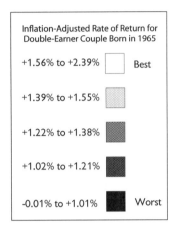

Inflation-Adjusted Rate of Return for Double-Earner Couple Born in 1965

+1.56% to +2.39% ☐ Best

+1.39% to +1.55%

+1.22% to +1.38%

+1.02% to +1.21%

-0.01% to +1.01% ■ Worst

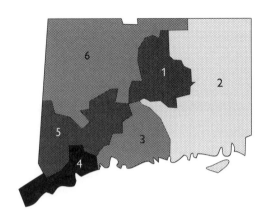

Lifetime Dollar Losses Under Social Security (OASI) Compared with Personal Retirement Accounts for Double-Earner Couples Born in 1965

District	Member of Congress	Loss Under Social Security (3)-(2)	Ranking from Lowest Loss to Highest Loss	Social Security Taxes Paid (1)	Social Security Benefits (2)	Personal Retirement Accounts (3)
Senate						
	Christopher J. Dodd (D)					
	Joseph I. Lieberman (D)					
Statewide		$ 724,659	49	$ 482,510	$ 662,799	$ 1,387,458
House of Representatives						
1	John B. Larson (D)	676,630	370 / 436	452,268	623,933	1,300,563
2	Sam Gejdenson (D)	540,561	269	386,812	571,774	1,112,335
3	Rosa L. DeLauro (D)	628,940	342	432,971	616,133	1,245,073
4	Christopher Shays (R)	1,003,567	433	590,928	741,955	1,745,522
5	James H. Maloney (D)	752,101	396	501,493	691,711	1,443,813
6	Nancy L. Johnson (R)	676,301	368	466,530	665,275	1,341,576

Note: Column (1) shows the total amount of Old-Age and Survivors Insurance (OASI) taxes paid during the individual's working life. Column (2) shows the total value of Old-Age and Survivors Insurance benefits collected by the worker and his or her spouse following retirement. Column (3) shows the amount accumulated in a Personal Retirement Account had the worker been able to place his or her OASI taxes in a Personal Retirement Account. The accumulation in this personal account has been reduced by the cost of purchasing life insurance coverage equivalent to the pre-retirement Survivors Insurance portion of Social Security. All amounts exclude both Disability Insurance benefits and taxes. All values include both the portion of the OASI tax paid directly by workers and the portion paid by the employer on a worker's behalf. The losses from not participating in a Personal Retirement Account (columns (3)-(2)) are for illustrative purposes only and do not reflect any specific plan for reforming Social Security. All amounts are expressed in inflation-adjusted dollars for the year 2000. Calculations are based on life expectancies and average earnings for each district. Because of non-linearity in the benefit function, amounts for each district may not sum to the state average.

Inflation-Adjusted Rate of Return from Social Security (OASI) by Birth Year

District	Member of Congress	Single Males			Single Females			Double-Earner Couples		
		1955	1965	1975	1955	1965	1975	1955	1965	1975
Senate										
	Christopher J. Dodd (D)									
	Joseph I. Lieberman (D)									
Statewide		0.35 %	0.07 %	-0.26 %	2.34 %	2.19 %	2.02 %	1.36 %	1.14 %	0.88 %
House of Representatives										
1	John B. Larson (D)	0.40	0.07	-0.30	2.38	2.22	2.04	1.41	1.17	0.88
2	Sam Gejdenson (D)	0.71	0.41	0.04	2.52	2.38	2.22	1.63	1.41	1.14
3	Rosa L. DeLauro (D)	0.54	0.27	-0.05	2.41	2.26	2.08	1.49	1.27	1.02
4	Christopher Shays (R)	0.05	-0.24	-0.55	1.89	1.73	1.54	1.03	0.82	0.57
5	James H. Maloney (D)	0.34	0.11	-0.19	2.31	2.17	2.00	1.34	1.15	0.91
6	Nancy L. Johnson (R)	0.50	0.27	-0.03	2.39	2.25	2.09	1.46	1.27	1.03

Note: Rates of return exclude both Disability Insurance benefits and taxes, but include all Old-Age and Survivors Insurance (OASI) benefits and taxes (including pre-retirement Survivors Insurance). All values include both the portion of the OASI tax paid directly by workers and the portion paid by the employer on a worker's behalf. All rates of return are net of inflation. Calculations are based on life expectancies and average earnings for each district. Because of non-linearity in the benefit function, amounts for each district may not sum to the state average.

DELAWARE

Lifetime Dollar Losses Under Social Security (OASI) Compared with Personal Retirement Accounts for Double-Earner Couples Born in 1965

District	Member of Congress	Loss Under Social Security (3)-(2)	Ranking from Lowest Loss to Highest Loss	Social Security Taxes Paid (1)	Social Security Benefits (2)	Personal Retirement Accounts (3)
Senate						
	William V. Roth, Jr. (R)					
	Joseph R. Biden, Jr. (D)					
Statewide		$ 528,313	37	$ 380,336	$ 565,401	$ 1,093,713
House of Representatives						
At large	Michael N. Castle (R)	528,313	258 / 436	380,336	565,401	1,093,713

Note: Column (1) shows the total amount of Old-Age and Survivors Insurance (OASI) taxes paid during the individual's working life. Column (2) shows the total value of Old-Age and Survivors Insurance benefits collected by the worker and his or her spouse following retirement. Column (3) shows the amount accumulated in a Personal Retirement Account had the worker been able to place his or her OASI taxes in a Personal Retirement Account. The accumulation in this personal account has been reduced by the cost of purchasing life insurance coverage equivalent to the pre-retirement Survivors Insurance portion of Social Security. All amounts exclude both Disability Insurance benefits and taxes. All values include both the portion of the OASI tax paid directly by workers and the portion paid by the employer on a worker's behalf. The losses from not participating in a Personal Retirement Account (columns (3)-(2)) are for illustrative purposes only and do not reflect any specific plan for reforming Social Security. All amounts are expressed in inflation-adjusted dollars for the year 2000. Calculations are based on life expectancies and average earnings for each district.

Inflation-Adjusted Rate of Return from Social Security (OASI) by Birth Year

District	Member of Congress	Single Males			Single Females			Double-Earner Couples		
		1955	1965	1975	1955	1965	1975	1955	1965	1975
Senate										
	William V. Roth, Jr. (R)									
	Joseph R. Biden, Jr. (D)									
Statewide		0.89 %	0.62 %	0.30 %	2.44 %	2.26 %	2.07 %	1.67 %	1.43 %	1.17 %
House of Representatives										
At large	Michael N. Castle (R)	0.89	0.62	0.30	2.44	2.26	2.07	1.67	1.43	1.17

Note: Rates of return exclude both Disability Insurance benefits and taxes, but include all Old-Age and Survivors Insurance (OASI) benefits and taxes (including pre-retirement Survivors Insurance). All values include both the portion of the OASI tax paid directly by workers and the portion paid by the employer on a worker's behalf. All rates of return are net of inflation. Calculations are based on life expectancies and average earnings for each district.

DISTRICT OF COLUMBIA

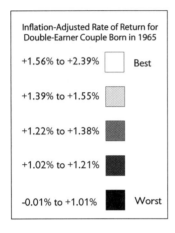

Inflation-Adjusted Rate of Return for
Double-Earner Couple Born in 1965

+1.56% to +2.39% ☐ Best

+1.39% to +1.55% ▨

+1.22% to +1.38% ▨

+1.02% to +1.21% ▨

-0.01% to +1.01% ■ Worst

Lifetime Dollar Losses Under Social Security (OASI) Compared with Personal Retirement Accounts for Double-Earner Couples Born in 1965

District	Member of Congress	Loss Under Social Security (3)-(2)	Ranking from Lowest Loss to Highest Loss	Social Security Taxes Paid (1)	Social Security Benefits (2)	Personal Retirement Accounts (3)
Statewide			51			
House of Representatives	Eleanor Holmes Norton (D)	$ 786,850	407 / 436	$ 429,064	$ 446,987	$ 1,233,837

Note: Column (1) shows the total amount of Old-Age and Survivors Insurance (OASI) taxes paid during the individual's working life. Column (2) shows the total value of Old-Age and Survivors Insurance benefits collected by the worker and his or her spouse following retirement. Column (3) shows the amount accumulated in a Personal Retirement Account had the worker been able to place his or her OASI taxes in a Personal Retirement Account. The accumulation in this personal account has been reduced by the cost of purchasing life insurance coverage equivalent to the pre-retirement Survivors Insurance portion of Social Security. All amounts exclude both Disability Insurance benefits and taxes. All values include both the portion of the OASI tax paid directly by workers and the portion paid by the employer on a worker's behalf. The losses from not participating in a Personal Retirement Account (columns (3)-(2)) are for illustrative purposes only and do not reflect any specific plan for reforming Social Security. All amounts are expressed in inflation-adjusted dollars for the year 2000. Calculations are based on life expectancies and average earnings for each district.

Inflation-Adjusted Rate of Return from Social Security (OASI) by Birth Year

District	Member of Congress	Single Males			Single Females			Double-Earner Couples		
		1955	1965	1975	1955	1965	1975	1955	1965	1975
House of Representatives										
	Eleanor Holmes Norton (D)	-0.55	-1.90	-3.27	2.11	1.82	1.57	0.85	0.16	-0.46

Note: Rates of return exclude both Disability Insurance benefits and taxes, but include all Old-Age and Survivors Insurance (OASI) benefits and taxes (including pre-retirement Survivors Insurance). All values include both the portion of the OASI tax paid directly by workers and the portion paid by the employer on a worker's behalf. All rates of return are net of inflation. Calculations are based on life expectancies and average earnings for each district.

FLORIDA

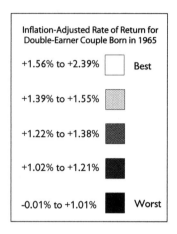

Inflation-Adjusted Rate of Return for
Double-Earner Couple Born in 1965

+1.56% to +2.39% □ Best

+1.39% to +1.55% ▨

+1.22% to +1.38% ▨

+1.02% to +1.21% ■

-0.01% to +1.01% ■ Worst

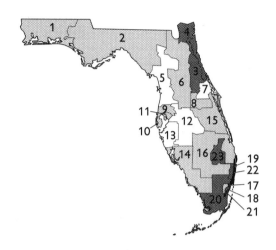

Lifetime Dollar Losses Under Social Security (OASI) Compared with Personal Retirement Accounts for Double-Earner Couples Born in 1965

District	Member of Congress	Loss Under Social Security (3)-(2)	Ranking from Lowest Loss to Highest Loss	Social Security Taxes Paid (1)	Social Security Benefits (2)	Personal Retirement Accounts (3)
Senate						
	Bob Graham (D)					
	Connie Mack (R)					
Statewide		$ 483,196	31	$ 345,486	$ 510,143	$ 993,340
House of Representatives						
1	Joe Scarborough (R)	407,535	98 / 436	296,481	445,041	852,576
2	F. Allen Boyd, Jr. (D)	399,431	87	294,789	448,278	847,709
3	Corrine Brown (D)	403,840	92	281,656	406,105	809,944
4	Tillie K. Fowler (R)	576,647	306	395,101	559,524	1,136,171
5	Karen L. Thurman (D)	384,838	64	292,552	456,438	841,276
6	Cliff Stearns (R)	424,304	122	314,053	478,804	903,108
7	John L. Mica (R)	474,664	186	357,053	552,094	1,026,758
8	Bill McCollum (R)	478,461	192	351,948	533,617	1,012,078
9	Michael Bilirakis (R)	506,348	229	369,960	557,526	1,063,875
10	C. W. Bill Young (R)	452,763	153	334,576	509,360	962,122
11	Jim Davis (D)	453,951	157	330,047	495,149	949,100
12	Charles T. Canady (R)	418,692	115	313,246	482,094	900,787
13	Dan Miller (R)	433,031	134	332,016	521,731	954,762
14	Porter J. Goss (R)	474,420	183	352,767	540,015	1,014,435
15	David Weldon (R)	470,346	177	347,161	527,968	998,315
16	Mark Foley (R)	534,441	262	385,176	573,189	1,107,631
17	Carrie P. Meek (D)	413,203	107	273,574	373,498	786,701
18	Ileana Ros-Lehtinen (R)	552,354	281	378,877	537,164	1,089,518
19	Robert Wexler (D)	639,199	348	442,149	632,267	1,271,466
20	Peter Deutsch (D)	626,229	340	432,736	618,169	1,244,398

Lifetime Dollar Losses Under Social Security (OASI) Compared with Personal Retirement Accounts for Double-Earner Couples Born in 1965

District	Member of Congress	Loss Under Social Security (3)-(2)	Ranking from Lowest to Highest	Social Security Taxes Paid (1)	Social Security Benefits (2)	Personal Retirement Accounts (3)
21	Lincoln Diaz-Balart (R)	485,727	201	354,214	532,866	1,018,594
22	E. Clay Shaw, Jr. (R)	768,519	401	493,277	650,791	1,419,310
23	Alcee L. Hastings (D)	413,267	108	281,777	397,024	810,291

Note: Column (1) shows the total amount of Old-Age and Survivors Insurance (OASI) taxes paid during the individual's working life. Column (2) shows the total value of Old-Age and Survivors Insurance benefits collected by the worker and his or her spouse following retirement. Column (3) shows the amount accumulated in a Personal Retirement Account had the worker been able to place his or her OASI taxes in a Personal Retirement Account. The accumulation in this personal account has been reduced by the cost of purchasing life insurance coverage equivalent to the pre-retirement Survivors Insurance portion of Social Security. All amounts exclude both Disability Insurance benefits and taxes. All values include both the portion of the OASI tax paid directly by workers and the portion paid by the employer on a worker's behalf. The losses from not participating in a Personal Retirement Account (columns (3)-(2)) are for illustrative purposes only and do not reflect any specific plan for reforming Social Security. All amounts are expressed in inflation-adjusted dollars for the year 2000. Calculations are based on life expectancies and average earnings for each district. Because of non-linearity in the benefit function, amounts for each district may not sum to the state average.

Inflation-Adjusted Rate of Return from Social Security (OASI) by Birth Year

District	Member of Congress	Single Males 1955	1965	1975	Single Females 1955	1965	1975	Double-Earner Couples 1955	1965	1975
Senate										
	Bob Graham (D)									
	Connie Mack (R)									
Statewide		0.80 %	0.33 %	-0.17 %	2.62 %	2.46 %	2.27 %	1.72 %	1.42 %	1.08 %
House of Representatives										
1	Joe Scarborough (R)	0.93	0.35	-0.30	2.72	2.56	2.38	1.84	1.50	1.10
2	F. Allen Boyd, Jr. (D)	0.99	0.48	-0.09	2.71	2.55	2.36	1.87	1.54	1.17
3	Corrine Brown (D)	0.80	0.13	-0.61	2.69	2.50	2.30	1.77	1.37	0.93
4	Tillie K. Fowler (R)	0.54	0.12	-0.36	2.51	2.35	2.17	1.54	1.27	0.94
5	Karen L. Thurman (D)	1.08	0.57	0.00	2.79	2.62	2.43	1.95	1.62	1.26
6	Cliff Stearns (R)	0.94	0.49	-0.03	2.70	2.54	2.35	1.83	1.54	1.19
7	John L. Mica (R)	0.92	0.64	0.28	2.62	2.47	2.29	1.78	1.56	1.29
8	Bill McCollum (R)	0.88	0.49	0.04	2.64	2.48	2.30	1.77	1.50	1.19
9	Michael Bilirakis (R)	0.80	0.47	0.09	2.60	2.45	2.26	1.72	1.48	1.19
10	C. W. Bill Young (R)	0.91	0.49	0.03	2.69	2.51	2.32	1.81	1.52	1.20
11	Jim Davis (D)	0.87	0.44	-0.05	2.65	2.47	2.28	1.77	1.48	1.14
12	Charles T. Canady (R)	0.97	0.60	0.16	2.67	2.51	2.33	1.83	1.57	1.26
13	Dan Miller (R)	1.02	0.67	0.28	2.71	2.55	2.37	1.88	1.63	1.33
14	Porter J. Goss (R)	0.89	0.53	0.11	2.66	2.50	2.32	1.79	1.53	1.23
15	David Weldon (R)	0.88	0.53	0.12	2.62	2.47	2.29	1.76	1.52	1.22
16	Mark Foley (R)	0.75	0.43	0.04	2.56	2.41	2.22	1.67	1.43	1.14
17	Carrie P. Meek (D)	0.68	-0.23	-1.17	2.65	2.44	2.22	1.69	1.19	0.67
18	Ileana Ros-Lehtinen (R)	0.68	0.00	-0.68	2.62	2.43	2.22	1.67	1.27	0.86
19	Robert Wexler (D)	0.54	0.21	-0.17	2.48	2.32	2.13	1.52	1.28	1.00
20	Peter Deutsch (D)	0.56	0.18	-0.24	2.49	2.33	2.15	1.54	1.28	0.98
21	Lincoln Diaz-Balart (R)	0.89	0.34	-0.26	2.70	2.53	2.34	1.81	1.47	1.09
22	E. Clay Shaw, Jr. (R)	0.25	-0.29	-0.81	2.39	2.20	2.00	1.35	1.01	0.66
23	Alcee L. Hastings (D)	0.74	-0.05	-0.87	2.69	2.49	2.28	1.74	1.29	0.83

Note: Rates of return exclude both Disability Insurance benefits and taxes, but include all Old-Age and Survivors Insurance (OASI) benefits and taxes (including pre-retirement Survivors Insurance). All values include both the portion of the OASI tax paid directly by workers and the portion paid by the employer on a worker's behalf. All rates of return are net of inflation. Calculations are based on life expectancies and average earnings for each district. Because of non-linearity in the benefit function, amounts for each district may not sum to the state average.

GEORGIA

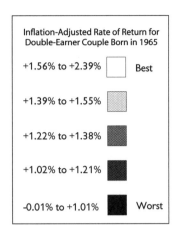

Inflation-Adjusted Rate of Return for
Double-Earner Couple Born in 1965

+1.56% to +2.39% ☐ Best

+1.39% to +1.55% ☐

+1.22% to +1.38% ☐

+1.02% to +1.21% ☐

-0.01% to +1.01% ■ Worst

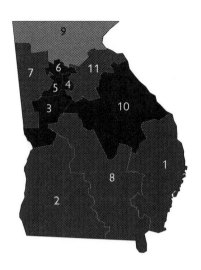

Lifetime Dollar Losses Under Social Security (OASI) Compared with Personal Retirement Accounts for Double-Earner Couples Born in 1965

District	Member of Congress	Loss Under Social Security (3)-(2)	Ranking from Lowest Loss to Highest Loss	Social Security Taxes Paid (1)	Social Security Benefits (2)	Personal Retirement Accounts (3)
Senate						
	Paul D. Coverdell (R)					
	Max Cleland (D)					
Statewide		$ 552,410	40	$ 346,606	$ 444,151	$ 996,562
House of Representatives						
1	Jack Kingston (R)	500,351	226 / 436	319,400	418,130	918,481
2	Sanford D. Bishop, Jr. (D)	411,661	105	272,903	373,113	784,774
3	Michael Collins (R)	573,674	304	358,765	458,008	1,031,683
4	Cynthia McKinney (D)	655,213	359	397,063	486,601	1,141,814
5	John Lewis (D)	680,228	373	382,499	419,705	1,099,933
6	Johnny Isakson (R)	842,551	415	506,852	617,607	1,460,158
7	Bob Barr (R)	496,718	220	325,132	438,248	934,965
8	Saxby Chambliss (R)	461,917	166	299,018	397,953	859,870
9	Nathan Deal (R)	434,610	135	299,071	425,411	860,022
10	Charles W. Norwood, Jr. (R)	498,256	223	314,683	406,662	904,917
11	John Linder (R)	549,757	275	355,292	471,938	1,021,695

Note: Column (1) shows the total amount of Old-Age and Survivors Insurance (OASI) taxes paid during the individual's working life. Column (2) shows the total value of Old-Age and Survivors Insurance benefits collected by the worker and his or her spouse following retirement. Column (3) shows the amount accumulated in a Personal Retirement Account had the worker been able to place his or her OASI taxes in a Personal Retirement Account. The accumulation in this personal account has been reduced by the cost of purchasing life insurance coverage equivalent to the pre-retirement Survivors Insurance portion of Social Security. All amounts exclude both Disability Insurance benefits and taxes. All values include both the portion of the OASI tax paid directly by workers and the portion paid by the employer on a worker's behalf. The losses from not participating in a Personal Retirement Account (columns (3)-(2)) are for illustrative purposes only and do not reflect any specific plan for reforming Social Security. All amounts are expressed in inflation-adjusted dollars for the year 2000. Calculations are based on life expectancies and average earnings for each district. Because of non-linearity in the benefit function, amounts for each district may not sum to the state average.

Inflation-Adjusted Rate of Return from Social Security (OASI) by Birth Year

District	Member of Congress	Single Males			Single Females			Double-Earner Couples		
		1955	1965	1975	1955	1965	1975	1955	1965	1975
Senate										
	Paul D. Coverdell (R)									
	Max Cleland (D)									
Statewide		0.13%	-0.35%	-0.89%	2.32%	2.14%	1.95%	1.25%	0.94%	0.59%
House of Representatives										
1	Jack Kingston (R)	0.25	-0.25	-0.80	2.37	2.20	2.02	1.34	1.03	0.67
2	Sanford D. Bishop, Jr. (D)	0.52	-0.04	-0.67	2.51	2.34	2.15	1.54	1.20	0.80
3	Michael Collins (R)	0.09	-0.35	-0.85	2.28	2.11	1.92	1.21	0.93	0.59
4	Cynthia McKinney (D)	-0.13	-0.63	-1.17	2.23	2.04	1.85	1.09	0.77	0.42
5	John Lewis (D)	-0.61	-1.46	-2.33	2.12	1.90	1.68	0.83	0.36	-0.10
6	Johnny Isakson (R)	-0.26	-0.57	-0.94	2.10	1.95	1.77	0.96	0.74	0.46
7	Bob Barr (R)	0.37	-0.04	-0.51	2.39	2.23	2.05	1.41	1.13	0.80
8	Saxby Chambliss (R)	0.37	-0.17	-0.77	2.43	2.26	2.06	1.43	1.09	0.71
9	Nathan Deal (R)	0.63	0.24	-0.21	2.51	2.35	2.18	1.59	1.32	1.01
10	Charles W. Norwood, Jr. (R)	0.21	-0.34	-0.96	2.37	2.19	2.00	1.32	0.98	0.60
11	John Linder (R)	0.26	-0.11	-0.54	2.34	2.18	2.00	1.32	1.07	0.76

Note: Rates of return exclude both Disability Insurance benefits and taxes, but include all Old-Age and Survivors Insurance (OASI) benefits and taxes (including pre-retirement Survivors Insurance). All values include both the portion of the OASI tax paid directly by workers and the portion paid by the employer on a worker's behalf. All rates of return are net of inflation. Calculations are based on life expectancies and average earnings for each district. Because of non-linearity in the benefit function, amounts for each district may not sum to the state average.

Hawaii

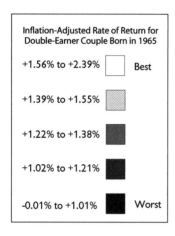

Inflation-Adjusted Rate of Return for Double-Earner Couple Born in 1965

+1.56% to +2.39% ▢ Best

+1.39% to +1.55% ▨

+1.22% to +1.38% ▨

+1.02% to +1.21% ▨

-0.01% to +1.01% ■ Worst

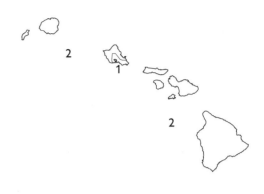

Lifetime Dollar Losses Under Social Security (OASI) Compared with Personal Retirement Accounts for Double-Earner Couples Born in 1965

District	Member of Congress	Loss Under Social Security (3)-(2)	Ranking from Lowest Loss to Highest Loss	Social Security Taxes Paid (1)	Social Security Benefits (2)	Personal Retirement Accounts (3)
Senate						
	Daniel K. Inouye (D)					
	Daniel K. Akaka (D)					
Statewide		$ 467,288	27	$ 374,258	$ 608,779	$ 1,076,067
House of Representatives						
1	Neil Abercrombie (D)	518,339	248 / 436	400,631	633,735	1,152,075
2	Patsy T. Mink (D)	414,717	110	347,263	583,888	998,605

Note: Column (1) shows the total amount of Old-Age and Survivors Insurance (OASI) taxes paid during the individual's working life. Column (2) shows the total value of Old-Age and Survivors Insurance benefits collected by the worker and his or her spouse following retirement. Column (3) shows the amount accumulated in a Personal Retirement Account had the worker been able to place his or her OASI taxes in a Personal Retirement Account. The accumulation in this personal account has been reduced by the cost of purchasing life insurance coverage equivalent to the pre-retirement Survivors Insurance portion of Social Security. All amounts exclude both Disability Insurance benefits and taxes. All values include both the portion of the OASI tax paid directly by workers and the portion paid by the employer on a worker's behalf. The losses from not participating in a Personal Retirement Account (columns (3)-(2)) are for illustrative purposes only and do not reflect any specific plan for reforming Social Security. All amounts are expressed in inflation-adjusted dollars for the year 2000. Calculations are based on life expectancies and average earnings for each district. Because of non-linearity in the benefit function, amounts for each district may not sum to the state average.

Inflation-Adjusted Rate of Return from Social Security (OASI) by Birth Year

District	Member of Congress	Single Males			Single Females			Double-Earner Couples		
		1955	1965	1975	1955	1965	1975	1955	1965	1975
Senate										
	Daniel K. Inouye (D)									
	Daniel K. Akaka (D)									
Statewide		0.98 %	0.90 %	0.61 %	2.65 %	2.53 %	2.37 %	1.82 %	1.71 %	1.47 %
House of Representatives										
1	Neil Abercrombie (D)	0.84	0.76	0.45	2.61	2.47	2.31	1.74	1.61	1.37
2	Patsy T. Mink (D)	1.14	1.06	0.78	2.71	2.59	2.44	1.93	1.82	1.59

Note: Rates of return exclude both Disability Insurance benefits and taxes, but include all Old-Age and Survivors Insurance (OASI) benefits and taxes (including pre-retirement Survivors Insurance). All values include both the portion of the OASI tax paid directly by workers and the portion paid by the employer on a worker's behalf. All rates of return are net of inflation. Calculations are based on life expectancies and average earnings for each district. Because of non-linearity in the benefit function, amounts for each district may not sum to the state average.

IDAHO

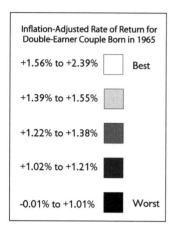

Inflation-Adjusted Rate of Return for
Double-Earner Couple Born in 1965

+1.56% to +2.39% ☐ Best

+1.39% to +1.55% ▨

+1.22% to +1.38% ▦

+1.02% to +1.21% ▪

-0.01% to +1.01% ■ Worst

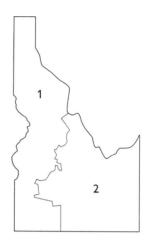

Lifetime Dollar Losses Under Social Security (OASI) Compared with Personal Retirement Accounts for Double-Earner Couples Born in 1965

District	Member of Congress	Loss Under Social Security (3)-(2)	Ranking from Lowest Loss to Highest Loss	Social Security Taxes Paid (1)	Social Security Benefits (2)	Personal Retirement Accounts (3)
Senate						
	Larry E. Craig (R)					
	Michael D. Crapo (R)					
Statewide		$ 323,263	4	$ 292,809	$ 518,622	$ 841,884
House of Representatives						
1	Helen P. Chenoweth (R)	318,918	16 / 436	288,378	510,355	829,273
2	Michael K. Simpson (R)	326,405	20	296,753	526,951	853,356

Note: Column (1) shows the total amount of Old-Age and Survivors Insurance (OASI) taxes paid during the individual's working life. Column (2) shows the total value of Old-Age and Survivors Insurance benefits collected by the worker and his or her spouse following retirement. Column (3) shows the amount accumulated in a Personal Retirement Account had the worker been able to place his or her OASI taxes in a Personal Retirement Account. The accumulation in this personal account has been reduced by the cost of purchasing life insurance coverage equivalent to the pre-retirement Survivors Insurance portion of Social Security. All amounts exclude both Disability Insurance benefits and taxes. All values include both the portion of the OASI tax paid directly by workers and the portion paid by the employer on a worker's behalf. The losses from not participating in a Personal Retirement Account (columns (3)-(2)) are for illustrative purposes only and do not reflect any specific plan for reforming Social Security. All amounts are expressed in inflation-adjusted dollars for the year 2000. Calculations are based on life expectancies and average earnings for each district. Because of non-linearity in the benefit function, amounts for each district may not sum to the state average.

Inflation-Adjusted Rate of Return from Social Security (OASI) by Birth Year

District	Member of Congress	Single Males 1955	Single Males 1965	Single Males 1975	Single Females 1955	Single Females 1965	Single Females 1975	Double-Earner Couples 1955	Double-Earner Couples 1965	Double-Earner Couples 1975
Senate										
	Larry E. Craig (R)									
	Michael D. Crapo (R)									
Statewide		1.49 %	1.34 %	1.07 %	2.81 %	2.71 %	2.56 %	2.16 %	2.02 %	1.80 %
House of Representatives										
1	Helen P. Chenoweth (R)	1.49	1.33	1.08	2.82	2.71	2.55	2.16	2.02	1.80
2	Michael K. Simpson (R)	1.50	1.34	1.07	2.81	2.71	2.57	2.16	2.02	1.81

Note: Rates of return exclude both Disability Insurance benefits and taxes, but include all Old-Age and Survivors Insurance (OASI) benefits and taxes (including pre-retirement Survivors Insurance). All values include both the portion of the OASI tax paid directly by workers and the portion paid by the employer on a worker's behalf. All rates of return are net of inflation. Calculations are based on life expectancies and average earnings for each district.

ILLINOIS

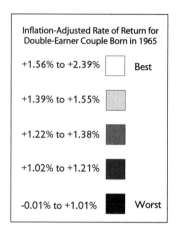

Inflation-Adjusted Rate of Return for
Double-Earner Couple Born in 1965

+1.56% to +2.39%   Best

+1.39% to +1.55%

+1.22% to +1.38%

+1.02% to +1.21%

-0.01% to +1.01%   Worst

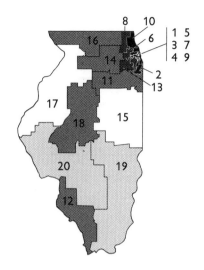

Lifetime Dollar Losses Under Social Security (OASI) Compared with Personal Retirement Accounts for Double-Earner Couples Born in 1965

District	Member of Congress	Loss Under Social Security (3)-(2)	Ranking from Lowest Loss to Highest Loss	Social Security Taxes Paid (1)	Social Security Benefits (2)	Personal Retirement Accounts (3)
Senate						
	Peter G. Fitzgerald (R)					
	Richard J. Durbin (D)					
Statewide		$ 596,105	44	$ 386,090	$ 513,982	$ 1,110,086
House of Representatives						
1	Bobby L. Rush (D)	592,699	317/ 436	338,362	380,311	973,010
2	Jessie L. Jackson, Jr. (D)	578,054	307	341,389	403,660	981,714
3	William O. Lipinski (D)	596,688	320	398,609	549,572	1,146,260
4	Luis V. Gutierrez (D)	383,956	60	266,213	381,578	765,534
5	Rod R. Blagojevich (D)	723,680	388	449,817	569,837	1,293,517
6	Henry J. Hyde (R)	695,312	379	460,822	629,852	1,325,164
7	Danny K. Davis (D)	728,526	389	395,425	408,579	1,137,104
8	Philip M. Crane (R)	768,164	400	501,033	674,265	1,442,429
9	Janice D. Schakowsky (D)	679,814	372	423,381	537,681	1,217,495
10	John Edward Porter (R)	988,303	432	574,221	697,362	1,685,666
11	Jerry Weller (R)	539,433	266	366,056	513,217	1,052,649
12	Jerry F. Costello (D)	446,567	148	302,536	423,419	869,987
13	Judy Biggert (R)	817,699	412	523,884	696,579	1,514,277
14	J. Dennis Hastert (R)	584,265	312	400,653	567,872	1,152,137
15	Thomas W. Ewing (R)	384,733	63	289,354	447,348	832,081
16	Donald A. Manzullo (R)	560,881	290	386,364	550,166	1,111,048
17	Lane Evans (D)	391,707	72	293,338	451,830	843,537
18	Ray LaHood (R)	496,513	219	347,773	503,559	1,000,073
19	David D. Phelps (D)	393,073	77	288,511	436,583	829,656
20	John Shimkus (R)	431,237	132	309,739	459,462	890,700

Note: Column (1) shows the total amount of Old-Age and Survivors Insurance (OASI) taxes paid during the individual's working life. Column (2) shows the total value of Old-Age and Survivors Insurance benefits collected by the worker and his or her spouse following retirement. Column (3) shows the amount accumulated in a Personal Retirement Account had the worker been able to place his or her OASI taxes in a Personal Retirement Account. The accumulation in this personal account has been reduced by the cost of purchasing life insurance coverage equivalent to the pre-retirement Survivors Insurance portion of Social Security. All amounts exclude both Disability Insurance benefits and taxes. All values include both the portion of the OASI tax paid directly by workers and the portion paid by the employer on a worker's behalf. The losses from not participating in a Personal Retirement Account (columns (3)-(2)) are for illustrative purposes only and do not reflect any specific plan for reforming Social Security. All amounts are expressed in inflation-adjusted dollars for the year 2000. Calculations are based on life expectancies and average earnings for each district. Because of non-linearity in the benefit function, amounts for each district may not sum to the state average.

Inflation-Adjusted Rate of Return from Social Security (OASI) by Birth Year

District	Member of Congress	Single Males			Single Females			Double-Earner Couples		
		1955	1965	1975	1955	1965	1975	1955	1965	1975
Senate										
	Peter G. Fitzgerald (R)									
	Richard J. Durbin (D)									
Statewide		0.28 %	-0.08 %	-0.47 %	2.32 %	2.16 %	1.99 %	1.32 %	1.07 %	0.78 %
House of Representatives										
1	Bobby L. Rush (D)	-0.43	-1.19	-1.92	2.13	1.90	1.69	0.91	0.46	0.04
2	Jessie L. Jackson, Jr. (D)	-0.23	-0.75	-1.36	2.14	1.94	1.74	1.00	0.65	0.27
3	William O. Lipinski (D)	0.43	0.14	-0.20	2.35	2.20	2.03	1.41	1.18	0.92
4	Luis V. Gutierrez (D)	0.84	0.29	-0.35	2.57	2.39	2.20	1.72	1.36	0.97
5	Rod R. Blagojevich (D)	0.09	-0.40	-0.86	2.26	2.07	1.89	1.20	0.88	0.56
6	Henry J. Hyde (R)	0.31	0.09	-0.18	2.30	2.16	1.99	1.32	1.14	0.90
7	Danny K. Davis (D)	-0.79	-1.71	-2.58	1.94	1.69	1.47	0.65	0.13	-0.34
8	Philip M. Crane (R)	0.21	0.02	-0.23	2.23	2.10	1.94	1.24	1.08	0.86
9	Janice D. Schakowsky (D)	0.11	-0.44	-0.92	2.31	2.12	1.93	1.24	0.89	0.57
10	John Edward Porter (R)	-0.21	-0.55	-0.92	1.92	1.78	1.61	0.93	0.71	0.45
11	Jerry Weller (R)	0.49	0.21	-0.12	2.40	2.25	2.08	1.46	1.25	0.99
12	Jerry F. Costello (D)	0.58	0.15	-0.33	2.49	2.32	2.15	1.55	1.27	0.95
13	Judy Biggert (R)	0.12	-0.05	-0.29	2.19	2.06	1.90	1.18	1.03	0.82
14	J. Dennis Hastert (R)	0.50	0.28	0.00	2.37	2.24	2.08	1.45	1.27	1.04
15	Thomas W. Ewing (R)	0.99	0.66	0.30	2.66	2.51	2.35	1.84	1.60	1.33
16	Donald A. Manzullo (R)	0.52	0.31	0.03	2.39	2.26	2.09	1.47	1.29	1.06
17	Lane Evans (D)	0.95	0.67	0.33	2.62	2.48	2.32	1.80	1.59	1.33
18	Ray LaHood (R)	0.63	0.36	0.02	2.48	2.34	2.17	1.57	1.36	1.10
19	David D. Phelps (D)	0.89	0.58	0.21	2.61	2.46	2.30	1.77	1.53	1.26
20	John Shimkus (R)	0.78	0.45	0.08	2.57	2.42	2.26	1.69	1.46	1.18

Note: Rates of return exclude both Disability Insurance benefits and taxes, but include all Old-Age and Survivors Insurance (OASI) benefits and taxes (including pre-retirement Survivors Insurance). All values include both the portion of the OASI tax paid directly by workers and the portion paid by the employer on a worker's behalf. All rates of return are net of inflation. Calculations are based on life expectancies and average earnings for each district. Because of non-linearity in the benefit function, amounts for each district may not sum to the state average.

INDIANA

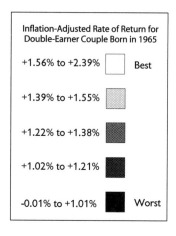

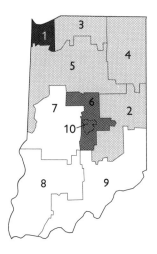

Lifetime Dollar Losses Under Social Security (OASI) Compared with Personal Retirement Accounts for Double-Earner Couples Born in 1965

District	Member of Congress	Loss Under Social Security (3)-(2)	Ranking from Lowest Loss to Highest Loss	Social Security Taxes Paid (1)	Social Security Benefits (2)	Personal Retirement Accounts (3)
Senate						
	Richard G. Lugar (R)					
	Evan Bayh (D)					
Statewide		$ 464,275	26	$ 332,402	$ 491,448	$ 955,723
House of Representatives						
1	Peter J. Visclosky (D)	555,283	285 / 436	366,732	499,309	1,054,591
2	David M. McIntosh (R)	415,444	111	306,714	466,558	882,002
3	Timothy J. Roemer (D)	458,235	163	329,852	490,302	948,537
4	Mark E. Souder (R)	466,350	173	338,964	508,390	974,740
5	Stephen E. Buyer (R)	426,572	128	315,901	481,850	908,422
6	Dan Burton (R)	650,230	356	443,858	626,151	1,276,381
7	Edward A. Pease (R)	391,584	71	301,261	474,737	866,321
8	John N. Hostettler (R)	385,216	65	294,505	461,677	846,893
9	Baron P. Hill (D)	406,648	96	305,209	471,027	877,675
10	Julia Carson (R)	474,648	185	318,261	440,558	915,206

Note: Column (1) shows the total amount of Old-Age and Survivors Insurance (OASI) taxes paid during the individual's working life. Column (2) shows the total value of Old-Age and Survivors Insurance benefits collected by the worker and his or her spouse following retirement. Column (3) shows the amount accumulated in a Personal Retirement Account had the worker been able to place his or her OASI taxes in a Personal Retirement Account. The accumulation in this personal account has been reduced by the cost of purchasing life insurance coverage equivalent to the pre-retirement Survivors Insurance portion of Social Security. All amounts exclude both Disability Insurance benefits and taxes. All values include both the portion of the OASI tax paid directly by workers and the portion paid by the employer on a worker's behalf. The losses from not participating in a Personal Retirement Account (columns (3)-(2)) are for illustrative purposes only and do not reflect any specific plan for reforming Social Security. All amounts are expressed in inflation-adjusted dollars for the year 2000. Calculations are based on life expectancies and average earnings for each district. Because of non-linearity in the benefit function, amounts for each district may not sum to the state average.

Inflation-Adjusted Rate of Return from Social Security (OASI) by Birth Year

District	Member of Congress	Single Males			Single Females			Double-Earner Couples		
		1955	1965	1975	1955	1965	1975	1955	1965	1975
Senate										
	Richard G. Lugar (R)									
	Evan Bayh (D)									
Statewide		0.73 %	0.51 %	0.21 %	2.49 %	2.35 %	2.19 %	1.62 %	1.44 %	1.19 %
House of Representatives										
1	Peter J. Visclosky (D)	0.38	0.14	-0.20	2.29	2.14	1.97	1.35	1.15	0.89
2	David M. McIntosh (R)	0.88	0.65	0.34	2.55	2.42	2.26	1.73	1.54	1.30
3	Timothy J. Roemer (D)	0.75	0.50	0.18	2.51	2.38	2.22	1.64	1.45	1.20
4	Mark E. Souder (R)	0.77	0.58	0.31	2.50	2.37	2.21	1.64	1.48	1.25
5	Stephen E. Buyer (R)	0.87	0.66	0.36	2.54	2.42	2.26	1.72	1.55	1.31
6	Dan Burton (R)	0.40	0.27	0.05	2.32	2.20	2.05	1.37	1.24	1.04
7	Edward A. Pease (R)	1.01	0.80	0.51	2.63	2.51	2.35	1.83	1.66	1.42
8	John N. Hostettler (R)	1.01	0.80	0.52	2.62	2.48	2.32	1.82	1.65	1.41
9	Baron P. Hill (D)	0.93	0.73	0.45	2.57	2.44	2.28	1.76	1.59	1.36
10	Julia Carson (R)	0.51	0.13	-0.29	2.43	2.27	2.09	1.49	1.22	0.92

Note: Rates of return exclude both Disability Insurance benefits and taxes, but include all Old-Age and Survivors Insurance (OASI) benefits and taxes (including pre-retirement Survivors Insurance). All values include both the portion of the OASI tax paid directly by workers and the portion paid by the employer on a worker's behalf. All rates of return are net of inflation. Calculations are based on life expectancies and average earnings for each district. Because of non-linearity in the benefit function, amounts for each district may not sum to the state average.

IOWA

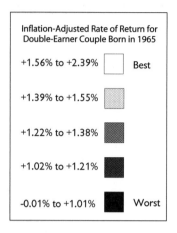

Inflation-Adjusted Rate of Return for Double-Earner Couple Born in 1965

+1.56% to +2.39% ☐ Best

+1.39% to +1.55% ▨

+1.22% to +1.38% ▨

+1.02% to +1.21% ▨

-0.01% to +1.01% ■ Worst

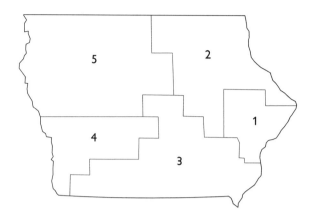

Lifetime Dollar Losses Under Social Security (OASI) Compared with Personal Retirement Accounts for Double-Earner Couples Born in 1965

District	Member of Congress	Loss Under Social Security (3)-(2)	Ranking from Lowest Loss to Highest Loss	Social Security Taxes Paid (1)	Social Security Benefits (2)	Personal Retirement Accounts (3)
Senate						
	Charles E. Grassley (R)					
	Tom Harkin (D)					
Statewide		$ 332,256	5	$ 295,430	$ 517,164	$ 849,421
House of Representatives						
1	James A. Leach (R)	390,035	70 / 436	324,538	543,221	933,256
2	Jim Nussle (R)	307,647	14	280,983	500,362	808,009
3	Leonard L. Boswell (D)	283,727	7	268,668	488,868	772,594
4	Greg Ganske (R)	395,107	81	328,062	548,283	943,390
5	Tom Latham (R)	283,944	8	273,671	503,039	786,983

Note: Column (1) shows the total amount of Old-Age and Survivors Insurance (OASI) taxes paid during the individual's working life. Column (2) shows the total value of Old-Age and Survivors Insurance benefits collected by the worker and his or her spouse following retirement. Column (3) shows the amount accumulated in a Personal Retirement Account had the worker been able to place his or her OASI taxes in a Personal Retirement Account. The accumulation in this personal account has been reduced by the cost of purchasing life insurance coverage equivalent to the pre-retirement Survivors Insurance portion of Social Security. All amounts exclude both Disability Insurance benefits and taxes. All values include both the portion of the OASI tax paid directly by workers and the portion paid by the employer on a worker's behalf. The losses from not participating in a Personal Retirement Account (columns (3)-(2)) are for illustrative purposes only and do not reflect any specific plan for reforming Social Security. All amounts are expressed in inflation-adjusted dollars for the year 2000. Calculations are based on life expectancies and average earnings for each district. Because of non-linearity in the benefit function, amounts for each district may not sum to the state average.

Inflation-Adjusted Rate of Return from Social Security (OASI) by Birth Year

District	Member of Congress	Single Males			Single Females			Double-Earner Couples		
		1955	1965	1975	1955	1965	1975	1955	1965	1975
Senate										
	Charles E. Grassley (R)									
	Tom Harkin (D)									
Statewide		1.37 %	1.22 %	0.99 %	2.85 %	2.74 %	2.59 %	2.12 %	1.98 %	1.78 %
House of Representatives										
1	James A. Leach (R)	1.17	1.02	0.79	2.74	2.62	2.47	1.96	1.83	1.62
2	Jim Nussle (R)	1.46	1.31	1.08	2.88	2.77	2.62	2.18	2.04	1.84
3	Leonard L. Boswell (D)	1.54	1.38	1.15	2.95	2.84	2.69	2.26	2.11	1.91
4	Greg Ganske (R)	1.16	1.00	0.77	2.75	2.63	2.47	1.96	1.82	1.61
5	Tom Latham (R)	1.55	1.40	1.18	2.97	2.86	2.72	2.27	2.14	1.94

Note: Rates of return exclude both Disability Insurance benefits and taxes, but include all Old-Age and Survivors Insurance (OASI) benefits and taxes (including pre-retirement Survivors Insurance). All values include both the portion of the OASI tax paid directly by workers and the portion paid by the employer on a worker's behalf. All rates of return are net of inflation. Calculations are based on life expectancies and average earnings for each district. Because of non-linearity in the benefit function, amounts for each district may not sum to the state average.

KANSAS

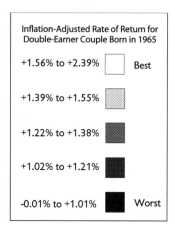

Inflation-Adjusted Rate of Return for
Double-Earner Couple Born in 1965

+1.56% to +2.39% Best

+1.39% to +1.55%

+1.22% to +1.38%

+1.02% to +1.21%

-0.01% to +1.01% Worst

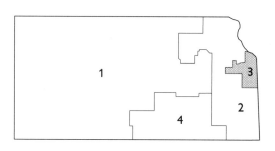

Lifetime Dollar Losses Under Social Security (OASI) Compared with Personal Retirement Accounts for Double-Earner Couples Born in 1965

District	Member of Congress	Loss Under Social Security (3)-(2)	Ranking from Lowest Loss to Highest Loss	Social Security Taxes Paid (1)	Social Security Benefits (2)	Personal Retirement Accounts (3)
Senate						
	Sam Brownback (R)					
	Pat Roberts (R)					
Statewide		$ 406,805	14	$ 324,208	$ 525,358	$ 932,163
House of Representatives						
1	Jerry Moran (R)	290,373	9 / 436	271,988	491,768	782,141
2	Jim Ryun (R)	339,497	29	276,703	456,205	795,701
3	Dennis Moore (D)	552,723	282	404,720	611,109	1,163,832
4	Todd Tiahrt (R)	440,334	141	342,342	544,121	984,455

Note: Column (1) shows the total amount of Old-Age and Survivors Insurance (OASI) taxes paid during the individual's working life. Column (2) shows the total value of Old-Age and Survivors Insurance benefits collected by the worker and his or her spouse following retirement. Column (3) shows the amount accumulated in a Personal Retirement Account had the worker been able to place his or her OASI taxes in a Personal Retirement Account. The accumulation in this personal account has been reduced by the cost of purchasing life insurance coverage equivalent to the pre-retirement Survivors Insurance portion of Social Security. All amounts exclude both Disability Insurance benefits and taxes. All values include both the portion of the OASI tax paid directly by workers and the portion paid by the employer on a worker's behalf. The losses from not participating in a Personal Retirement Account (columns (3)-(2)) are for illustrative purposes only and do not reflect any specific plan for reforming Social Security. All amounts are expressed in inflation-adjusted dollars for the year 2000. Calculations are based on life expectancies and average earnings for each district. Because of non-linearity in the benefit function, amounts for each district may not sum to the state average.

Inflation-Adjusted Rate of Return from Social Security (OASI) by Birth Year

District	Member of Congress	Single Males			Single Females			Double-Earner Couples		
		1955	1965	1975	1955	1965	1975	1955	1965	1975
Senate										
	Sam Brownback (R)									
	Pat Roberts (R)									
Statewide		1.07 %	0.86 %	0.57 %	2.70 %	2.58 %	2.43 %	1.89 %	1.73 %	1.49 %
House of Representatives										
1	Jerry Moran (R)	1.54	1.36	1.10	2.93	2.82	2.67	2.24	2.09	1.88
2	Jim Ryun (R)	1.21	0.86	0.42	2.84	2.72	2.56	2.04	1.81	1.51
3	Dennis Moore (D)	0.71	0.56	0.32	2.50	2.37	2.22	1.61	1.47	1.26
4	Todd Tiahrt (R)	0.98	0.80	0.54	2.63	2.50	2.35	1.81	1.66	1.43

Note: Rates of return exclude both Disability Insurance benefits and taxes, but include all Old-Age and Survivors Insurance (OASI) benefits and taxes (including pre-retirement Survivors Insurance). All values include both the portion of the OASI tax paid directly by workers and the portion paid by the employer on a worker's behalf. All rates of return are net of inflation. Calculations are based on life expectancies and average earnings for each district. Because of non-linearity in the benefit function, amounts for each district may not sum to the state average.

KENTUCKY

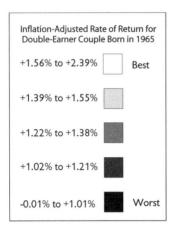

Inflation-Adjusted Rate of Return for
Double-Earner Couple Born in 1965

+1.56% to +2.39% ☐ Best

+1.39% to +1.55% ☐

+1.22% to +1.38% ☐

+1.02% to +1.21% ☐

-0.01% to +1.01% ☐ Worst

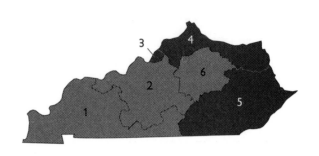

Lifetime Dollar Losses Under Social Security (OASI) Compared with Personal Retirement Accounts for Double-Earner Couples Born in 1965

District	Member of Congress	Loss Under Social Security (3)-(2)	Ranking from Lowest Loss to Highest Loss	Social Security Taxes Paid (1)	Social Security Benefits (2)	Personal Retirement Accounts (3)
Senate						
	Mitch McConnell (R)					
	Jim Bunning (R)					
Statewide		$ 439,514	19	$ 297,613	$ 416,184	$ 855,698
House of Representatives						
1	Edward Whitfield (R)	381,248	59 / 436	265,854	383,256	764,503
2	Ron Lewis (R)	398,772	86	278,229	401,317	800,089
3	Anne M. Northup (R)	549,884	276	352,118	462,683	1,012,568
4	Ken Lucas (D)	483,503	198	323,305	446,209	929,712
5	Harold Rogers (R)	410,743	104	273,004	374,320	785,064
6	Ernest L. Fletcher (R)	435,625	138	303,747	437,846	873,471

Note: Column (1) shows the total amount of Old-Age and Survivors Insurance (OASI) taxes paid during the individual's working life. Column (2) shows the total value of Old-Age and Survivors Insurance benefits collected by the worker and his or her spouse following retirement. Column (3) shows the amount accumulated in a Personal Retirement Account had the worker been able to place his or her OASI taxes in a Personal Retirement Account. The accumulation in this personal account has been reduced by the cost of purchasing life insurance coverage equivalent to the pre-retirement Survivors Insurance portion of Social Security. All amounts exclude both Disability Insurance benefits and taxes. All values include both the portion of the OASI tax paid directly by workers and the portion paid by the employer on a worker's behalf. The losses from not participating in a Personal Retirement Account (columns (3)-(2)) are for illustrative purposes only and do not reflect any specific plan for reforming Social Security. All amounts are expressed in inflation-adjusted dollars for the year 2000. Calculations are based on life expectancies and average earnings for each district. Because of non-linearity in the benefit function, amounts for each district may not sum to the state average.

Inflation-Adjusted Rate of Return from Social Security (OASI) by Birth Year

District	Member of Congress	Single Males			Single Females			Double-Earner Couples		
		1955	1965	1975	1955	1965	1975	1955	1965	1975
Senate										
	Mitch McConnell (R)									
	Jim Bunning (R)									
Statewide		0.53 %	0.14 %	-0.28 %	2.48 %	2.33 %	2.16 %	1.53 %	1.26 %	0.97 %
House of Representatives										
1	Edward Whitfield (R)	0.66	0.22	-0.27	2.61	2.46	2.30	1.66	1.38	1.06
2	Ron Lewis (R)	0.69	0.28	-0.17	2.56	2.42	2.25	1.65	1.38	1.07
3	Anne M. Northup (R)	0.17	-0.17	-0.56	2.33	2.16	1.99	1.28	1.03	0.75
4	Ken Lucas (D)	0.42	0.11	-0.24	2.41	2.26	2.09	1.44	1.21	0.95
5	Harold Rogers (R)	0.55	0.00	-0.52	2.49	2.33	2.15	1.54	1.21	0.86
6	Ernest L. Fletcher (R)	0.62	0.31	-0.04	2.52	2.37	2.20	1.59	1.36	1.10

Note: Rates of return exclude both Disability Insurance benefits and taxes, but include all Old-Age and Survivors Insurance (OASI) benefits and taxes (including pre-retirement Survivors Insurance). All values include both the portion of the OASI tax paid directly by workers and the portion paid by the employer on a worker's behalf. All rates of return are net of inflation. Calculations are based on life expectancies and average earnings for each district. Because of non-linearity in the benefit function, amounts for each district may not sum to the state average.

LOUISIANA

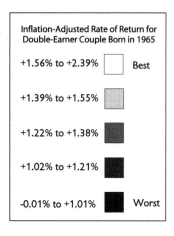

Inflation-Adjusted Rate of Return for
Double-Earner Couple Born in 1965

+1.56% to +2.39% ☐ Best

+1.39% to +1.55% ▨

+1.22% to +1.38% ▦

+1.02% to +1.21% ■

-0.01% to +1.01% ■ Worst

Lifetime Dollar Losses Under Social Security (OASI) Compared with Personal Retirement Accounts for Double-Earner Couples Born in 1965

District	Member of Congress	Loss Under Social Security (3)-(2)	Ranking from Lowest Loss to Highest Loss	Social Security Taxes Paid (1)	Social Security Benefits (2)	Personal Retirement Accounts (3)
Senate						
	John B. Breaux (D)					
	Mary Landrieu (D)					
Statewide		$ 514,566	35	$ 311,241	$ 380,314	$ 894,880
House of Representatives						
1	David Vitter (R)	604,840	327 / 436	364,583	443,574	1,048,414
2	William J. Jefferson (D)	554,199	283	309,589	336,071	890,270
3	W. J. Tauzin (R)	510,401	235	311,452	385,227	895,628
4	Jim McCrery (R)	525,005	252	315,820	383,182	908,187
5	John Cooksey (R)	447,896	149	280,347	358,285	806,181
6	Richard H. Baker (R)	567,983	298	339,768	409,072	977,055
7	Christopher John (D)	496,888	221	305,641	382,027	878,915

Note: Column (1) shows the total amount of Old-Age and Survivors Insurance (OASI) taxes paid during the individual's working life. Column (2) shows the total value of Old-Age and Survivors Insurance benefits collected by the worker and his or her spouse following retirement. Column (3) shows the amount accumulated in a Personal Retirement Account had the worker been able to place his or her OASI taxes in a Personal Retirement Account. The accumulation in this personal account has been reduced by the cost of purchasing life insurance coverage equivalent to the pre-retirement Survivors Insurance portion of Social Security. All amounts exclude both Disability Insurance benefits and taxes. All values include both the portion of the OASI tax paid directly by workers and the portion paid by the employer on a worker's behalf. The losses from not participating in a Personal Retirement Account (columns (3)-(2)) are for illustrative purposes only and do not reflect any specific plan for reforming Social Security. All amounts are expressed in inflation-adjusted dollars for the year 2000. Calculations are based on life expectancies and average earnings for each district. Because of non-linearity in the benefit function, amounts for each district may not sum to the state average.

Inflation-Adjusted Rate of Return from Social Security (OASI) by Birth Year

District	Member of Congress	Single Males			Single Females			Double-Earner Couples		
		1955	1965	1975	1955	1965	1975	1955	1965	1975
Senate										
	John B. Breaux (D)									
	Mary Landrieu (D)									
Statewide		0.05 %	-0.59 %	-1.31 %	2.23 %	2.04 %	1.85 %	1.17 %	0.78 %	0.36 %
House of Representatives										
1	David Vitter (R)	-0.06	-0.59	-1.20	2.18	1.99	1.81	1.09	0.75	0.38
2	William J. Jefferson (D)	-0.48	-1.51	-2.67	2.11	1.88	1.65	0.88	0.33	-0.24
3	W. J. Tauzin (R)	0.12	-0.47	-1.15	2.21	2.03	1.84	1.19	0.83	0.42
4	Jim McCrery (R)	0.00	-0.63	-1.34	2.21	2.02	1.82	1.14	0.75	0.33
5	John Cooksey (R)	0.30	-0.36	-1.10	2.35	2.16	1.97	1.35	0.95	0.52
6	Richard H. Baker (R)	-0.07	-0.63	-1.28	2.16	1.97	1.78	1.07	0.72	0.33
7	Christopher John (D)	0.17	-0.44	-1.13	2.25	2.07	1.89	1.24	0.87	0.46

Note: Rates of return exclude both Disability Insurance benefits and taxes, but include all Old-Age and Survivors Insurance (OASI) benefits and taxes (including pre-retirement Survivors Insurance). All values include both the portion of the OASI tax paid directly by workers and the portion paid by the employer on a worker's behalf. All rates of return are net of inflation. Calculations are based on life expectancies and average earnings for each district. Because of non-linearity in the benefit function, amounts for each district may not sum to the state average.

MAINE

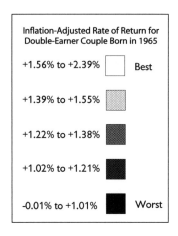

Inflation-Adjusted Rate of Return for
Double-Earner Couple Born in 1965

+1.56% to +2.39% — Best

+1.39% to +1.55%

+1.22% to +1.38%

+1.02% to +1.21%

-0.01% to +1.01% — Worst

Lifetime Dollar Losses Under Social Security (OASI) Compared with Personal Retirement Accounts for Double-Earner Couples Born in 1965

District	Member of Congress	Loss Under Social Security (3)-(2)	Ranking from Lowest Loss to Highest Loss	Social Security Taxes Paid (1)	Social Security Benefits (2)	Personal Retirement Accounts (3)
Senate						
	Olympia J. Snowe (R)					
	Susan M. Collins (R)					
Statewide		$ 406,268	13	$ 310,342	$ 486,028	$ 892,296
House of Representatives						
1	Thomas H. Allen (D)	453,081	154 / 436	337,735	518,127	971,208
2	John Elias Baldacci (D)	357,475	44	282,432	454,701	812,176

Note: Column (1) shows the total amount of Old-Age and Survivors Insurance (OASI) taxes paid during the individual's working life. Column (2) shows the total value of Old-Age and Survivors Insurance benefits collected by the worker and his or her spouse following retirement. Column (3) shows the amount accumulated in a Personal Retirement Account had the worker been able to place his or her OASI taxes in a Personal Retirement Account. The accumulation in this personal account has been reduced by the cost of purchasing life insurance coverage equivalent to the pre-retirement Survivors Insurance portion of Social Security. All amounts exclude both Disability Insurance benefits and taxes. All values include both the portion of the OASI tax paid directly by workers and the portion paid by the employer on a worker's behalf. The losses from not participating in a Personal Retirement Account (columns (3)-(2)) are for illustrative purposes only and do not reflect any specific plan for reforming Social Security. All amounts are expressed in inflation-adjusted dollars for the year 2000. Calculations are based on life expectancies and average earnings for each district. Because of non-linearity in the benefit function, amounts for each district may not sum to the state average.

Inflation-Adjusted Rate of Return from Social Security (OASI) by Birth Year

District	Member of Congress	Single Males			Single Females			Double-Earner Couples		
		1955	1965	1975	1955	1965	1975	1955	1965	1975
Senate										
	Olympia J. Snowe (R)									
	Susan M. Collins (R)									
Statewide		0.96 %	0.74 %	0.47 %	2.63 %	2.51 %	2.36 %	1.80 %	1.63 %	1.41 %
House of Representatives										
1	Thomas H. Allen (D)	0.84	0.64	0.37	2.57	2.45	2.30	1.71	1.55	1.33
2	John Elias Baldacci (D)	1.10	0.87	0.58	2.70	2.58	2.43	1.91	1.74	1.51

Note: Rates of return exclude both Disability Insurance benefits and taxes, but include all Old-Age and Survivors Insurance (OASI) benefits and taxes (including pre-retirement Survivors Insurance). All values include both the portion of the OASI tax paid directly by workers and the portion paid by the employer on a worker's behalf. All rates of return are net of inflation. Calculations are based on life expectancies and average earnings for each district. Because of non-linearity in the benefit function, amounts for each district may not sum to the state average.

MARYLAND

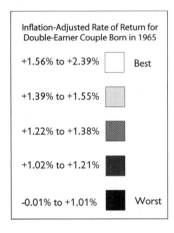

Inflation-Adjusted Rate of Return for
Double-Earner Couple Born in 1965

+1.56% to +2.39% Best

+1.39% to +1.55%

+1.22% to +1.38%

+1.02% to +1.21%

-0.01% to +1.01% Worst

Lifetime Dollar Losses Under Social Security (OASI) Compared with Personal Retirement Accounts for Double-Earner Couples Born in 1965

District	Member of Congress	Loss Under Social Security (3)-(2)	Ranking from Lowest Loss to Highest Loss	Social Security Taxes Paid (1)	Social Security Benefits (2)	Personal Retirement Accounts (3)
Senate						
	Paul S. Sarbanes (D)					
	Barbara A. Mikulski (D)					
Statewide		$ 680,169	47	$ 427,232	$ 548,207	$ 1,228,377
House of Representatives						
1	Wayne T. Gilchrest (R)	582,589	309 / 436	383,810	521,112	1,103,701
2	Robert L. Ehrlich, Jr. (R)	666,800	364	435,581	585,780	1,252,580
3	Benjamin L. Cardin (D)	685,412	374	430,559	552,725	1,238,137
4	Albert R. Wynn (D)	676,559	369	411,287	506,159	1,182,718
5	Steny H. Hoyer (D)	655,394	360	425,465	568,093	1,223,487
6	Roscoe G. Bartlett (R)	602,468	325	401,810	552,998	1,155,465
7	Elijah Cummings (D)	551,113	278	319,681	368,176	919,289
8	Constance A. Morella (R)	944,813	429	567,623	717,904	1,662,717

Note: Column (1) shows the total amount of Old-Age and Survivors Insurance (OASI) taxes paid during the individual's working life. Column (2) shows the total value of Old-Age and Survivors Insurance benefits collected by the worker and his or her spouse following retirement. Column (3) shows the amount accumulated in a Personal Retirement Account had the worker been able to place his or her OASI taxes in a Personal Retirement Account. The accumulation in this personal account has been reduced by the cost of purchasing life insurance coverage equivalent to the pre-retirement Survivors Insurance portion of Social Security. All amounts exclude both Disability Insurance benefits and taxes. All values include both the portion of the OASI tax paid directly by workers and the portion paid by the employer on a worker's behalf. The losses from not participating in a Personal Retirement Account (columns (3)-(2)) are for illustrative purposes only and do not reflect any specific plan for reforming Social Security. All amounts are expressed in inflation-adjusted dollars for the year 2000. Calculations are based on life expectancies and average earnings for each district. Because of non-linearity in the benefit function, amounts for each district may not sum to the state average.

Inflation-Adjusted Rate of Return from Social Security (OASI) by Birth Year

District	Member of Congress	Single Males			Single Females			Double-Earner Couples		
		1955	1965	1975	1955	1965	1975	1955	1965	1975
Senate										
	Paul S. Sarbanes (D)									
	Barbara A. Mikulski (D)									
Statewide		0.13 %	-0.26 %	-0.72 %	2.23 %	2.07 %	1.89 %	1.20 %	0.93 %	0.61 %
House of Representatives										
1	Wayne T. Gilchrest (R)	0.39	0.04	-0.39	2.34	2.18	2.01	1.38	1.13	0.83
2	Robert L. Ehrlich, Jr. (R)	0.30	0.03	-0.33	2.27	2.12	1.95	1.30	1.09	0.82
3	Benjamin L. Cardin (D)	0.15	-0.25	-0.71	2.23	2.06	1.88	1.21	0.93	0.61
4	Albert R. Wynn (D)	-0.05	-0.57	-1.13	2.21	2.03	1.83	1.11	0.79	0.42
5	Steny H. Hoyer (D)	0.28	-0.03	-0.42	2.27	2.13	1.95	1.29	1.07	0.78
6	Roscoe G. Bartlett (R)	0.41	0.12	-0.26	2.34	2.20	2.03	1.39	1.17	0.89
7	Elijah Cummings (D)	-0.20	-1.11	-2.08	2.23	2.00	1.77	1.07	0.56	0.04
8	Constance A. Morella (R)	0.03	-0.22	-0.52	1.95	1.81	1.64	1.04	0.85	0.61

Note: Rates of return exclude both Disability Insurance benefits and taxes, but include all Old-Age and Survivors Insurance (OASI) benefits and taxes (including pre-retirement Survivors Insurance). All values include both the portion of the OASI tax paid directly by workers and the portion paid by the employer on a worker's behalf. All rates of return are net of inflation. Calculations are based on life expectancies and average earnings for each district. Because of non-linearity in the benefit function, amounts for each district may not sum to the state average.

MASSACHUSETTS

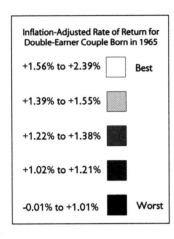

Inflation-Adjusted Rate of Return for
Double-Earner Couple Born in 1965

+1.56% to +2.39% **Best**

+1.39% to +1.55%

+1.22% to +1.38%

+1.02% to +1.21%

-0.01% to +1.01% **Worst**

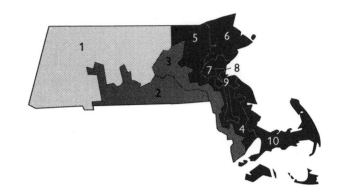

Lifetime Dollar Losses Under Social Security (OASI) Compared with Personal Retirement Accounts for Double-Earner Couples Born in 1965

District	Member of Congress	Loss Under Social Security (3)-(2)	Ranking from Lowest Loss to Highest Loss	Social Security Taxes Paid (1)	Social Security Benefits (2)	Personal Retirement Accounts (3)
Senate						
	Edward M. Kennedy (D)					
	John F. Kerry (D)					
Statewide		$ 620,524	45	$ 414,242	$ 570,505	$ 1,191,029
House of Representatives						
1	John W. Olver (D)	462,497	168 / 436	340,242	515,920	978,417
2	Richard E. Neal (D)	519,719	250	365,728	531,985	1,051,704
3	James P. McGovern (D)	566,092	295	392,630	562,973	1,129,065
4	Barney Frank (D)	702,390	382	456,688	610,884	1,313,274
5	Martin T. Meehan (D)	714,732	385	462,124	614,174	1,328,906
6	John F. Tierney (D)	670,812	365	448,083	617,718	1,288,530
7	Edward J. Markey (D)	694,678	378	455,587	615,430	1,310,109
8	Michael E. Capuano (D)	563,670	292	361,694	476,434	1,040,104
9	John Joseph Moakley (D)	678,240	371	437,867	580,912	1,259,152
10	William D. Delahunt (D)	619,787	336	418,331	583,186	1,202,973

Note: Column (1) shows the total amount of Old-Age and Survivors Insurance (OASI) taxes paid during the individual's working life. Column (2) shows the total value of Old-Age and Survivors Insurance benefits collected by the worker and his or her spouse following retirement. Column (3) shows the amount accumulated in a Personal Retirement Account had the worker been able to place his or her OASI taxes in a Personal Retirement Account. The accumulation in this personal account has been reduced by the cost of purchasing life insurance coverage equivalent to the pre-retirement Survivors Insurance portion of Social Security. All amounts exclude both Disability Insurance benefits and taxes. All values include both the portion of the OASI tax paid directly by workers and the portion paid by the employer on a worker's behalf. The losses from not participating in a Personal Retirement Account (columns (3)-(2)) are for illustrative purposes only and do not reflect any specific plan for reforming Social Security. All amounts are expressed in inflation-adjusted dollars for the year 2000. Calculations are based on life expectancies and average earnings for each district. Because of non-linearity in the benefit function, amounts for each district may not sum to the state average.

Inflation-Adjusted Rate of Return from Social Security (OASI) by Birth Year

District	Member of Congress	Single Males 1955	1965	1975	Single Females 1955	1965	1975	Double-Earner Couples 1955	1965	1975
Senate										
	Edward M. Kennedy (D)									
	John F. Kerry (D)									
Statewide		0.40 %	0.08 %	-0.24 %	2.38 %	2.23 %	2.07 %	1.40 %	1.17 %	0.93 %
House of Representatives										
1	John W. Olver (D)	0.83	0.58	0.32	2.56	2.42	2.27	1.71	1.51	1.29
2	Richard E. Neal (D)	0.63	0.36	0.07	2.48	2.34	2.18	1.57	1.37	1.13
3	James P. McGovern (D)	0.56	0.31	0.04	2.42	2.29	2.13	1.51	1.31	1.09
4	Barney Frank (D)	0.23	-0.10	-0.42	2.31	2.17	2.01	1.29	1.06	0.82
5	Martin T. Meehan (D)	0.21	-0.09	-0.42	2.27	2.13	1.97	1.26	1.04	0.79
6	John F. Tierney (D)	0.37	0.11	-0.16	2.33	2.19	2.04	1.36	1.17	0.94
7	Edward J. Markey (D)	0.29	-0.02	-0.33	2.33	2.17	2.01	1.33	1.10	0.85
8	Michael E. Capuano (D)	0.37	-0.28	-0.76	2.43	2.23	2.06	1.42	1.03	0.72
9	John Joseph Moakley (D)	0.23	-0.16	-0.52	2.33	2.17	2.01	1.31	1.04	0.77
10	William D. Delahunt (D)	0.43	0.15	-0.13	2.38	2.23	2.08	1.42	1.21	0.98

Note: Rates of return exclude both Disability Insurance benefits and taxes, but include all Old-Age and Survivors Insurance (OASI) benefits and taxes (including pre-retirement Survivors Insurance). All values include both the portion of the OASI tax paid directly by workers and the portion paid by the employer on a worker's behalf. All rates of return are net of inflation. Calculations are based on life expectancies and average earnings for each district. Because of non-linearity in the benefit function, amounts for each district may not sum to the state average.

MICHIGAN

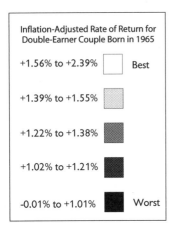

Inflation-Adjusted Rate of Return for
Double-Earner Couple Born in 1965

+1.56% to +2.39% ☐ Best

+1.39% to +1.55%

+1.22% to +1.38%

+1.02% to +1.21%

-0.01% to +1.01% ■ Worst

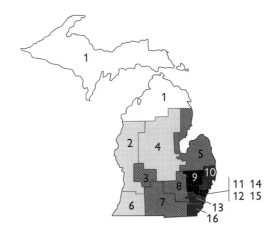

Lifetime Dollar Losses Under Social Security (OASI) Compared with Personal Retirement Accounts for Double-Earner Couples Born in 1965

District	Member of Congress	Loss Under Social Security (3)-(2)	Ranking from Lowest Loss to Highest Loss	Social Security Taxes Paid (1)	Social Security Benefits (2)	Personal Retirement Accounts (3)
Senate						
	Carl Levin (D)					
	Spencer Abraham (R)					
Statewide		$ 565,674	42	$ 370,564	$ 499,771	$ 1,065,445
House of Representatives						
1	Bart T. Stupak (D)	368,342	51 / 436	276,185	425,868	794,210
2	Peter Hoekstra (R)	450,855	152	324,280	481,659	932,514
3	Vernon J. Ehlers (R)	517,928	246	356,965	508,578	1,026,505
4	Dave Camp (R)	415,446	112	304,078	458,975	874,420
5	James A. Barcia (D)	481,399	195	326,468	457,409	938,809
6	Fred S. Upton (R)	462,774	170	328,759	482,622	945,396
7	Nick Smith (R)	486,063	203	335,227	477,932	963,995
8	Debbie Stabenow (D)	552,291	280	380,292	541,294	1,093,585
9	Dale E. Kildee (D)	658,323	362	412,238	527,130	1,185,453
10	David E. Bonior (D)	603,408	326	401,883	552,266	1,155,674
11	Joseph Knollenberg (R)	922,425	426	558,521	708,591	1,631,016
12	Sander M. Levin (D)	646,163	352	425,080	576,219	1,222,381
13	Lynn N. Rivers (D)	587,571	315	392,679	541,635	1,129,206
14	John Conyers, Jr. (D)	613,970	331	349,388	390,748	1,004,717
15	Carolyn C. Kilpatrick (D)	598,572	322	318,706	317,914	916,487
16	John D. Dingell (D)	605,487	328	401,292	548,486	1,153,974

Note: Column (1) shows the total amount of Old-Age and Survivors Insurance (OASI) taxes paid during the individual's working life. Column (2) shows the total value of Old-Age and Survivors Insurance benefits collected by the worker and his or her spouse following retirement. Column (3) shows the amount accumulated in a Personal Retirement Account had the worker been able to place his or her OASI taxes in a Personal Retirement Account. The accumulation in this personal account has been reduced by the cost of purchasing life insurance coverage equivalent to the pre-retirement Survivors Insurance portion of Social Security. All amounts exclude both Disability Insurance benefits and taxes. All values include both the portion of the OASI tax paid directly by workers and the portion paid by the employer on a worker's behalf. The losses from not participating in a Personal Retirement Account (columns (3)-(2)) are for illustrative purposes only and do not reflect any specific plan for reforming Social Security. All amounts are expressed in inflation-adjusted dollars for the year 2000. Calculations are based on life expectancies and average earnings for each district. Because of non-linearity in the benefit function, amounts for each district may not sum to the state average.

Inflation-Adjusted Rate of Return from Social Security (OASI) by Birth Year

District	Member of Congress	Single Males 1955	1965	1975	Single Females 1955	1965	1975	Double-Earner Couples 1955	1965	1975
Senate										
	Carl Levin (D)									
	Spencer Abraham (R)									
Statewide		0.39 %	0.07 %	-0.30 %	2.30 %	2.14 %	1.97 %	1.35 %	1.12 %	0.84 %
House of Representatives										
1	Bart T. Stupak (D)	1.00	0.68	0.30	2.65	2.50	2.35	1.84	1.60	1.33
2	Peter Hoekstra (R)	0.81	0.57	0.25	2.47	2.34	2.18	1.65	1.46	1.21
3	Vernon J. Ehlers (R)	0.61	0.32	-0.02	2.41	2.27	2.10	1.52	1.30	1.04
4	Dave Camp (R)	0.90	0.65	0.33	2.52	2.38	2.22	1.72	1.52	1.27
5	James A. Barcia (D)	0.59	0.29	-0.08	2.37	2.22	2.05	1.49	1.26	0.99
6	Fred S. Upton (R)	0.76	0.50	0.18	2.47	2.32	2.15	1.62	1.42	1.16
7	Nick Smith (R)	0.62	0.29	-0.11	2.45	2.30	2.14	1.55	1.31	1.03
8	Debbie Stabenow (D)	0.58	0.36	0.06	2.36	2.22	2.06	1.48	1.29	1.05
9	Dale E. Kildee (D)	0.15	-0.16	-0.53	2.15	1.98	1.81	1.16	0.92	0.64
10	David E. Bonior (D)	0.41	0.16	-0.15	2.30	2.16	1.99	1.37	1.17	0.92
11	Joseph Knollenberg (R)	0.02	-0.17	-0.39	1.96	1.81	1.64	1.03	0.86	0.65
12	Sander M. Levin (D)	0.36	0.09	-0.22	2.28	2.13	1.96	1.33	1.12	0.87
13	Lynn N. Rivers (D)	0.46	0.19	-0.12	2.32	2.16	1.99	1.40	1.19	0.93
14	John Conyers, Jr. (D)	-0.36	-1.05	-1.76	2.03	1.79	1.58	0.87	0.44	0.01
15	Carolyn C. Kilpatrick (D)	-0.80	-2.00	-3.18	1.91	1.63	1.41	0.62	-0.01	-0.58
16	John D. Dingell (D)	0.41	0.14	-0.18	2.30	2.15	1.98	1.36	1.15	0.90

Note: Rates of return exclude both Disability Insurance benefits and taxes, but include all Old-Age and Survivors Insurance (OASI) benefits and taxes (including pre-retirement Survivors Insurance). All values include both the portion of the OASI tax paid directly by workers and the portion paid by the employer on a worker's behalf. All rates of return are net of inflation. Calculations are based on life expectancies and average earnings for each district. Because of non-linearity in the benefit function, amounts for each district may not sum to the state average.

MINNESOTA

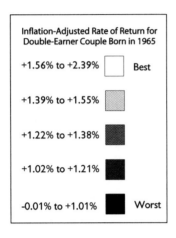

Inflation-Adjusted Rate of Return for
Double-Earner Couple Born in 1965

+1.56% to +2.39% ☐ Best

+1.39% to +1.55% ▨

+1.22% to +1.38% ▨

+1.02% to +1.21% ▨

-0.01% to +1.01% ■ Worst

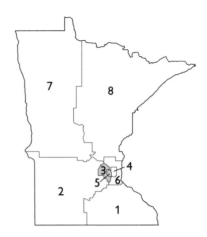

Lifetime Dollar Losses Under Social Security (OASI) Compared with Personal Retirement Accounts for Double-Earner Couples Born in 1965

District	Member of Congress	Loss Under Social Security (3)-(2)	Ranking from Lowest Loss to Highest Loss	Social Security Taxes Paid (1)	Social Security Benefits (2)	Personal Retirement Accounts (3)
Senate						
	Paul David Wellstone (D)					
	Rod Grams (R)					
Statewide		$ 427,655	17	$ 349,164	$ 576,262	$ 1,003,917
House of Representatives						
1	Gil Gutknecht (R)	333,875	27 / 436	305,231	543,863	877,738
2	David Minge (D)	321,462	17	299,312	539,254	860,716
3	Jim Ramstad (R)	661,625	363	487,842	741,669	1,403,294
4	Bruce F. Vento (D)	498,833	224	379,748	593,190	1,092,023
5	Martin Olav Sabo (D)	488,591	207	362,249	553,111	1,041,702
6	William P. Luther (D)	513,345	240	407,018	657,096	1,170,441
7	Collin C. Peterson (D)	254,244	3	254,175	476,673	730,917
8	James L. Oberstar (D)	341,917	31	294,756	505,699	847,616

Note: Column (1) shows the total amount of Old-Age and Survivors Insurance (OASI) taxes paid during the individual's working life. Column (2) shows the total value of Old-Age and Survivors Insurance benefits collected by the worker and his or her spouse following retirement. Column (3) shows the amount accumulated in a Personal Retirement Account had the worker been able to place his or her OASI taxes in a Personal Retirement Account. The accumulation in this personal account has been reduced by the cost of purchasing life insurance coverage equivalent to the pre-retirement Survivors Insurance portion of Social Security. All amounts exclude both Disability Insurance benefits and taxes. All values include both the portion of the OASI tax paid directly by workers and the portion paid by the employer on a worker's behalf. The losses from not participating in a Personal Retirement Account (columns (3)-(2)) are for illustrative purposes only and do not reflect any specific plan for reforming Social Security. All amounts are expressed in inflation-adjusted dollars for the year 2000. Calculations are based on life expectancies and average earnings for each district. Because of non-linearity in the benefit function, amounts for each district may not sum to the state average.

Inflation-Adjusted Rate of Return from Social Security (OASI) by Birth Year

District	Member of Congress	Single Males 1955	Single Males 1965	Single Males 1975	Single Females 1955	Single Females 1965	Single Females 1975	Double-Earner Couples 1955	Double-Earner Couples 1965	Double-Earner Couples 1975
Senate										
	Paul David Wellstone (D)									
	Rod Grams (R)									
Statewide		1.11 %	0.95 %	0.72 %	2.71 %	2.59 %	2.44 %	1.91 %	1.77 %	1.57 %
House of Representatives										
1	Gil Gutknecht (R)	1.40	1.27	1.06	2.88	2.77	2.63	2.15	2.02	1.83
2	David Minge (D)	1.46	1.33	1.12	2.89	2.78	2.64	2.18	2.06	1.87
3	Jim Ramstad (R)	0.67	0.57	0.39	2.47	2.35	2.21	1.58	1.46	1.28
4	Bruce F. Vento (D)	0.91	0.69	0.44	2.61	2.47	2.31	1.77	1.59	1.37
5	Martin Olav Sabo (D)	0.88	0.56	0.25	2.62	2.46	2.30	1.76	1.52	1.28
6	William P. Luther (D)	0.95	0.86	0.68	2.60	2.49	2.34	1.78	1.67	1.49
7	Collin C. Peterson (D)	1.62	1.48	1.25	3.04	2.93	2.80	2.34	2.21	2.02
8	James L. Oberstar (D)	1.30	1.14	0.89	2.81	2.70	2.55	2.06	1.92	1.71

Note: Rates of return exclude both Disability Insurance benefits and taxes, but include all Old-Age and Survivors Insurance (OASI) benefits and taxes (including pre-retirement Survivors Insurance). All values include both the portion of the OASI tax paid directly by workers and the portion paid by the employer on a worker's behalf. All rates of return are net of inflation. Calculations are based on life expectancies and average earnings for each district. Because of non-linearity in the benefit function, amounts for each district may not sum to the state average.

MISSISSIPPI

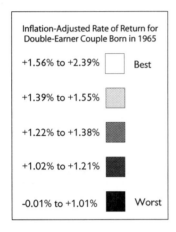

Inflation-Adjusted Rate of Return for
Double-Earner Couple Born in 1965

+1.56% to +2.39% ☐ Best

+1.39% to +1.55% ▢

+1.22% to +1.38% ▨

+1.02% to +1.21% ▨

-0.01% to +1.01% ■ Worst

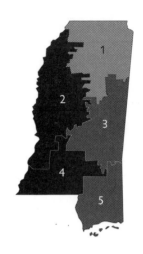

Lifetime Dollar Losses Under Social Security (OASI) Compared with Personal Retirement Accounts for Double-Earner Couples Born in 1965

District	Member of Congress	Loss Under Social Security (3)-(2)	Ranking from Lowest Loss to Highest Loss	Social Security Taxes Paid (1)	Social Security Benefits (2)	Personal Retirement Accounts (3)
Senate						
	Thad Cochran (R)					
	Trent Lott (R)					
Statewide		$ 436,249	18	$ 277,138	$ 360,578	$ 796,827
House of Representatives						
1	Roger F. Wicker (R)	393,505	78 / 436	268,627	378,972	772,477
2	Bennie G. Thompson (D)	422,973	120	250,594	297,647	720,620
3	Charles Pickering, Jr. (R)	457,456	162	291,909	381,972	839,428
4	Ronnie Shows (D)	478,130	191	295,613	371,949	850,079
5	Gene Taylor (D)	431,283	133	277,794	367,556	798,839

Note: Column (1) shows the total amount of Old-Age and Survivors Insurance (OASI) taxes paid during the individual's working life. Column (2) shows the total value of Old-Age and Survivors Insurance benefits collected by the worker and his or her spouse following retirement. Column (3) shows the amount accumulated in a Personal Retirement Account had the worker been able to place his or her OASI taxes in a Personal Retirement Account. The accumulation in this personal account has been reduced by the cost of purchasing life insurance coverage equivalent to the pre-retirement Survivors Insurance portion of Social Security. All amounts exclude both Disability Insurance benefits and taxes. All values include both the portion of the OASI tax paid directly by workers and the portion paid by the employer on a worker's behalf. The losses from not participating in a Personal Retirement Account (columns (3)-(2)) are for illustrative purposes only and do not reflect any specific plan for reforming Social Security. All amounts are expressed in inflation-adjusted dollars for the year 2000. Calculations are based on life expectancies and average earnings for each district. Because of non-linearity in the benefit function, amounts for each district may not sum to the state average.

Inflation-Adjusted Rate of Return from Social Security (OASI) by Birth Year

District	Member of Congress	Single Males			Single Females			Double-Earner Couples		
		1955	1965	1975	1955	1965	1975	1955	1965	1975
Senate										
	Thad Cochran (R)									
	Trent Lott (R)									
Statewide		0.33 %	-0.30 %	-0.98 %	2.42 %	2.23 %	2.02 %	1.40 %	1.02 %	0.60 %
House of Representatives										
1	Roger F. Wicker (R)	0.65	0.21	-0.30	2.53	2.35	2.16	1.61	1.31	0.96
2	Bennie G. Thompson (D)	-0.05	-1.00	-2.06	2.36	2.14	1.91	1.21	0.69	0.14
3	Charles Pickering, Jr. (R)	0.30	-0.26	-0.89	2.42	2.22	2.02	1.39	1.03	0.64
4	Ronnie Shows (D)	0.14	-0.49	-1.17	2.35	2.14	1.93	1.28	0.89	0.47
5	Gene Taylor (D)	0.38	-0.25	-0.95	2.47	2.29	2.09	1.46	1.08	0.66

Note: Rates of return exclude both Disability Insurance benefits and taxes, but include all Old-Age and Survivors Insurance (OASI) benefits and taxes (including pre-retirement Survivors Insurance). All values include both the portion of the OASI tax paid directly by workers and the portion paid by the employer on a worker's behalf. All rates of return are net of inflation. Calculations are based on life expectancies and average earnings for each district. Because of non-linearity in the benefit function, amounts for each district may not sum to the state average.

MISSOURI

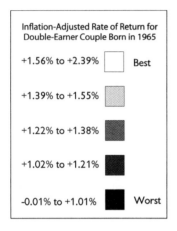

Inflation-Adjusted Rate of Return for
Double-Earner Couple Born in 1965

+1.56% to +2.39% ☐ Best

+1.39% to +1.55% ☐

+1.22% to +1.38% ☐

+1.02% to +1.21% ☐

-0.01% to +1.01% ■ Worst

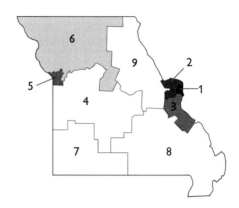

Lifetime Dollar Losses Under Social Security (OASI) Compared with Personal Retirement Accounts for Double-Earner Couples Born in 1965

District	Member of Congress	Loss Under Social Security (3)-(2)	Ranking from Lowest Loss to Highest Loss	Social Security Taxes Paid (1)	Social Security Benefits (2)	Personal Retirement Accounts (3)
Senate						
	Christopher S. Bond (R)					
	John Ashcroft (R)					
Statewide		$ 457,169	24	$ 324,386	$ 475,506	$ 932,675
House of Representatives						
1	William Clay (D)	529,400	259 / 436	329,602	418,421	947,821
2	James M. Talent (R)	760,316	399	496,798	669,403	1,429,719
3	Richard A. Gephardt (D)	507,232	230	355,580	515,293	1,022,524
4	Ike Skelton (D)	349,384	38	266,960	418,298	767,682
5	Karen McCarthy (D)	502,747	228	338,623	471,014	973,761
6	Pat Danner (D)	428,597	130	318,233	486,530	915,127
7	Roy Blunt (R)	329,213	22	267,840	441,000	770,213
8	Jo Ann Emerson (R)	324,980	19	251,143	397,218	722,199
9	Kenny C. Hulshof (R)	373,314	54	290,498	462,055	835,369

Note: Column (1) shows the total amount of Old-Age and Survivors Insurance (OASI) taxes paid during the individual's working life. Column (2) shows the total value of Old-Age and Survivors Insurance benefits collected by the worker and his or her spouse following retirement. Column (3) shows the amount accumulated in a Personal Retirement Account had the worker been able to place his or her OASI taxes in a Personal Retirement Account. The accumulation in this personal account has been reduced by the cost of purchasing life insurance coverage equivalent to the pre-retirement Survivors Insurance portion of Social Security. All amounts exclude both Disability Insurance benefits and taxes. All values include both the portion of the OASI tax paid directly by workers and the portion paid by the employer on a worker's behalf. The losses from not participating in a Personal Retirement Account (columns (3)-(2)) are for illustrative purposes only and do not reflect any specific plan for reforming Social Security. All amounts are expressed in inflation-adjusted dollars for the year 2000. Calculations are based on life expectancies and average earnings for each district. Because of non-linearity in the benefit function, amounts for each district may not sum to the state average.

Inflation-Adjusted Rate of Return from Social Security (OASI) by Birth Year

District	Member of Congress	Single Males			Single Females			Double-Earner Couples		
		1955	1965	1975	1955	1965	1975	1955	1965	1975
Senate										
	Christopher S. Bond (R)									
	John Ashcroft (R)									
Statewide		0.69 %	0.40 %	0.03 %	2.53 %	2.39 %	2.23 %	1.63 %	1.41 %	1.14 %
House of Representatives										
1	William Clay (D)	0.10	-0.43	-0.98	2.33	2.14	1.95	1.25	0.91	0.56
2	James M. Talent (R)	0.15	-0.01	-0.28	2.26	2.14	1.98	1.23	1.08	0.86
3	Richard A. Gephardt (D)	0.61	0.36	0.04	2.47	2.33	2.17	1.56	1.36	1.11
4	Ike Skelton (D)	1.01	0.62	0.15	2.77	2.63	2.48	1.91	1.65	1.34
5	Karen McCarthy (D)	0.46	0.11	-0.31	2.46	2.29	2.12	1.48	1.23	0.93
6	Pat Danner (D)	0.84	0.60	0.27	2.60	2.47	2.31	1.74	1.55	1.30
7	Roy Blunt (R)	1.22	0.98	0.66	2.77	2.64	2.48	2.00	1.82	1.57
8	Jo Ann Emerson (R)	1.08	0.74	0.33	2.76	2.62	2.46	1.93	1.70	1.41
9	Kenny C. Hulshof (R)	1.05	0.81	0.49	2.68	2.55	2.40	1.88	1.69	1.45

Note: Rates of return exclude both Disability Insurance benefits and taxes, but include all Old-Age and Survivors Insurance (OASI) benefits and taxes (including pre-retirement Survivors Insurance). All values include both the portion of the OASI tax paid directly by workers and the portion paid by the employer on a worker's behalf. All rates of return are net of inflation. Calculations are based on life expectancies and average earnings for each district. Because of non-linearity in the benefit function, amounts for each district may not sum to the state average.

MONTANA

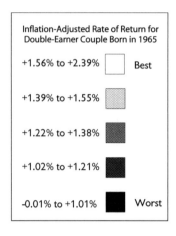

Inflation-Adjusted Rate of Return for
Double-Earner Couple Born in 1965

+1.56% to +2.39%	Best
+1.39% to +1.55%	
+1.22% to +1.38%	
+1.02% to +1.21%	
-0.01% to +1.01%	Worst

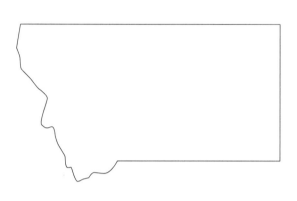

Lifetime Dollar Losses Under Social Security (OASI) Compared to Personal Retirement Accounts for Double-Earner Couples Born in 1965

District	Member of Congress	Loss Under Social Security (3)-(2)	Ranking from Lowest Loss to Highest Loss	Social Security Taxes Paid (1)	Social Security Benefits (2)	Personal Retirement Accounts (3)
Senate						
	Max Baucus (D)					
	Conrad Burns (R)					
Statewide		$ 265,016	3	$ 273,437	$ 521,294	$ 786,310
House of Representatives						
At large	Rick Hill (R)	265,016	5 / 436	273,437	521,294	786,310

Note: Column (1) shows the total amount of Old-Age and Survivors Insurance (OASI) taxes paid during the individual's working life. Column (2) shows the total value of Old-Age and Survivors Insurance benefits collected by the worker and his or her spouse following retirement. Column (3) shows the amount accumulated in a Personal Retirement Account had the worker been able to place his or her OASI taxes in a Personal Retirement Account. The accumulation in this personal account has been reduced by the cost of purchasing life insurance coverage equivalent to the pre-retirement Survivors Insurance portion of Social Security. All amounts exclude both Disability Insurance benefits and taxes. All values include both the portion of the OASI tax paid directly by workers and the portion paid by the employer on a worker's behalf. The losses from not participating in a Personal Retirement Account (columns (3)-(2)) are for illustrative purposes only and do not reflect any specific plan for reforming Social Security. All amounts are expressed in inflation-adjusted dollars for the year 2000. Calculations are based on life expectancies and average earnings for each district.

Inflation-Adjusted Rate of Return from Social Security (OASI) by Birth Year

District	Member of Congress	Single Males			Single Females			Double-Earner Couples		
		1955	1965	1975	1955	1965	1975	1955	1965	1975
Senate										
	Max Baucus (D)									
	Conrad Burns (R)									
Statewide		1.91 %	1.71 %	1.41 %	2.96 %	2.79 %	2.61 %	2.44 %	2.25 %	2.00 %
House of Representatives										
At large	Rick Hill (R)	1.91	1.71	1.41	2.96	2.79	2.61	2.44	2.25	2.00

Note: Rates of return exclude both Disability Insurance benefits and taxes, but include all Old-Age and Survivors Insurance (OASI) benefits and taxes (including pre-retirement Survivors Insurance). All values include both the portion of the OASI tax paid directly by workers and the portion paid by the employer on a worker's behalf. All rates of return are net of inflation. Calculations are based on life expectancies and average earnings for each district.

NEBRASKA

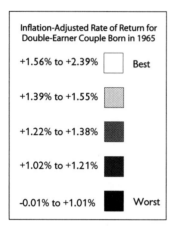

Inflation-Adjusted Rate of Return for Double-Earner Couple Born in 1965

+1.56% to +2.39% ☐ Best

+1.39% to +1.55% ▢

+1.22% to +1.38% ▨

+1.02% to +1.21% ■

-0.01% to +1.01% ■ Worst

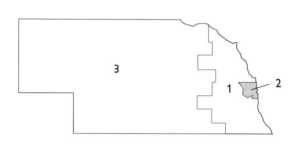

Lifetime Dollar Losses Under Social Security (OASI) Compared with Personal Retirement Accounts for Double-Earner Couples Born in 1965

District	Member of Congress	Loss Under Social Security (3)-(2)	Ranking from Lowest Loss to Highest Loss	Social Security Taxes Paid (1)	Social Security Benefits (2)	Personal Retirement Accounts (3)
Senate						
	J. Robert Kerrey (D)					
	Chuck Hagel (R)					
Statewide		$ 345,699	8	$ 298,029	$ 511,195	$ 856,894
House of Representatives						
1	Doug Bereuter (R)	304,908	11 / 436	280,827	502,653	807,561
2	Lee Terry (R)	467,057	174	348,577	535,328	1,002,385
3	Bill Barrett (R)	269,581	6	263,940	489,417	758,998

Note: Column (1) shows the total amount of Old-Age and Survivors Insurance (OASI) taxes paid during the individual's working life. Column (2) shows the total value of Old-Age and Survivors Insurance benefits collected by the worker and his or her spouse following retirement. Column (3) shows the amount accumulated in a Personal Retirement Account had the worker been able to place his or her OASI taxes in a Personal Retirement Account. The accumulation in this personal account has been reduced by the cost of purchasing life insurance coverage equivalent to the pre-retirement Survivors Insurance portion of Social Security. All amounts exclude both Disability Insurance benefits and taxes. All values include both the portion of the OASI tax paid directly by workers and the portion paid by the employer on a worker's behalf. The losses from not participating in a Personal Retirement Account (columns (3)-(2)) are for illustrative purposes only and do not reflect any specific plan for reforming Social Security. All amounts are expressed in inflation-adjusted dollars for the year 2000. Calculations are based on life expectancies and average earnings for each district. Because of non-linearity in the benefit function, amounts for each district may not sum to the state average.

Inflation-Adjusted Rate of Return from Social Security (OASI) by Birth Year

District	Member of Congress	Single Males			Single Females			Double-Earner Couples		
		1955	1965	1975	1955	1965	1975	1955	1965	1975
Senate										
	J. Robert Kerrey (D)									
	Chuck Hagel (R)									
Statewide		1.30 %	1.11 %	0.86 %	2.82 %	2.71 %	2.56 %	2.07 %	1.92 %	1.70 %
House of Representatives										
1	Doug Bereuter (R)	1.47	1.33	1.10	2.89	2.78	2.64	2.19	2.06	1.86
2	Lee Terry (R)	0.83	0.56	0.22	2.63	2.50	2.34	1.74	1.55	1.29
3	Bill Barrett (R)	1.58	1.45	1.23	2.99	2.89	2.75	2.30	2.17	1.98

Note: Rates of return exclude both Disability Insurance benefits and taxes, but include all Old-Age and Survivors Insurance (OASI) benefits and taxes (including pre-retirement Survivors Insurance). All values include both the portion of the OASI tax paid directly by workers and the portion paid by the employer on a worker's behalf. All rates of return are net of inflation. Calculations are based on life expectancies and average earnings for each district. Because of non-linearity in the benefit function, amounts for each district may not sum to the state average.

NEVADA

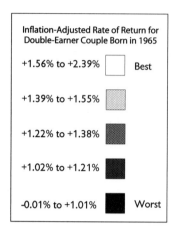

Inflation-Adjusted Rate of Return for Double-Earner Couple Born in 1965

+1.56% to +2.39%	☐	Best
+1.39% to +1.55%	▨	
+1.22% to +1.38%	▨	
+1.02% to +1.21%	■	
-0.01% to +1.01%	■	Worst

Lifetime Dollar Losses Under Social Security (OASI) Compared with Personal Retirement Accounts for Double-Earner Couples Born in 1965

District	Member of Congress	Loss Under Social Security (3)-(2)	Ranking from Lowest Loss to Highest Loss	Social Security Taxes Paid (1)	Social Security Benefits (2)	Personal Retirement Accounts (3)
Senate						
	Harry Reid (D)					
	Richard H. Bryan (D)					
Statewide		$ 547,313	39	$ 363,779	$ 498,623	$ 1,045,936
House of Representatives						
1	Shelley Berkley (D)	545,187	271 / 436	358,977	487,106	1,032,293
2	James A. Gibbons (R)	547,913	274	367,975	510,252	1,058,166

Note: Column (1) shows the total amount of Old-Age and Survivors Insurance (OASI) taxes paid during the individual's working life. Column (2) shows the total value of Old-Age and Survivors Insurance benefits collected by the worker and his or her spouse following retirement. Column (3) shows the amount accumulated in a Personal Retirement Account had the worker been able to place his or her OASI taxes in a Personal Retirement Account. The accumulation in this personal account has been reduced by the cost of purchasing life insurance coverage equivalent to the pre-retirement Survivors Insurance portion of Social Security. All amounts exclude both Disability Insurance benefits and taxes. All values include both the portion of the OASI tax paid directly by workers and the portion paid by the employer on a worker's behalf. The losses from not participating in a Personal Retirement Account (columns (3)-(2)) are for illustrative purposes only and do not reflect any specific plan for reforming Social Security. All amounts are expressed in inflation-adjusted dollars for the year 2000. Calculations are based on life expectancies and average earnings for each district. Because of non-linearity in the benefit function, amounts for each district may not sum to the state average.

Inflation-Adjusted Rate of Return from Social Security (OASI) by Birth Year

District	Member of Congress	Single Males			Single Females			Double-Earner Couples		
		1955	1965	1975	1955	1965	1975	1955	1965	1975
Senate										
	Harry Reid (D)									
	Richard H. Bryan (D)									
Statewide		0.47 %	0.12 %	-0.30 %	2.35 %	2.20 %	2.03 %	1.42 %	1.17 %	0.88 %
House of Representatives										
1	Shelley Berkley (D)	0.44	0.07	-0.35	2.33	2.17	1.99	1.40	1.14	0.83
2	James A. Gibbons (R)	0.50	0.16	-0.24	2.38	2.23	2.06	1.45	1.21	0.92

Note: Rates of return exclude both Disability Insurance benefits and taxes, but include all Old-Age and Survivors Insurance (OASI) benefits and taxes (including pre-retirement Survivors Insurance). All values include both the portion of the OASI tax paid directly by workers and the portion paid by the employer on a worker's behalf. All rates of return are net of inflation. Calculations are based on life expectancies and average earnings for each district. Because of non-linearity in the benefit function, amounts for each district may not sum to the state average.

New Hampshire

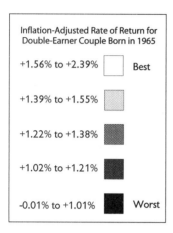

Inflation-Adjusted Rate of Return for
Double-Earner Couple Born in 1965

+1.56% to +2.39%		Best
+1.39% to +1.55%		
+1.22% to +1.38%		
+1.02% to +1.21%		
-0.01% to +1.01%		Worst

Lifetime Dollar Losses Under Social Security (OASI) Compared with Personal Retirement Accounts for Double-Earner Couples Born in 1965

District	Member of Congress	Loss Under Social Security (3)-(2)	Ranking from Lowest Loss to Highest Loss	Social Security Taxes Paid (1)	Social Security Benefits (2)	Personal Retirement Accounts (3)
Senate						
	Robert C. Smith (I)					
	Judd Gregg (R)					
Statewide		$ 515,871	36	$ 378,741	$ 573,085	$ 1,088,956
House of Representatives						
1	John E. Sununu (R)	516,902	244 / 436	378,006	570,111	1,087,013
2	Charles F. Bass (R)	513,363	241	378,845	576,062	1,089,426

Note: Column (1) shows the total amount of Old-Age and Survivors Insurance (OASI) taxes paid during the individual's working life. Column (2) shows the total value of Old-Age and Survivors Insurance benefits collected by the worker and his or her spouse following retirement. Column (3) shows the amount accumulated in a Personal Retirement Account had the worker been able to place his or her OASI taxes in a Personal Retirement Account. The accumulation in this personal account has been reduced by the cost of purchasing life insurance coverage equivalent to the pre-retirement Survivors Insurance portion of Social Security. All amounts exclude both Disability Insurance benefits and taxes. All values include both the portion of the OASI tax paid directly by workers and the portion paid by the employer on a worker's behalf. The losses from not participating in a Personal Retirement Account (columns (3)-(2)) are for illustrative purposes only and do not reflect any specific plan for reforming Social Security. All amounts are expressed in inflation-adjusted dollars for the year 2000. Calculations are based on life expectancies and average earnings for each district. Because of non-linearity in the benefit function, amounts for each district may not sum to the state average.

Inflation-Adjusted Rate of Return from Social Security (OASI) by Birth Year

District	Member of Congress	Single Males			Single Females			Double-Earner Couples		
		1955	1965	1975	1955	1965	1975	1955	1965	1975
Senate										
	Robert C. Smith (I)									
	Judd Gregg (R)									
Statewide		0.77%	0.63%	0.44%	2.47%	2.35%	2.21%	1.62%	1.49%	1.30%
House of Representatives										
1	John E. Sununu (R)	0.75	0.61	0.41	2.46	2.35	2.20	1.61	1.48	1.29
2	Charles F. Bass (R)	0.78	0.65	0.47	2.47	2.36	2.21	1.63	1.50	1.32

Note: Rates of return exclude both Disability Insurance benefits and taxes, but include all Old-Age and Survivors Insurance (OASI) benefits and taxes (including pre-retirement Survivors Insurance). All values include both the portion of the OASI tax paid directly by workers and the portion paid by the employer on a worker's behalf. All rates of return are net of inflation. Calculations are based on life expectancies and average earnings for each district. Because of non-linearity in the benefit function, amounts for each district may not sum to the state average.

NEW JERSEY

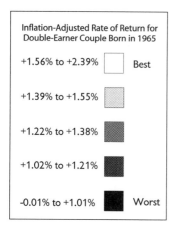

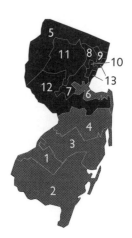

Lifetime Dollar Losses Under Social Security (OASI) Compared with Personal Retirement Accounts for Double-Earner Couples Born in 1965

District	Member of Congress	Loss Under Social Security (3)-(2)	Ranking from Lowest Loss to Highest Loss	Social Security Taxes Paid (1)	Social Security Benefits (2)	Personal Retirement Accounts (3)
Senate						
	Frank R. Lautenberg (D)					
	Robert G. Torricelli (D)					
Statewide		$ 747,933	50	$ 467,721	$ 596,858	$ 1,344,791
House of Representatives						
1	Robert E. Andrews (D)	595,035	318 / 436	389,064	523,777	1,118,812
2	Frank A.J. LoBiondo (R)	568,646	299	373,314	504,873	1,073,519
3	Jim Saxton (R)	708,602	383	456,534	604,229	1,312,831
4	Christopher H. Smith (R)	640,156	350	413,259	548,231	1,188,387
5	Marge Roukema (R)	919,350	425	561,904	723,450	1,642,800
6	Frank Pallone, Jr. (D)	674,017	366	437,201	583,220	1,257,237
7	Bob Franks (R)	887,814	420	542,435	687,995	1,575,809
8	William Pascrell, Jr. (D)	750,905	394	463,333	581,479	1,332,384
9	Steven R. Rothman (D)	779,553	403	483,838	612,013	1,391,566
10	Donald M. Payne (D)	597,678	321	350,270	409,575	1,007,254
11	Rodney P. Frelinghuysen (R)	927,584	428	565,795	728,771	1,656,354
12	Rush D. Holt (D)	910,778	424	556,809	714,275	1,625,053
13	Robert Menendez (D)	563,918	293	357,275	463,479	1,027,398

Note: Column (1) shows the total amount of Old-Age and Survivors Insurance (OASI) taxes paid during the individual's working life. Column (2) shows the total value of Old-Age and Survivors Insurance benefits collected by the worker and his or her spouse following retirement. Column (3) shows the amount accumulated in a Personal Retirement Account had the worker been able to place his or her OASI taxes in a Personal Retirement Account. The accumulation in this personal account has been reduced by the cost of purchasing life insurance coverage equivalent to the pre-retirement Survivors Insurance portion of Social Security. All amounts exclude both Disability Insurance benefits and taxes. All values include both the portion of the OASI tax paid directly by workers and the portion paid by the employer on a worker's behalf. The losses from not participating in a Personal Retirement Account (columns (3)-(2)) are for illustrative purposes only and do not reflect any specific plan for reforming Social Security. All amounts are expressed in inflation-adjusted dollars for the year 2000. Calculations are based on life expectancies and average earnings for each district. Because of non-linearity in the benefit function, amounts for each district may not sum to the state average.

Inflation-Adjusted Rate of Return from Social Security (OASI) by Birth Year

District	Member of Congress	Single Males			Single Females			Double-Earner Couples		
		1955	1965	1975	1955	1965	1975	1955	1965	1975
Senate										
	Frank R. Lautenberg (D)									
	Robert G. Torricelli (D)									
Statewide		0.11%	-0.27%	-0.69%	2.21%	2.04%	1.84%	1.18%	0.90%	0.59%
House of Representatives										
1	Robert E. Andrews (D)	0.39	0.02	-0.40	2.32	2.15	1.96	1.37	1.10	0.80
2	Frank A.J. LoBiondo (R)	0.43	0.02	-0.43	2.36	2.18	1.99	1.41	1.12	0.80
3	Jim Saxton (R)	0.23	-0.10	-0.48	2.26	2.11	1.93	1.26	1.03	0.74
4	Christopher H. Smith (R)	0.28	-0.10	-0.53	2.31	2.14	1.96	1.31	1.05	0.74
5	Marge Roukema (R)	0.11	-0.11	-0.37	1.99	1.84	1.66	1.09	0.91	0.68
6	Frank Pallone, Jr. (D)	0.31	-0.01	-0.37	2.27	2.11	1.92	1.31	1.06	0.78
7	Bob Franks (R)	0.04	-0.26	-0.59	2.07	1.91	1.72	1.09	0.87	0.60
8	William Pascrell, Jr. (D)	0.07	-0.38	-0.86	2.20	2.01	1.81	1.16	0.85	0.51
9	Steven R. Rothman (D)	0.11	-0.35	-0.78	2.21	2.03	1.83	1.18	0.87	0.55
10	Donald M. Payne (D)	-0.11	-0.95	-1.75	2.22	1.98	1.76	1.10	0.61	0.14
11	Rodney P. Frelinghuysen (R)	0.12	-0.10	-0.36	1.98	1.83	1.65	1.09	0.91	0.68
12	Rush D. Holt (D)	0.08	-0.17	-0.46	2.03	1.88	1.70	1.10	0.90	0.66
13	Robert Menendez (D)	0.39	-0.24	-0.89	2.34	2.13	1.92	1.38	0.98	0.57

Note: Rates of return exclude both Disability Insurance benefits and taxes, but include all Old-Age and Survivors Insurance (OASI) benefits and taxes (including pre-retirement Survivors Insurance). All values include both the portion of the OASI tax paid directly by workers and the portion paid by the employer on a worker's behalf. All rates of return are net of inflation. Calculations are based on life expectancies and average earnings for each district. Because of non-linearity in the benefit function, amounts for each district may not sum to the state average.

NEW MEXICO

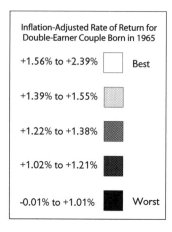

Inflation-Adjusted Rate of Return for
Double-Earner Couple Born in 1965

+1.56% to +2.39% ☐ Best

+1.39% to +1.55%

+1.22% to +1.38%

+1.02% to +1.21%

-0.01% to +1.01% ■ Worst

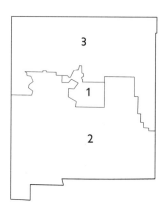

Lifetime Dollar Losses Under Social Security (OASI) Compared with Personal Retirement Accounts for Double-Earner Couples Born in 1965

District	Member of Congress	Loss Under Social Security (3)-(2)	Ranking from Lowest Loss to Highest Loss	Social Security Taxes Paid (1)	Social Security Benefits (2)	Personal Retirement Accounts (3)
Senate						
	Pete V. Domenici (R)					
	Jeff Bingaman (D)					
Statewide		$ 381,163	10	$ 299,583	$ 480,197	$ 861,360
House of Representatives						
1	Heather Wilson (R)	425,031	126 / 436	328,883	520,720	945,751
2	Joe Skeen (R)	327,891	21	272,260	455,033	782,924
3	Tom Udall (D)	388,496	69	296,857	465,162	853,657

Note: Column (1) shows the total amount of Old-Age and Survivors Insurance (OASI) taxes paid during the individual's working life. Column (2) shows the total value of Old-Age and Survivors Insurance benefits collected by the worker and his or her spouse following retirement. Column (3) shows the amount accumulated in a Personal Retirement Account had the worker been able to place his or her OASI taxes in a Personal Retirement Account. The accumulation in this personal account has been reduced by the cost of purchasing life insurance coverage equivalent to the pre-retirement Survivors Insurance portion of Social Security. All amounts exclude both Disability Insurance benefits and taxes. All values include both the portion of the OASI tax paid directly by workers and the portion paid by the employer on a worker's behalf. The losses from not participating in a Personal Retirement Account (columns (3)-(2)) are for illustrative purposes only and do not reflect any specific plan for reforming Social Security. All amounts are expressed in inflation-adjusted dollars for the year 2000. Calculations are based on life expectancies and average earnings for each district. Because of non-linearity in the benefit function, amounts for each district may not sum to the state average.

Inflation-Adjusted Rate of Return from Social Security (OASI) by Birth Year

District	Member of Congress	Single Males			Single Females			Double-Earner Couples		
		1955	1965	1975	1955	1965	1975	1955	1965	1975
Senate										
	Pete V. Domenici (R)									
	Jeff Bingaman (D)									
Statewide		1.21 %	0.91 %	0.42 %	2.67 %	2.51 %	2.33 %	1.94 %	1.71 %	1.37 %
House of Representatives										
1	Heather Wilson (R)	1.10	0.83	0.39	2.63	2.47	2.29	1.87	1.66	1.34
2	Joe Skeen (R)	1.40	1.10	0.60	2.76	2.62	2.44	2.09	1.86	1.52
3	Tom Udall (D)	1.14	0.81	0.28	2.64	2.47	2.27	1.90	1.64	1.28

Note: Rates of return exclude both Disability Insurance benefits and taxes, but include all Old-Age and Survivors Insurance (OASI) benefits and taxes (including pre-retirement Survivors Insurance). All values include both the portion of the OASI tax paid directly by workers and the portion paid by the employer on a worker's behalf. All rates of return are net of inflation. Calculations are based on life expectancies and average earnings for each district. Because of non-linearity in the benefit function, amounts for each district may not sum to the state average.

NEW YORK

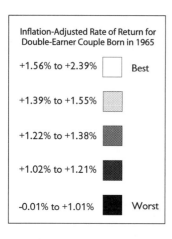

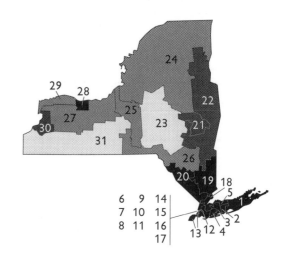

Lifetime Dollar Losses under Social Security (OASI) Compared with Personal Retirement Accounts for Double-Earner Couples Born in 1965

District	Member of Congress	Loss Under Social Security (3)-(2)	Ranking from Lowest Loss to Highest Loss	Social Security Taxes Paid (1)	Social Security Benefits (2)	Personal Retirement Accounts (3)
Senate						
	Daniel Patrick Moynihan (D)					
	Charles E. Schumer (D)					
Statewide		$ 694,799	48	$ 421,696	$ 517,661	$ 1,212,460
House of Representatives						
1	Michael P. Forbes (D)	715,642	386 / 436	458,759	603,587	1,319,229
2	Rick A. Lazio (R)	712,219	384	454,302	594,193	1,306,412
3	Peter T. King (R)	909,953	423	551,870	697,993	1,607,946
4	Carolyn McCarthy (D)	810,496	411	498,845	625,354	1,435,850
5	Gary L. Ackerman (D)	961,996	430	562,950	684,449	1,646,446
6	Gregory M. Meeks (D)	624,813	339	366,494	429,096	1,053,908
7 *	Joseph Crowley (D)	631,986	345	387,282	481,702	1,113,688
8	Jerrold L. Nadler (D)	1,094,797	434	579,059	608,031	1,702,827
9 *	Anthony D. Weiner (D)	785,565	405	470,629	567,800	1,353,365
10 *	Edolphus Towns (D)	692,773	376	374,194	383,277	1,076,050
11 *	Major R. Owens (D)	647,241	354	354,173	371,236	1,018,476
12 *	Nydia M. Velazquez (D)	424,401	124	275,478	367,776	792,177
13	Vito Fossella (R)	786,883	408	474,617	577,978	1,364,861
14 *	Carolyn B. Maloney (D)	1,369,748	436	672,414	685,602	2,055,350
15	Charles B. Rangel (D)	574,063	305	316,768	336,851	910,914
16	Jose E. Serrano (D)	481,459	196	276,339	313,195	794,654
17	Eliot L. Engel (D)	631,763	344	368,537	428,020	1,059,783
18	Nita M. Lowey (D)	977,038	431	560,673	661,475	1,638,513
19	Sue W. Kelly (R)	893,874	421	531,438	645,065	1,538,939
20	Benjamin A. Gilman (R)	825,521	413	506,840	634,601	1,460,121
21	Michael R. McNulty (D)	539,911	268	361,073	498,408	1,038,319
22	John E. Sweeney (R)	535,730	264	360,038	499,613	1,035,343
23	Sherwood L. Boehlert (R)	410,412	103	292,653	431,157	841,569
24	John M. McHugh (R)	405,655	93	280,633	401,347	807,002

Lifetime Dollar Losses under Social Security (OASI) Compared to Personal Retirement Accounts for Double-Earner Couples Born in 1965

District	Member of Congress	Loss Under Social Security (3)-(2)	Ranking from Lowest Loss to Highest Loss	Social Security Taxes Paid (1)	Social Security Benefits (2)	Personal Retirement Accounts (3)
25	James T. Walsh (R)	512,450	237	349,242	491,846	1,004,296
26	Maurice D. Hinchey (D)	480,302	194	330,716	470,721	951,023
27	Thomas M. Reynolds (R)	550,125	277	371,219	517,372	1,067,497
28	Louise McIntosh Slaughter (D)	630,806	343	401,695	524,328	1,155,134
29	John J. LaFalce (D)	490,050	210	333,784	469,797	959,847
30	Jack Quinn (R)	476,622	189	315,993	432,063	908,686
31	Amo Houghton, Jr. (R)	401,711	88	288,397	427,617	829,328

Note: Column (1) shows the total amount of Old-Age and Survivors Insurance (OASI) taxes paid during the individual's working life. Column (2) shows the total value of Old-Age and Survivors Insurance benefits collected by the worker and his or her spouse following retirement. Column (3) shows the amount accumulated in a Personal Retirement Account had the worker been able to place his or her OASI taxes in a Personal Retirement Account. The accumulation in this personal account has been reduced by the cost of purchasing life insurance coverage equivalent to the pre-retirement Survivors Insurance portion of Social Security. All amounts exclude both Disability Insurance benefits and taxes. All values include both the portion of the OASI tax paid directly by workers and the portion paid by the employer on a worker's behalf. The losses from not participating in a Personal Retirement Account (columns (3)-(2)) are for illustrative purposes only and do not reflect any specific plan for reforming Social Security. Districts marked * have been subject to boundary changes since publication of data used in this analysis. All amounts are expressed in inflation-adjusted dollars for the year 2000. Calculations are based on life expectancies and average earnings for each district. Because of non-linearity in the benefit function, amounts for each district may not sum to the state average.

Inflation-Adjusted Rate of Return from Social Security (OASI) by Birth Year

District	Member of Congress	Single Males			Single Females			Double-Earner Couples		
		1955	1965	1975	1955	1965	1975	1955	1965	1975
Senate										
	Daniel Patrick Moynihan (D)									
	Charles E. Schumer (D)									
Statewide		0.03 %	-0.63 %	-1.24 %	2.25 %	2.05 %	1.85 %	1.17 %	0.77 %	0.39 %
House of Representatives										
1	Michael P. Forbes (D)	0.26	-0.11	-0.51	2.25	2.09	1.91	1.27	1.01	0.72
2	Rick A. Lazio (R)	0.24	-0.13	-0.54	2.24	2.07	1.89	1.25	0.99	0.69
3	Peter T. King (R)	0.08	-0.25	-0.60	2.03	1.87	1.68	1.09	0.85	0.59
4	Carolyn McCarthy (D)	0.04	-0.42	-0.88	2.19	2.01	1.82	1.14	0.84	0.51
5	Gary L. Ackerman (D)	-0.08	-0.51	-0.92	1.97	1.79	1.60	1.00	0.72	0.42
6	Gregory M. Meeks (D)	-0.14	-1.03	-1.90	2.25	2.03	1.80	1.10	0.61	0.13
7 *	Joseph Crowley (D)	0.17	-0.63	-1.37	2.35	2.13	1.91	1.29	0.83	0.39
8	Jerrold L. Nadler (D)	-0.54	-1.57	-2.35	1.79	1.54	1.32	0.72	0.18	-0.23
9 *	Anthony D. Weiner (D)	-0.03	-0.75	-1.36	2.22	2.02	1.81	1.13	0.70	0.32
10 *	Edolphus Towns (D)	-0.65	-2.05	-3.39	2.07	1.80	1.55	0.78	0.10	-0.52
11 *	Major R. Owens (D)	-0.50	-2.08	-3.49	2.19	1.93	1.68	0.92	0.19	-0.43
12 *	Nydia M. Velazquez (D)	0.66	-0.17	-1.06	2.52	2.29	2.06	1.61	1.11	0.60
13	Vito Fossella (R)	-0.04	-0.63	-1.17	2.19	1.99	1.79	1.10	0.74	0.38
14 *	Carolyn B. Maloney (D)	-0.55	-1.46	-2.07	1.35	1.08	0.86	0.57	0.07	-0.28
15	Charles B. Rangel (D)	-0.44	-2.10	-3.90	2.28	2.01	1.77	1.01	0.25	-0.46
16	Jose E. Serrano (D)	0.01	-1.25	-2.68	2.27	1.99	1.74	1.18	0.50	-0.18
17	Eliot L. Engel (D)	-0.17	-1.13	-2.02	2.27	2.03	1.80	1.10	0.58	0.09
18	Nita M. Lowey (D)	-0.20	-0.76	-1.25	1.98	1.78	1.58	0.95	0.61	0.29
19	Sue W. Kelly (R)	-0.15	-0.70	-1.23	2.14	1.97	1.77	1.04	0.72	0.38
20	Benjamin A. Gilman (R)	0.00	-0.46	-0.92	2.18	2.02	1.84	1.12	0.83	0.51
21	Michael R. McNulty (D)	0.54	0.05	-0.42	2.46	2.28	2.09	1.52	1.19	0.87
22	John E. Sweeney (R)	0.53	0.05	-0.43	2.46	2.30	2.13	1.52	1.21	0.88
23	Sherwood L. Boehlert (R)	0.86	0.33	-0.20	2.65	2.48	2.31	1.77	1.44	1.09
24	John M. McHugh (R)	0.79	0.13	-0.54	2.63	2.46	2.29	1.73	1.35	0.95
25	James T. Walsh (R)	0.64	0.18	-0.26	2.48	2.31	2.12	1.57	1.27	0.95
26	Maurice D. Hinchey (D)	0.71	0.21	-0.29	2.53	2.36	2.17	1.63	1.31	0.98
27	Thomas M. Reynolds (R)	0.55	0.12	-0.32	2.44	2.28	2.10	1.51	1.22	0.92
28	Louise McIntosh Slaughter (D)	0.29	-0.23	-0.73	2.33	2.14	1.95	1.33	0.99	0.65
29	John J. LaFalce (D)	0.67	0.18	-0.29	2.49	2.31	2.13	1.59	1.27	0.94
30	Jack Quinn (R)	0.60	0.01	-0.57	2.47	2.28	2.09	1.55	1.18	0.81
31	Amo Houghton, Jr. (R)	0.91	0.40	-0.11	2.63	2.47	2.30	1.79	1.46	1.13

Note: Rates of return exclude both Disability Insurance benefits and taxes, but include all Old-Age and Survivors Insurance (OASI) benefits and taxes (including pre-retirement Survivors Insurance). All values include both the portion of the OASI tax paid directly by workers and the portion paid by the employer on a worker's behalf. All rates of return are net of inflation. Districts marked * have been subject to boundary changes since publication of data used in this analysis. Calculations are based on life expectancies and average earnings for each district. Because of non-linearity in the benefit function, amounts for each district may not sum to the state average.

NORTH CAROLINA

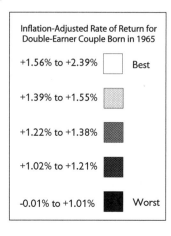

Inflation-Adjusted Rate of Return for
Double-Earner Couple Born in 1965

+1.56% to +2.39% Best

+1.39% to +1.55%

+1.22% to +1.38%

+1.02% to +1.21%

-0.01% to +1.01% Worst

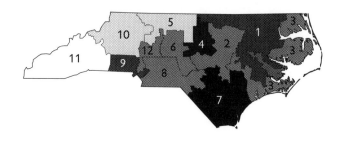

Lifetime Dollar Losses Under Social Security (OASI) Compared with Personal Retirement Accounts for Double-Earner Couples Born in 1965

District	Member of Congress	Loss Under Social Security (3)-(2)	Ranking from Lowest Loss to Highest Loss	Social Security Taxes Paid (1)	Social Security Benefits (2)	Personal Retirement Accounts (3)
Senate						
	Jesse Helms (R)					
	John Edwards (D)					
Statewide		$ 450,887	20	$ 308,452	$ 435,973	$ 886,860
House of Representatives						
1 *	Eva M. Clayton (D)	371,360	52 / 436	244,444	331,575	702,935
2 *	Bob Etheridge (D)	459,223	164	316,399	450,629	909,851
3 *	Walter B. Jones, Jr. (R)	393,918	80	273,698	393,142	787,060
4 *	David E. Price (D)	565,923	294	376,593	517,027	1,082,950
5 *	Richard M. Burr (R)	424,396	123	302,431	445,290	869,686
6 *	Howard Coble (R)	491,226	214	345,887	503,425	994,650
7 *	Mike McIntyre (D)	395,244	82	250,722	325,745	720,989
8 *	Robin Hayes (R)	429,659	131	296,214	422,150	851,809
9 *	Sue Myrick (R)	617,839	333	409,823	560,666	1,178,506
10 *	Cass Ballenger (R)	453,440	155	325,717	483,209	936,649
11 *	Charles H. Taylor (R)	380,640	57	282,544	431,857	812,496
12 *	Melvin Watt (D)	408,168	100	273,865	379,371	787,539

Note: Column (1) shows the total amount of Old-Age and Survivors Insurance (OASI) taxes paid during the individual's working life. Column (2) shows the total value of Old-Age and Survivors Insurance benefits collected by the worker and his or her spouse following retirement. Column (3) shows the amount accumulated in a Personal Retirement Account had the worker been able to place his or her OASI taxes in a Personal Retirement Account. The accumulation in this personal account has been reduced by the cost of purchasing life insurance coverage equivalent to the pre-retirement Survivors Insurance portion of Social Security. All amounts exclude both Disability Insurance benefits and taxes. All values include both the portion of the OASI tax paid directly by workers and the portion paid by the employer on a worker's behalf. The losses from not participating in a Personal Retirement Account (columns (3)-(2)) are for illustrative purposes only and do not reflect any specific plan for reforming Social Security. Districts marked * have been subject to boundary changes since publication of data used in this analysis. All amounts are expressed in inflation-adjusted dollars for the year 2000. Calculations are based on life expectancies and average earnings for each district. Because of non-linearity in the benefit function, amounts for each district may not sum to the state average.

Inflation-Adjusted Rate of Return from Social Security (OASI) by Birth Year

District	Member of Congress	Single Males			Single Females			Double-Earner Couples		
		1955	1965	1975	1955	1965	1975	1955	1965	1975
Senate										
	Jesse Helms (R)									
	John Edwards (D)									
Statewide		0.56%	0.15%	-0.31%	2.54%	2.38%	2.20%	1.57%	1.29%	0.98%
House of Representatives										
1 *	Eva M. Clayton (D)	0.45	-0.20	-0.89	2.61	2.41	2.22	1.57	1.18	0.76
2 *	Bob Etheridge (D)	0.57	0.20	-0.21	2.53	2.37	2.19	1.58	1.32	1.02
3 *	Walter B. Jones, Jr. (R)	0.71	0.16	-0.43	2.64	2.47	2.30	1.70	1.36	1.00
4 *	David E. Price (D)	0.34	0.03	-0.31	2.41	2.25	2.08	1.40	1.17	0.91
5 *	Richard M. Burr (R)	0.72	0.40	0.03	2.59	2.43	2.25	1.67	1.43	1.16
6 *	Howard Coble (R)	0.59	0.35	0.04	2.52	2.37	2.20	1.58	1.38	1.13
7 *	Mike McIntyre (D)	0.26	-0.93	-2.29	2.71	2.54	2.36	1.55	1.01	0.44
8 *	Robin Hayes (R)	0.59	0.17	-0.31	2.57	2.41	2.23	1.61	1.33	1.00
9 *	Sue Myrick (R)	0.29	0.05	-0.24	2.36	2.21	2.03	1.35	1.15	0.91
10 *	Cass Ballenger (R)	0.71	0.46	0.15	2.56	2.41	2.23	1.65	1.45	1.20
11 *	Charles H. Taylor (R)	0.92	0.60	0.25	2.67	2.50	2.33	1.81	1.57	1.30
12 *	Melvin Watt (D)	0.51	0.03	-0.49	2.55	2.36	2.17	1.56	1.24	0.89

Note: Rates of return exclude both Disability Insurance benefits and taxes, but include all Old Age and Survivors Insurance (OASI) benefits and taxes (including pre-retirement Survivors Insurance). All values include both the portion of the OASI tax paid directly by workers and the portion paid by the employer on a worker's behalf. All rates of return are net of inflation. Districts marked * have been subject to boundary changes since publication of data used in this analysis. Calculations are based on life expectancies and average earnings for each district. Because of non-linearity in the benefit function, amounts for each district may not sum to the state average.

NORTH DAKOTA

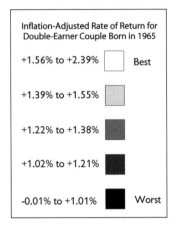

Inflation-Adjusted Rate of Return for
Double-Earner Couple Born in 1965

+1.56% to +2.39% ☐ Best

+1.39% to +1.55% ☐

+1.22% to +1.38% ☐

+1.02% to +1.21% ☐

-0.01% to +1.01% ■ Worst

Lifetime Dollar Losses Under Social Security (OASI) Compared with Personal Retirement Accounts for Double-Earner Couples Born in 1965

District	Member of Congress	Loss Under Social Security (3)-(2)	Ranking from Lowest Loss to Highest Loss	Social Security Taxes Paid (1)	Social Security Benefits (2)	Personal Retirement Accounts (3)
Senate						
	Kent Conrad (D)					
	Byron L. Dorgan (D)					
Statewide		$ 230,288	I	$ 262,760	$ 525,317	$ 755,605
House of Representatives						
At large	Earl Pomeroy (D)	230,288	I / 436	262,760	525,317	755,605

Note: Column (1) shows the total amount of Old-Age and Survivors Insurance (OASI) taxes paid during the individual's working life. Column (2) shows the total value of Old-Age and Survivors Insurance benefits collected by the worker and his or her spouse following retirement. Column (3) shows the amount accumulated in a Personal Retirement Account had the worker been able to place his or her OASI taxes in a Personal Retirement Account. The accumulation in this personal account has been reduced by the cost of purchasing life insurance coverage equivalent to the pre-retirement Survivors Insurance portion of Social Security. All amounts exclude both Disability Insurance benefits and taxes. All values include both the portion of the OASI tax paid directly by workers and the portion paid by the employer on a worker's behalf. The losses from not participating in a Personal Retirement Account (columns (3)-(2)) are for illustrative purposes only and do not reflect any specific plan for reforming Social Security. All amounts are expressed in inflation-adjusted dollars for the year 2000. Calculations are based on life expectancies and average earnings for each district.

Inflation-Adjusted Rate of Return from Social Security (OASI) by Birth Year

District	Member of Congress	Single Males			Single Females			Double-Earner Couples		
		1955	1965	1975	1955	1965	1975	1955	1965	1975
Senate										
	Kent Conrad (D)									
	Byron L. Dorgan (D)									
Statewide		1.97 %	1.81 %	1.58 %	3.12 %	2.96 %	2.80 %	2.55 %	2.39 %	2.18 %
House of Representatives										
At large	Earl Pomeroy (D)	1.97	1.81	1.58	3.12	2.96	2.80	2.55	2.39	2.18

Note: Rates of return exclude both Disability Insurance benefits and taxes, but include all Old-Age and Survivors Insurance (OASI) benefits and taxes (including pre-retirement Survivors Insurance). All values include both the portion of the OASI tax paid directly by workers and the portion paid by the employer on a worker's behalf. All rates of return are net of inflation. Calculations are based on life expectancies and average earnings for each district.

OHIO

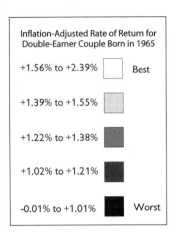

Inflation-Adjusted Rate of Return for
Double-Earner Couple Born in 1965

+1.56% to +2.39%	Best
+1.39% to +1.55%	
+1.22% to +1.38%	
+1.02% to +1.21%	
-0.01% to +1.01%	Worst

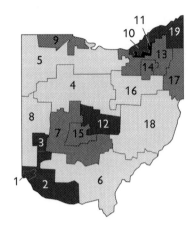

Lifetime Dollar Losses Under Social Security (OASI) Compared with Personal Retirement Accounts for Double-Earner Couples Born in 1965

District	Member of Congress	Loss Under Social Security (3)-(2)	Ranking from Lowest Loss to Highest Loss	Social Security Taxes Paid (1)	Social Security Benefits (2)	Personal Retirement Accounts (3)
	George V. Voinovich (R) Mike DeWine (R)					
Statewide		$ 512,714	34	$ 349,000	$ 490,730	$ 1,003,443
House of Representatives						
1	Steven J. Chabot (R)	490,671	212 / 436	324,673	442,973	933,644
2	Rob Portman (R)	651,316	358	429,209	582,938	1,234,254
3	Tony P. Hall (D)	558,259	287	367,880	499,635	1,057,894
4	Michael G. Oxley (R)	438,556	139	314,583	466,074	904,631
5	Paul E. Gillmor (R)	454,205	158	329,848	494,322	948,527
6	Ted Strickland (D)	407,497	97	292,210	432,796	840,293
7	David L. Hobson (R)	470,394	178	330,673	480,505	950,898
8	John A. Boehner (R)	473,545	181	342,124	510,282	983,827
9	Marcy Kaptur (D)	518,336	247	349,289	486,097	1,004,433
10	Dennis J. Kucinich (D)	566,830	297	377,855	519,749	1,086,579
11	Stephanie Tubbs Jones (D)	595,884	319	349,229	408,376	1,004,260
12	John R. Kasich (R)	572,658	303	377,068	511,657	1,084,316
13	Sherrod Brown (D)	559,473	288	383,803	544,210	1,103,682
14	Thomas C. Sawyer (D)	518,923	249	353,681	498,138	1,017,061
15	Deborah Pryce (R)	495,384	217	346,683	501,555	996,939
16	Ralph Regula (R)	453,784	156	324,120	478,272	932,056
17	James A. Traficant, Jr. (D)	478,894	193	327,567	463,074	941,968
18	Robert W. Ney (R)	396,702	84	290,960	439,997	836,699
19	Steven C. LaTourette (R)	618,213	334	414,018	572,357	1,190,569

Note: Column (1) shows the total amount of Old-Age and Survivors Insurance (OASI) taxes paid during the individual's working life. Column (2) shows the total value of Old-Age and Survivors Insurance benefits collected by the worker and his or her spouse following retirement. Column (3) shows the amount accumulated in a Personal Retirement Account had the worker been able to place his or her OASI taxes in a Personal Retirement Account. The accumulation in this personal account has been reduced by the cost of purchasing life insurance coverage equivalent to the pre-retirement Survivors Insurance portion of Social Security. All amounts exclude both Disability Insurance benefits and taxes. All values include both the portion of the OASI tax paid directly by workers and the portion paid by the employer on a worker's behalf. The losses from not participating in a Personal Retirement Account (columns (3)-(2)) are for illustrative purposes only and do not reflect any specific plan for reforming Social Security. All amounts are expressed in inflation-adjusted dollars for the year 2000. Calculations are based on life expectancies and average earnings for each district. Because of non-linearity in the benefit function, amounts for each district may not sum to the state average.

Inflation-Adjusted Rate of Return from Social Security (OASI) by Birth Year

District	Member of Congress	Single Males			Single Females			Double-Earner Couples		
		1955	1965	1975	1955	1965	1975	1955	1965	1975
Senate										
	George V. Voinovich (R)									
	Mike DeWine (R)									
Statewide		0.53 %	0.26 %	-0.06 %	2.39 %	2.25 %	2.08 %	1.47 %	1.26 %	1.01 %
House of Representatives										
1	Steven J. Chabot (R)	0.46	0.05	-0.36	2.40	2.23	2.06	1.45	1.17	0.87
2	Rob Portman (R)	0.29	0.08	-0.19	2.27	2.14	1.98	1.29	1.12	0.89
3	Tony P. Hall (D)	0.37	0.06	-0.30	2.33	2.18	2.01	1.37	1.14	0.87
4	Michael G. Oxley (R)	0.76	0.52	0.19	2.50	2.37	2.21	1.64	1.45	1.20
5	Paul E. Gillmor (R)	0.79	0.62	0.37	2.46	2.34	2.18	1.63	1.48	1.26
6	Ted Strickland (D)	0.82	0.51	0.15	2.53	2.39	2.23	1.69	1.46	1.19
7	David L. Hobson (R)	0.66	0.40	0.06	2.47	2.34	2.18	1.58	1.38	1.12
8	John A. Boehner (R)	0.75	0.58	0.34	2.46	2.33	2.18	1.61	1.46	1.24
9	Marcy Kaptur (D)	0.50	0.24	-0.08	2.35	2.20	2.04	1.44	1.23	0.98
10	Dennis J. Kucinich (D)	0.43	0.13	-0.20	2.35	2.20	2.03	1.41	1.18	0.92
11	Stephanie Tubbs Jones (D)	-0.25	-0.87	-1.48	2.15	1.94	1.74	1.00	0.61	0.23
12	John R. Kasich (R)	0.35	0.07	-0.26	2.31	2.16	1.99	1.35	1.13	0.88
13	Sherrod Brown (D)	0.52	0.35	0.09	2.33	2.21	2.05	1.44	1.28	1.06
14	Thomas C. Sawyer (D)	0.54	0.29	-0.02	2.38	2.23	2.07	1.47	1.27	1.02
15	Deborah Pryce (R)	0.65	0.35	0.00	2.48	2.34	2.18	1.58	1.36	1.10
16	Ralph Regula (R)	0.74	0.51	0.22	2.48	2.34	2.18	1.62	1.43	1.20
17	James A. Traficant, Jr. (D)	0.59	0.30	-0.03	2.41	2.25	2.09	1.51	1.29	1.03
18	Robert W. Ney (R)	0.88	0.64	0.33	2.55	2.41	2.25	1.73	1.53	1.29
19	Steven C. LaTourette (R)	0.37	0.17	-0.10	2.32	2.18	2.02	1.36	1.19	0.96

Note: Rates of return exclude both Disability Insurance benefits and taxes, but include all Old-Age and Survivors Insurance (OASI) benefits and taxes (including pre-retirement Survivors Insurance). All values include both the portion of the OASI tax paid directly by workers and the portion paid by the employer on a worker's behalf. All rates of return are net of inflation. Calculations are based on life expectancies and average earnings for each district. Because of non-linearity in the benefit function, amounts for each district may not sum to the state average.

OKLAHOMA

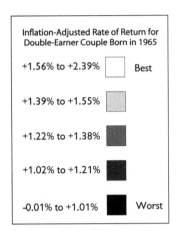

Inflation-Adjusted Rate of Return for
Double-Earner Couple Born in 1965

+1.56% to +2.39% Best

+1.39% to +1.55%

+1.22% to +1.38%

+1.02% to +1.21%

-0.01% to +1.01% Worst

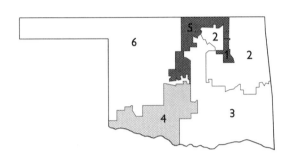

Lifetime Dollar Losses Under Social Security (OASI) Compared with Personal Retirement Accounts for Double-Earner Couples Born in 1965

District	Member of Congress	Loss Under Social Security (3)-(2)	Ranking from Lowest Loss to Highest Loss	Social Security Taxes Paid (1)	Social Security Benefits (2)	Personal Retirement Accounts (3)
Senate						
	Don Nickles (R)					
	James M. Inhofe (R)					
Statewide		$ 419,994	16	$ 301,456	$ 446,751	$ 866,745
House of Representatives						
1	Steve Largent (R)	535,662	263 / 436	364,648	512,937	1,048,599
2	Tom A. Coburn (R)	361,512	48	270,014	414,954	776,466
3	Wes Watkins (R)	333,626	25	252,161	391,500	725,125
4	J.C. Watts, Jr. (R)	403,809	91	287,294	422,347	826,156
5	Ernest J. Istook, Jr. (R)	527,639	257	366,198	525,418	1,053,057
6	Frank D. Lucas (R)	358,354	45	266,915	409,198	767,553

Note: Column (1) shows the total amount of Old-Age and Survivors Insurance (OASI) taxes paid during the individual's working life. Column (2) shows the total value of Old-Age and Survivors Insurance benefits collected by the worker and his or her spouse following retirement. Column (3) shows the amount accumulated in a Personal Retirement Account had the worker been able to place his or her OASI taxes in a Personal Retirement Account. The accumulation in this personal account has been reduced by the cost of purchasing life insurance coverage equivalent to the pre-retirement Survivors Insurance portion of Social Security. All amounts exclude both Disability Insurance benefits and taxes. All values include both the portion of the OASI tax paid directly by workers and the portion paid by the employer on a worker's behalf. The losses from not participating in a Personal Retirement Account (columns (3)-(2)) are for illustrative purposes only and do not reflect any specific plan for reforming Social Security. All amounts are expressed in inflation-adjusted dollars for the year 2000. Calculations are based on life expectancies and average earnings for each district. Because of non-linearity in the benefit function, amounts for each district may not sum to the state average.

Inflation-Adjusted Rate of Return from Social Security (OASI) by Birth Year

District	Member of Congress	Single Males			Single Females			Double-Earner Couples		
		1955	1965	1975	1955	1965	1975	1955	1965	1975
Senate										
	Don Nickles (R)									
	James M. Inhofe (R)									
Statewide		0.82 %	0.49 %	0.11 %	2.56 %	2.40 %	2.23 %	1.70 %	1.46 %	1.17 %
House of Representatives										
1	Steve Largent (R)	0.51	0.24	-0.08	2.41	2.25	2.08	1.47	1.26	1.00
2	Tom A. Coburn (R)	1.01	0.69	0.32	2.64	2.48	2.30	1.84	1.60	1.31
3	Wes Watkins (R)	1.04	0.69	0.29	2.72	2.56	2.38	1.89	1.64	1.35
4	J.C. Watts, Jr. (R)	0.80	0.35	-0.17	2.61	2.46	2.29	1.72	1.44	1.10
5	Ernest J. Istook, Jr. (R)	0.58	0.34	0.04	2.44	2.28	2.11	1.52	1.32	1.08
6	Frank D. Lucas (R)	0.98	0.63	0.20	2.67	2.52	2.34	1.84	1.59	1.29

Note: Rates of return exclude both Disability Insurance benefits and taxes, but include all Old-Age and Survivors Insurance (OASI) benefits and taxes (including pre-retirement Survivors Insurance). All values include both the portion of the OASI tax paid directly by workers and the portion paid by the employer on a worker's behalf. All rates of return are net of inflation. Calculations are based on life expectancies and average earnings for each district. Because of non-linearity in the benefit function, amounts for each district may not sum to the state average.

OREGON

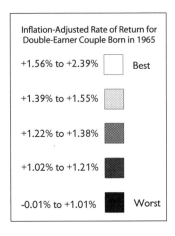

Inflation-Adjusted Rate of Return for
Double-Earner Couple Born in 1965

+1.56% to +2.39% Best

+1.39% to +1.55%

+1.22% to +1.38%

+1.02% to +1.21%

-0.01% to +1.01% Worst

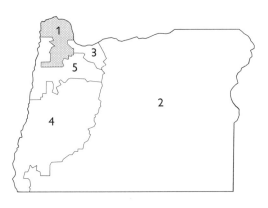

Lifetime Dollar Losses Under Social Security (OASI) Compared with Personal Retirement Accounts for Double-Earner Couples Born in 1965

District	Member of Congress	Loss Under Social Security (3)-(2)	Ranking from Lowest Loss to Highest Loss	Social Security Taxes Paid (1)	Social Security Benefits (2)	Personal Retirement Accounts (3)
Senate						
	Ron Wyden (D)					
	Gordon Smith (D)					
Statewide		$ 413,085	15	$ 324,498	$ 519,911	$ 932,996
House of Representatives						
1	David Wu (D)	557,169	286 / 436	406,101	610,635	1,167,805
2	Greg Walden (R)	343,452	34	287,135	482,248	825,701
3	Earl Blumenauer (D)	413,989	109	320,853	508,671	922,660
4	Peter A. DeFazio (D)	351,643	39	291,949	487,899	839,542
5	Darlene Hooley (D)	392,924	75	315,100	513,193	906,117

Note: Column (1) shows the total amount of Old-Age and Survivors Insurance (OASI) taxes paid during the individual's working life. Column (2) shows the total value of Old-Age and Survivors Insurance benefits collected by the worker and his or her spouse following retirement. Column (3) shows the amount accumulated in a Personal Retirement Account had the worker been able to place his or her OASI taxes in a Personal Retirement Account. The accumulation in this personal account has been reduced by the cost of purchasing life insurance coverage equivalent to the pre-retirement Survivors Insurance portion of Social Security. All amounts exclude both Disability Insurance benefits and taxes. All values include both the portion of the OASI tax paid directly by workers and the portion paid by the employer on a worker's behalf. The losses from not participating in a Personal Retirement Account (columns (3)-(2)) are for illustrative purposes only and do not reflect any specific plan for reforming Social Security. All amounts are expressed in inflation-adjusted dollars for the year 2000. Calculations are based on life expectancies and average earnings for each district. Because of non-linearity in the benefit function, amounts for each district may not sum to the state average.

Inflation-Adjusted Rate of Return from Social Security (OASI) by Birth Year

District	Member of Congress	Single Males			Single Females			Double-Earner Couples		
		1955	1965	1975	1955	1965	1975	1955	1965	1975
Senate										
	Ron Wyden (D)									
	Gordon Smith (D)									
Statewide		1.12 %	0.90 %	0.60 %	2.62 %	2.49 %	2.34 %	1.87 %	1.69 %	1.45 %
House of Representatives										
1	David Wu (D)	0.78	0.57	0.30	2.47	2.34	2.18	1.63	1.46	1.23
2	Greg Walden (R)	1.33	1.13	0.84	2.72	2.60	2.44	2.03	1.87	1.63
3	Earl Blumenauer (D)	1.10	0.85	0.53	2.62	2.48	2.31	1.87	1.66	1.41
4	Peter A. DeFazio (D)	1.32	1.12	0.82	2.70	2.58	2.42	2.02	1.85	1.61
5	Darlene Hooley (D)	1.18	0.95	0.63	2.67	2.55	2.39	1.93	1.75	1.50

Note: Rates of return exclude both Disability Insurance benefits and taxes, but include all Old-Age and Survivors Insurance (OASI) benefits and taxes (including pre-retirement Survivors Insurance). All values include both the portion of the OASI tax paid directly by workers and the portion paid by the employer on a worker's behalf. All rates of return are net of inflation. Calculations are based on life expectancies and average earnings for each district. Because of non-linearity in the benefit function, amounts for each district may not sum to the state average.

PENNSYLVANIA

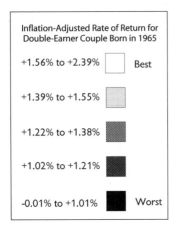

Inflation-Adjusted Rate of Return for
Double-Earner Couple Born in 1965

+1.56% to +2.39%	Best
+1.39% to +1.55%	
+1.22% to +1.38%	
+1.02% to +1.21%	
-0.01% to +1.01%	Worst

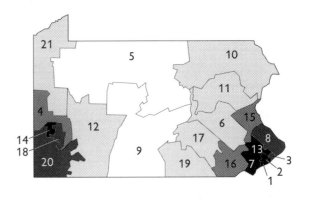

Lifetime Dollar Losses Under Social Security (OASI) Compared with Personal Retirement Accounts for Double-Earner Couples Born in 1965

District	Member of Congress	Loss Under Social Security (3)-(2)	Ranking from Lowest Loss to Highest Loss	Social Security Taxes Paid (1)	Social Security Benefits (2)	Personal Retirement Accounts (3)
Senate						
	Arlen Specter (R)					
	Rick Santorum (R)					
Statewide		$ 530,040	38	$ 357,030	$ 496,492	$ 1,026,533
House of Representatives						
1	Robert A. Brady (D)	490,623	211/ 436	292,058	349,235	839,857
2	Chaka Fattah (D)	586,062	314	341,543	396,095	982,157
3	Robert A. Borski (D)	539,766	267	354,760	480,398	1,020,164
4	Ron Klink (D)	489,543	208	341,224	491,698	981,241
5	John E. Peterson (R)	349,240	37	270,297	428,040	777,281
6	Tim Holden (D)	468,896	176	335,362	495,487	964,383
7	Curt Weldon (R)	751,532	395	480,887	631,439	1,382,971
8	James C. Greenwood (R)	697,101	380	459,257	623,560	1,320,661
9	Bud Shuster (R)	393,047	76	291,472	445,124	838,171
10	Don Sherwood (R)	425,336	127	311,179	469,506	894,842
11	Paul E. Kanjorski (D)	417,305	113	303,596	455,730	873,035
12	John P. Murtha (D)	393,743	79	286,570	430,330	824,074
13	Joseph M. Hoeffel III (D)	840,222	414	521,657	666,903	1,507,125
14	William J. Coyne (D)	566,121	296	358,582	465,034	1,031,156
15	Patrick J. Toomey (R)	532,055	261	370,752	534,096	1,066,152
16	Joseph R. Pitts (R)	602,393	324	409,901	576,339	1,178,732
17	George W. Gekas (R)	499,147	225	353,166	516,435	1,015,582
18	Michael F. Doyle (D)	583,840	311	385,358	524,316	1,108,156
19	William F. Goodling (R)	472,377	180	343,674	515,908	988,285
20	Frank Mascara (D)	547,216	273	363,894	499,216	1,046,433
21	Philip S. English (R)	421,540	118	306,332	459,364	880,904

Note: Column (1) shows the total amount of Old-Age and Survivors Insurance (OASI) taxes paid during the individual's working life. Column (2) shows the total value of Old-Age and Survivors Insurance benefits collected by the worker and his or her spouse following retirement. Column (3) shows the amount accumulated in a Personal Retirement Account had the worker been able to place his or her OASI taxes in a Personal Retirement Account. The accumulation in this personal account has been reduced by the cost of purchasing life insurance coverage equivalent to the pre-retirement Survivors Insurance portion of Social Security. All amounts exclude both Disability Insurance benefits and taxes. All values include both the portion of the OASI tax paid directly by workers and the portion paid by the employer on a worker's behalf. The losses from not participating in a Personal Retirement Account (columns (3)-(2)) are for illustrative purposes only and do not reflect any specific plan for reforming Social Security. All amounts are expressed in inflation-adjusted dollars for the year 2000. Calculations are based on life expectancies and average earnings for each district. Because of non-linearity in the benefit function, amounts for each district may not sum to the state average.

Inflation-Adjusted Rate of Return from Social Security (OASI) by Birth Year

District	Member of Congress	Single Males			Single Females			Double-Earner Couples		
		1955	1965	1975	1955	1965	1975	1955	1965	1975
Senate										
	Arlen Specter (R)									
	Rick Santorum (R)									
Statewide		0.47 %	0.16 %	-0.20 %	2.40 %	2.25 %	2.09 %	1.45 %	1.22 %	0.95 %
House of Representatives										
1	Robert A. Brady (D)	-0.01	-0.85	-1.72	2.30	2.07	1.86	1.19	0.70	0.23
2	Chaka Fattah (D)	-0.28	-1.04	-1.75	2.22	1.99	1.78	1.03	0.58	0.16
3	Robert A. Borski (D)	0.42	-0.02	-0.48	2.39	2.22	2.05	1.43	1.13	0.82
4	Ron Klink (D)	0.61	0.35	0.04	2.46	2.32	2.15	1.55	1.35	1.10
5	John E. Peterson (R)	1.09	0.81	0.47	2.69	2.56	2.40	1.90	1.69	1.44
6	Tim Holden (D)	0.72	0.48	0.17	2.51	2.36	2.20	1.63	1.43	1.18
7	Curt Weldon (R)	0.12	-0.14	-0.44	2.24	2.09	1.93	1.20	1.00	0.75
8	James C. Greenwood (R)	0.26	0.07	-0.20	2.26	2.14	1.98	1.28	1.11	0.88
9	Bud Shuster (R)	0.93	0.65	0.30	2.60	2.46	2.30	1.77	1.56	1.30
10	Don Sherwood (R)	0.84	0.58	0.26	2.56	2.42	2.26	1.71	1.51	1.26
11	Paul E. Kanjorski (D)	0.81	0.52	0.17	2.59	2.45	2.29	1.72	1.50	1.23
12	John P. Murtha (D)	0.87	0.56	0.21	2.58	2.43	2.27	1.74	1.51	1.25
13	Joseph M. Hoeffel III (D)	-0.05	-0.32	-0.63	2.17	2.03	1.87	1.10	0.90	0.66
14	William J. Coyne (D)	0.21	-0.29	-0.77	2.35	2.16	1.98	1.31	0.98	0.66
15	Patrick J. Toomey (R)	0.58	0.36	0.07	2.43	2.29	2.13	1.52	1.33	1.09
16	Joseph R. Pitts (R)	0.43	0.23	-0.05	2.36	2.23	2.07	1.41	1.24	1.01
17	George W. Gekas (R)	0.66	0.43	0.13	2.47	2.33	2.17	1.58	1.39	1.15
18	Michael F. Doyle (D)	0.34	0.04	-0.31	2.36	2.20	2.03	1.37	1.14	0.88
19	William F. Goodling (R)	0.76	0.56	0.27	2.52	2.39	2.23	1.65	1.48	1.25
20	Frank Mascara (D)	0.39	0.09	-0.26	2.37	2.22	2.05	1.40	1.17	0.91
21	Philip S. English (R)	0.84	0.57	0.24	2.54	2.40	2.24	1.70	1.50	1.24

Note: Rates of return exclude both Disability Insurance benefits and taxes, but include all Old-Age and Survivors Insurance (OASI) benefits and taxes (including pre-retirement Survivors Insurance). All values include both the portion of the OASI tax paid directly by workers and the portion paid by the employer on a worker's behalf. All rates of return are net of inflation. Calculations are based on life expectancies and average earnings for each district. Because of non-linearity in the benefit function, amounts for each district may not sum to the state average.

RHODE ISLAND

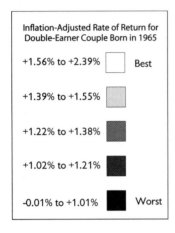

Inflation-Adjusted Rate of Return for
Double-Earner Couple Born in 1965

+1.56% to +2.39% ☐ Best

+1.39% to +1.55%

+1.22% to +1.38%

+1.02% to +1.21%

-0.01% to +1.01% ■ Worst

Lifetime Dollar Losses Under Social Security (OASI) Compared with Personal Retirement Accounts for Double-Earner Couples Born in 1965

District	Member of Congress	Loss Under Social Security (3)-(2)	Ranking from Lowest Loss to Highest Loss	Social Security Taxes Paid (1)	Social Security Benefits (2)	Personal Retirement Accounts (3)
Senate						
	John H. Chafee (R)					
	Jack Reed (D)					
Statewide		$ 510,159	33	$ 358,129	$ 519,534	$ 1,029,693
House of Representatives						
1	Patrick J. Kennedy (D)	509,268	233 / 436	355,948	514,315	1,023,583
2	Robert Weygand (D)	509,642	234	359,714	524,768	1,034,410

Note: Column (1) shows the total amount of Old-Age and Survivors Insurance (OASI) taxes paid during the individual's working life. Column (2) shows the total value of Old-Age and Survivors Insurance benefits collected by the worker and his or her spouse following retirement. Column (3) shows the amount accumulated in a Personal Retirement Account had the worker been able to place his or her OASI taxes in a Personal Retirement Account. The accumulation in this personal account has been reduced by the cost of purchasing life insurance coverage equivalent to the pre-retirement Survivors Insurance portion of Social Security. All amounts exclude both Disability Insurance benefits and taxes. All values include both the portion of the OASI tax paid directly by workers and the portion paid by the employer on a worker's behalf. The losses from not participating in a Personal Retirement Account (columns (3)-(2)) are for illustrative purposes only and do not reflect any specific plan for reforming Social Security. All amounts are expressed in inflation-adjusted dollars for the year 2000. Calculations are based on life expectancies and average earnings for each district. Because of non-linearity in the benefit function, amounts for each district may not sum to the state average.

Inflation-Adjusted Rate of Return from Social Security (OASI) by Birth Year

District	Member of Congress	Single Males			Single Females			Double-Earner Couples		
		1955	1965	1975	1955	1965	1975	1955	1965	1975
Senate										
	John H. Chafee (R)									
	Jack Reed (D)									
Statewide		0.64 %	0.32 %	-0.02 %	2.51 %	2.36 %	2.20 %	1.59 %	1.36 %	1.10 %
House of Representatives										
1	Patrick J. Kennedy (D)	0.62	0.27	-0.08	2.52	2.37	2.21	1.59	1.35	1.08
2	Robert Weygand (D)	0.67	0.37	0.05	2.50	2.35	2.19	1.60	1.38	1.13

Note: Rates of return exclude both Disability Insurance benefits and taxes, but include all Old-Age and Survivors Insurance (OASI) benefits and taxes (including pre-retirement Survivors Insurance). All values include both the portion of the OASI tax paid directly by workers and the portion paid by the employer on a worker's behalf. All rates of return are net of inflation. Calculations are based on life expectancies and average earnings for each district. Because of non-linearity in the benefit function, amounts for each district may not sum to the state average.

SOUTH CAROLINA

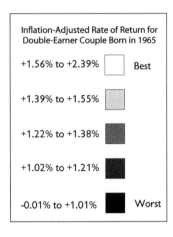

Inflation-Adjusted Rate of Return for
Double-Earner Couple Born in 1965

+1.56% to +2.39% ☐ Best

+1.39% to +1.55% ☐

+1.22% to +1.38% ☐

+1.02% to +1.21% ☐

-0.01% to +1.01% ☐ Worst

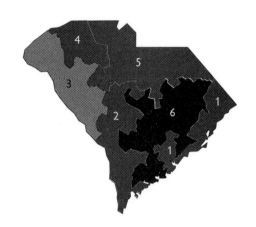

Lifetime Dollar Losses Under Social Security (OASI) Compared with Personal Retirement Accounts for Double-Earner Couples Born in 1965

District	Member of Congress	Loss Under Social Security (3)-(2)	Ranking from Lowest Loss to Highest Loss	Social Security Taxes Paid (1)	Social Security Benefits (2)	Personal Retirement Accounts (3)
Senate						
	Strom Thurmond (R)					
	Ernest F. Hollings (D)					
Statewide		$ 463,985	25	$ 299,497	$ 397,128	$ 861,113
House of Representatives						
1	Marshall Sanford (R)	485,913	202 / 436	309,380	403,755	889,668
2	Floyd Spence (R)	514,181	242	327,175	426,659	940,841
3	Lindsey O. Graham (R)	443,638	145	299,058	416,350	859,987
4	Jim DeMint (R)	497,358	222	326,102	440,398	937,756
5	John M. Spratt, Jr. (D)	442,697	144	288,512	386,963	829,660
6	James E. Clyburn (D)	397,460	85	245,258	307,815	705,275

Note: Column (1) shows the total amount of Old-Age and Survivors Insurance (OASI) taxes paid during the individual's working life. Column (2) shows the total value of Old-Age and Survivors Insurance benefits collected by the worker and his or her spouse following retirement. Column (3) shows the amount accumulated in a Personal Retirement Account had the worker been able to place his or her OASI taxes in a Personal Retirement Account. The accumulation in this personal account has been reduced by the cost of purchasing life insurance coverage equivalent to the pre-retirement Survivors Insurance portion of Social Security. All amounts exclude both Disability Insurance benefits and taxes. All values include both the portion of the OASI tax paid directly by workers and the portion paid by the employer on a worker's behalf. The losses from not participating in a Personal Retirement Account (columns (3)-(2)) are for illustrative purposes only and do not reflect any specific plan for reforming Social Security. All amounts are expressed in inflation-adjusted dollars for the year 2000. Calculations are based on life expectancies and average earnings for each district. Because of non-linearity in the benefit function, amounts for each district may not sum to the state average.

Inflation-Adjusted Rate of Return from Social Security (OASI) by Birth Year

District	Member of Congress	Single Males			Single Females			Double-Earner Couples		
		1955	1965	1975	1955	1965	1975	1955	1965	1975
Senate										
	Strom Thurmond (R)									
	Ernest F. Hollings (D)									
Statewide		0.37%	-0.19%	-0.79%	2.44%	2.26%	2.06%	1.43%	1.08%	0.70%
House of Representatives										
1	Marshall Sanford (R)	0.29	-0.41	-1.14	2.46	2.29	2.10	1.41	1.02	0.60
2	Floyd Spence (R)	0.23	-0.36	-0.99	2.42	2.25	2.06	1.36	1.01	0.63
3	Lindsey O. Graham (R)	0.55	0.16	-0.27	2.47	2.29	2.11	1.53	1.25	0.94
4	Jim DeMint (R)	0.39	-0.01	-0.45	2.40	2.22	2.04	1.42	1.13	0.82
5	John M. Spratt, Jr. (D)	0.45	-0.10	-0.69	2.45	2.26	2.07	1.47	1.12	0.75
6	James E. Clyburn (D)	0.20	-0.67	-1.58	2.48	2.26	2.05	1.38	0.89	0.40

Note: Rates of return exclude both Disability Insurance benefits and taxes, but include all Old-Age and Survivors Insurance (OASI) benefits and taxes (including pre-retirement Survivors Insurance). All values include both the portion of the OASI tax paid directly by workers and the portion paid by the employer on a worker's behalf. All rates of return are net of inflation. Calculations are based on life expectancies and average earnings for each district. Because of non-linearity in the benefit function, amounts for each district may not sum to the state average.

SOUTH DAKOTA

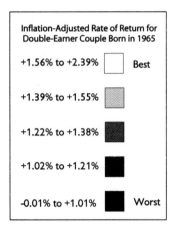

Inflation-Adjusted Rate of Return for
Double-Earner Couple Born in 1965

+1.56% to +2.39% ☐ Best

+1.39% to +1.55% ☐

+1.22% to +1.38% ☐

+1.02% to +1.21% ☐

-0.01% to +1.01% ☐ Worst

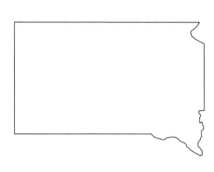

Lifetime Dollar Losses Under Social Security (OASI) Compared with Personal Retirement Accounts for Double-Earner Couples Born in 1965

District	Member of Congress	Loss Under Social Security (3)-(2)	Ranking from Lowest Loss to Highest Loss	Social Security Taxes Paid (1)	Social Security Benefits (2)	Personal Retirement Accounts (3)
Senate						
	Thomas A. Daschle (D)					
	Tim Johnson (D)					
Statewide		$ 238,972	2	$ 259,801	$ 508,124	$ 747,096
House of Representatives						
At large	John R. Thune (R)	238,972	2 / 436	259,801	508,124	747,096

Note: Column (1) shows the total amount of Old-Age and Survivors Insurance (OASI) taxes paid during the individual's working life. Column (2) shows the total value of Old-Age and Survivors Insurance benefits collected by the worker and his or her spouse following retirement. Column (3) shows the amount accumulated in a Personal Retirement Account had the worker been able to place his or her OASI taxes in a Personal Retirement Account. The accumulation in this personal account has been reduced by the cost of purchasing life insurance coverage equivalent to the pre-retirement Survivors Insurance portion of Social Security. All amounts exclude both Disability Insurance benefits and taxes. All values include both the portion of the OASI tax paid directly by workers and the portion paid by the employer on a worker's behalf. The losses from not participating in a Personal Retirement Account (columns (3)-(2)) are for illustrative purposes only and do not reflect any specific plan for reforming Social Security. All amounts are expressed in inflation-adjusted dollars for the year 2000. Calculations are based on life expectancies and average earnings for each district.

Inflation-Adjusted Rate of Return from Social Security (OASI) by Birth Year

District	Member of Congress	Single Males			Single Females			Double-Earner Couples		
		1955	1965	1975	1955	1965	1975	1955	1965	1975
Senate										
	Thomas A. Daschle (D)									
	Tim Johnson (D)									
Statewide		1.92 %	1.73 %	1.47 %	3.09 %	2.92 %	2.76 %	2.51 %	2.33 %	2.10 %
House of Representatives										
At large	John R. Thune (R)	1.92	1.73	1.47	3.09	2.92	2.76	2.51	2.33	2.10

Note: Rates of return exclude both Disability Insurance benefits and taxes, but include all Old Age and Survivors Insurance (OASI) benefits and taxes (including pre-retirement Survivors Insurance). All values include both the portion of the OASI tax paid directly by workers and the portion paid by the employer on a worker's behalf. All rates of return are net of inflation. Calculations are based on life expectancies and average earnings for each district.

TENNESSEE

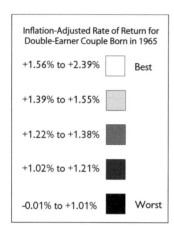

Inflation-Adjusted Rate of Return for
Double-Earner Couple Born in 1965

+1.56% to +2.39% ☐ Best

+1.39% to +1.55%

+1.22% to +1.38%

+1.02% to +1.21%

-0.01% to +1.01% ■ Worst

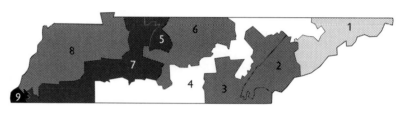

Lifetime Dollar Losses Under Social Security (OASI) Compared with Personal Retirement Accounts for Double-Earner Couples Born in 1965

District	Member of Congress	Loss Under Social Security (3)-(2)	Ranking from Lowest Loss to Highest Loss	Social Security Taxes Paid (1)	Social Security Benefits (2)	Personal Retirement Accounts (3)
Senate						
	Fred Thompson (R)					
	Bill Frist (R)					
Statewide		$ 470,315	28	$ 316,449	$ 439,540	$ 909,855
House of Representatives						
1	William L. Jenkins (R)	392,571	74 / 436	282,287	419,189	811,760
2	John J. Duncan, Jr. (R)	475,551	188	325,736	461,152	936,703
3	Zachary P. Wamp (R)	481,764	197	323,116	447,405	929,169
4	Van Hilleary (R)	359,675	47	265,690	404,356	764,031
5	Bob Clement (D)	552,206	279	355,344	469,639	1,021,845
6	Bart Gordon (D)	494,124	216	342,403	490,508	984,632
7	Ed Bryant (R)	555,272	284	359,660	478,984	1,034,256
8	John S. Tanner (D)	402,997	90	280,600	403,910	806,907
9	Harold E. Ford, Jr. (D)	513,216	239	310,838	380,645	893,860

Note: Column (1) shows the total amount of Old-Age and Survivors Insurance (OASI) taxes paid during the individual's working life. Column (2) shows the total value of Old-Age and Survivors Insurance benefits collected by the worker and his or her spouse following retirement. Column (3) shows the amount accumulated in a Personal Retirement Account had the worker been able to place his or her OASI taxes in a Personal Retirement Account. The accumulation in this personal account has been reduced by the cost of purchasing life insurance coverage equivalent to the pre-retirement Survivors Insurance portion of Social Security. All amounts exclude both Disability Insurance benefits and taxes. All values include both the portion of the OASI tax paid directly by workers and the portion paid by the employer on a worker's behalf. The losses from not participating in a Personal Retirement Account (columns (3)-(2)) are for illustrative purposes only and do not reflect any specific plan for reforming Social Security. All amounts are expressed in inflation-adjusted dollars for the year 2000. Calculations are based on life expectancies and average earnings for each district. Because of non-linearity in the benefit function, amounts for each district may not sum to the state average.

Inflation-Adjusted Rate of Return from Social Security (OASI) by Birth Year

District	Member of Congress	Single Males			Single Females			Double-Earner Couples		
		1955	1965	1975	1955	1965	1975	1955	1965	1975
Senate										
	Fred Thompson (R)									
	Bill Frist (R)									
Statewide		0.48%	0.11%	-0.33%	2.47%	2.31%	2.13%	1.50%	1.23%	0.92%
House of Representatives										
1	William L. Jenkins (R)	0.81	0.48	0.09	2.60	2.43	2.26	1.72	1.48	1.19
2	John J. Duncan, Jr. (R)	0.55	0.25	-0.12	2.46	2.30	2.13	1.52	1.29	1.01
3	Zachary P. Wamp (R)	0.45	0.09	-0.34	2.45	2.29	2.11	1.48	1.22	0.92
4	Van Hilleary (R)	0.91	0.58	0.18	2.67	2.51	2.34	1.80	1.56	1.27
5	Bob Clement (D)	0.21	-0.21	-0.67	2.39	2.21	2.03	1.33	1.05	0.73
6	Bart Gordon (D)	0.54	0.31	-0.01	2.46	2.31	2.14	1.52	1.33	1.07
7	Ed Bryant (R)	0.24	-0.16	-0.63	2.37	2.22	2.05	1.34	1.07	0.75
8	John S. Tanner (D)	0.67	0.26	-0.25	2.58	2.42	2.24	1.65	1.37	1.03
9	Harold E. Ford, Jr. (D)	-0.03	-0.70	-1.42	2.31	2.11	1.91	1.19	0.79	0.37

Note: Rates of return exclude both Disability Insurance benefits and taxes, but include all Old-Age and Survivors Insurance (OASI) benefits and taxes (including pre-retirement Survivors Insurance). All values include both the portion of the OASI tax paid directly by workers and the portion paid by the employer on a worker's behalf. All rates of return are net of inflation. Calculations are based on life expectancies and average earnings for each district. Because of non-linearity in the benefit function, amounts for each district may not sum to the state average.

TEXAS

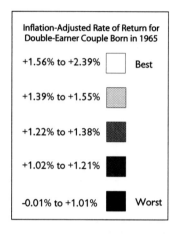

Inflation-Adjusted Rate of Return for
Double-Earner Couple Born in 1965

+1.56% to +2.39%	⬜	Best
+1.39% to +1.55%	▨	
+1.22% to +1.38%	▨	
+1.02% to +1.21%	⬛	
-0.01% to +1.01%	⬛	Worst

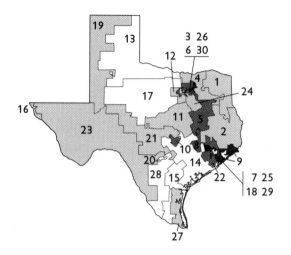

Lifetime Dollar Losses Under Social Security (OASI) Compared with Personal Retirement Accounts for Double-Earner Couples Born in 1965

District	Member of Congress	Loss Under Social Security (3)-(2)	Ranking from Lowest Loss to Highest Loss	Social Security Taxes Paid (1)	Social Security Benefits (2)	Personal Retirement Accounts (3)
Senate						
	Phil Gramm (R)					
	Kay Bailey Hutchison (R)					
Statewide		$ 485,897	32	$ 338,701	$ 487,936	$ 973,833
House of Representatives						
1	Max Sandlin (D)	395,637	83 / 436	291,918	443,817	839,454
2	Jim Turner (D)	407,636	99	288,623	422,342	829,978
3	Sam Johnson (R)	675,137	367	453,441	628,800	1,303,937
4	Ralph M. Hall (D)	455,886	161	333,520	503,201	959,087
5	Pete Sessions (R)	474,033	182	332,047	480,819	954,852
6	Joe L. Barton (R)	637,611	346	436,166	616,650	1,254,261
7	Bill Archer (R)	780,436	404	499,038	655,994	1,436,430
8	Kevin Brady (R)	611,701	330	418,870	592,822	1,204,522
9	Nicholas V. Lampson (D)	570,045	301	379,810	522,155	1,092,200
10	Lloyd Doggett (D)	488,066	205	342,857	497,871	985,937
11	Chet Edwards (D)	372,619	53	262,244	381,502	754,121
12	Kay Granger (R)	448,435	150	322,905	480,127	928,562
13	William M. Thornberry (R)	342,554	32	266,910	424,985	767,539
14	Ron Paul (R)	387,403	67	294,203	458,621	846,024
15	Ruben Hinojosa (D)	305,633	13	237,599	377,618	683,251
16	Silvestre Reyes (D)	376,728	55	273,902	410,917	787,645
17	Charles W. Stenholm (D)	358,420	46	276,710	437,301	795,721
18	Sheila Jackson-Lee (D)	477,786	190	309,817	413,140	890,926
19	Larry Combest (R)	450,756	151	336,308	516,349	967,105
20	Charles A. Gonzalez (D)	343,545	35	256,881	395,154	738,699
21	Lamar S. Smith (R)	530,305	260	376,296	551,791	1,082,096
22	Tom DeLay (R)	623,389	338	421,935	589,946	1,213,336
23	Henry Bonilla (R)	420,744	116	303,657	452,466	873,210
24	Martin Frost (D)	438,730	140	314,893	466,791	905,520

Lifetime Dollar Losses Under Social Security (OASI) Compared to Personal Retirement Accounts for Double-Earner Couples Born in 1965

District	Member of Congress	Loss Under Social Security (3)-(2)	Ranking from Lowest Loss to Highest Loss	Social Security Taxes Paid (1)	Social Security Benefits (2)	Personal Retirement Accounts (3)
25	Kenneth E. Bentsen, Jr. (D)	571,803	302	379,825	520,441	1,092,244
26	Richard K. Armey (R)	770,591	402	496,224	657,429	1,428,020
27	Solomon P. Ortiz (D)	384,513	61	283,675	431,236	815,749
28	Ciro D. Rodriguez (D)	314,104	15	242,006	381,822	695,926
29	Gene Green (D)	387,680	68	286,482	436,143	823,823
30	Eddie Bernice Johnson (D)	463,493	171	310,106	428,262	891,755

Note: Column (1) shows the total amount of Old-Age and Survivors Insurance (OASI) taxes paid during the individual's working life. Column (2) shows the total value of Old-Age and Survivors Insurance benefits collected by the worker and his or her spouse following retirement. Column (3) shows the amount accumulated in a Personal Retirement Account had the worker been able to place his or her OASI taxes in a Personal Retirement Account. The accumulation in this personal account has been reduced by the cost of purchasing life insurance coverage equivalent to the pre-retirement Survivors Insurance portion of Social Security. All amounts exclude both Disability Insurance benefits and taxes. All values include both the portion of the OASI tax paid directly by workers and the portion paid by the employer on a worker's behalf. The losses from not participating in a Personal Retirement Account (columns (3)-(2)) are for illustrative purposes only and do not reflect any specific plan for reforming Social Security. All amounts are expressed in inflation-adjusted dollars for the year 2000. Calculations are based on life expectancies and average earnings for each district. Because of non-linearity in the benefit function, amounts for each district may not sum to the state average.

Inflation-Adjusted Rate of Return from Social Security (OASI) by Birth Year

District	Member of Congress	Single Males			Single Females			Double-Earner Couples		
		1955	1965	1975	1955	1965	1975	1955	1965	1975
Senate										
	Phil Gramm (R)									
	Kay Bailey Hutchison (R)									
Statewide		0.64 %	0.32 %	-0.13 %	2.49 %	2.34 %	2.17 %	1.58 %	1.35 %	1.04 %
House of Representatives										
1	Max Sandlin (D)	0.94	0.61	0.20	2.60	2.46	2.29	1.78	1.55	1.25
2	Jim Turner (D)	0.78	0.30	-0.29	2.61	2.47	2.30	1.72	1.42	1.05
3	Sam Johnson (R)	0.35	0.16	-0.15	2.32	2.19	2.03	1.35	1.18	0.94
4	Ralph M. Hall (D)	0.82	0.58	0.24	2.54	2.40	2.24	1.69	1.50	1.24
5	Pete Sessions (R)	0.71	0.33	-0.12	2.52	2.36	2.19	1.63	1.37	1.05
6	Joe L. Barton (R)	0.45	0.27	-0.03	2.35	2.22	2.06	1.41	1.25	1.01
7	Bill Archer (R)	0.14	-0.15	-0.51	2.24	2.09	1.93	1.21	1.00	0.73
8	Kevin Brady (R)	0.48	0.27	-0.05	2.36	2.24	2.07	1.43	1.26	1.01
9	Nicholas V. Lampson (D)	0.39	0.08	-0.33	2.37	2.23	2.05	1.40	1.18	0.88
10	Lloyd Doggett (D)	0.68	0.34	-0.08	2.52	2.36	2.19	1.61	1.37	1.07
11	Chet Edwards (D)	0.76	0.09	-0.75	2.73	2.59	2.42	1.78	1.41	0.96
12	Kay Granger (R)	0.79	0.47	0.06	2.55	2.41	2.24	1.68	1.46	1.16
13	William M. Thornberry (R)	1.13	0.80	0.35	2.73	2.60	2.43	1.94	1.71	1.40
14	Ron Paul (R)	0.98	0.72	0.32	2.64	2.51	2.35	1.82	1.63	1.34
15	Ruben Hinojosa (D)	1.09	0.77	0.25	2.77	2.64	2.47	1.94	1.72	1.38
16	Silvestre Reyes (D)	0.92	0.47	-0.18	2.65	2.51	2.33	1.80	1.51	1.12
17	Charles W. Stenholm (D)	1.07	0.75	0.30	2.72	2.58	2.42	1.91	1.68	1.37
18	Sheila Jackson-Lee (D)	0.39	-0.16	-0.81	2.43	2.26	2.06	1.44	1.09	0.70
19	Larry Combest (R)	0.88	0.67	0.34	2.55	2.43	2.27	1.73	1.55	1.30
20	Charles A. Gonzalez (D)	0.93	0.54	-0.07	2.75	2.60	2.43	1.86	1.60	1.22
21	Lamar S. Smith (R)	0.62	0.38	0.02	2.50	2.37	2.20	1.58	1.39	1.12
22	Tom DeLay (R)	0.43	0.22	-0.12	2.34	2.21	2.04	1.40	1.22	0.96
23	Henry Bonilla (R)	0.82	0.50	0.00	2.55	2.42	2.25	1.70	1.47	1.15
24	Martin Frost (D)	0.78	0.48	0.06	2.54	2.40	2.22	1.67	1.45	1.15
25	Kenneth E. Bentsen, Jr. (D)	0.42	0.06	-0.40	2.38	2.23	2.05	1.42	1.16	0.85
26	Richard K. Armey (R)	0.16	-0.11	-0.45	2.25	2.11	1.94	1.23	1.02	0.76
27	Solomon P. Ortiz (D)	0.93	0.62	0.12	2.61	2.46	2.29	1.78	1.55	1.22
28	Ciro D. Rodriguez (D)	1.03	0.75	0.24	2.76	2.61	2.44	1.91	1.69	1.36
29	Gene Green (D)	0.98	0.62	0.11	2.61	2.47	2.29	1.81	1.56	1.21
30	Eddie Bernice Johnson (D)	0.52	0.05	-0.50	2.47	2.31	2.12	1.52	1.22	0.86

Note: Rates of return exclude both Disability Insurance benefits and taxes, but include all Old-Age and Survivors Insurance (OASI) benefits and taxes (including pre-retirement Survivors Insurance). All values include both the portion of the OASI tax paid directly by workers and the portion paid by the employer on a worker's behalf. All rates of return are net of inflation. Calculations are based on life expectancies and average earnings for each district. Because of non-linearity in the benefit function, amounts for each district may not sum to the state average.

UTAH

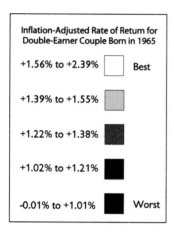

Inflation-Adjusted Rate of Return for Double-Earner Couple Born in 1965

+1.56% to +2.39%	☐	Best
+1.39% to +1.55%	▤	
+1.22% to +1.38%	▦	
+1.02% to +1.21%	▪	
-0.01% to +1.01%	■	Worst

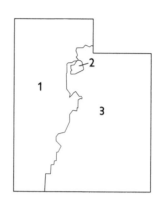

Lifetime Dollar Losses Under Social Security (OASI) Compared with Personal Retirement Accounts for Double-Earner Couples Born in 1965

District	Member of Congress	Loss Under Social Security (3)-(2)	Ranking from Lowest Loss to Highest Loss	Social Security Taxes Paid (1)	Social Security Benefits (2)	Personal Retirement Accounts (3)
Senate						
	Orrin G. Hatch (R)					
	Robert Bennett (R)					
Statewide		$ 334,146	6	$ 308,669	$ 553,338	$ 887,484
House of Representatives						
1	James V. Hansen (R)	331,147	24 / 436	307,686	553,652	884,798
2	Merrill Cook (R)	406,540	94	348,290	595,019	1,001,559
3	Christopher Cannon (R)	264,150	4	269,259	510,144	774,294

Note: Column (1) shows the total amount of Old-Age and Survivors Insurance (OASI) taxes paid during the individual's working life. Column (2) shows the total value of Old-Age and Survivors Insurance benefits collected by the worker and his or her spouse following retirement. Column (3) shows the amount accumulated in a Personal Retirement Account had the worker been able to place his or her OASI taxes in a Personal Retirement Account. The accumulation in this personal account has been reduced by the cost of purchasing life insurance coverage equivalent to the pre-retirement Survivors Insurance portion of Social Security. All amounts exclude both Disability Insurance benefits and taxes. All values include both the portion of the OASI tax paid directly by workers and the portion paid by the employer on a worker's behalf. The losses from not participating in a Personal Retirement Account (columns (3)-(2)) are for illustrative purposes only and do not reflect any specific plan for reforming Social Security. All amounts are expressed in inflation-adjusted dollars for the year 2000. Calculations are based on life expectancies and average earnings for each district. Because of non-linearity in the benefit function, amounts for each district may not sum to the state average.

Inflation-Adjusted Rate of Return from Social Security (OASI) by Birth Year

District	Member of Congress	Single Males			Single Females			Double-Earner Couples		
		1955	1965	1975	1955	1965	1975	1955	1965	1975
Senate										
	Orrin G. Hatch (R)									
	Robert Bennett (R)									
Statewide		1.57 %	1.40 %	1.16 %	2.80 %	2.69 %	2.55 %	2.19 %	2.04 %	1.84 %
House of Representatives										
1	James V. Hansen (R)	1.57	1.41	1.18	2.80	2.70	2.56	2.19	2.05	1.85
2	Merrill Cook (R)	1.34	1.15	0.91	2.71	2.60	2.45	2.03	1.87	1.66
3	Christopher Cannon (R)	1.82	1.66	1.42	2.91	2.81	2.67	2.37	2.24	2.04

Note: Rates of return exclude both Disability Insurance benefits and taxes, but include all Old-Age and Survivors Insurance (OASI) benefits and taxes (including pre-retirement Survivors Insurance). All values include both the portion of the OASI tax paid directly by workers and the portion paid by the employer on a worker's behalf. All rates of return are net of inflation. Calculations are based on life expectancies and average earnings for each district. Because of non-linearity in the benefit function, amounts for each district may not sum to the state average.

VERMONT

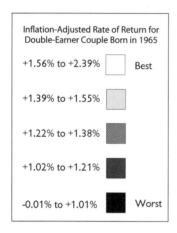

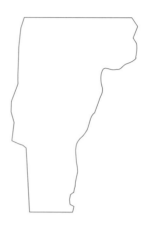

Inflation-Adjusted Rate of Return for Double-Earner Couple Born in 1965

+1.56% to +2.39% Best

+1.39% to +1.55%

+1.22% to +1.38%

+1.02% to +1.21%

-0.01% to +1.01% Worst

Lifetime Dollar Losses Under Social Security (OASI) Compared with Personal Retirement Accounts for Double-Earner Couples Born in 1965

District	Member of Congress	Loss Under Social Security (3)-(2)	Ranking from Lowest Loss to Highest Loss	Social Security Taxes Paid (1)	Social Security Benefits (2)	Personal Retirement Accounts (3)
Senate						
	Patrick J. Leahy (D)					
	Jim M. Jeffords (R)					
Statewide		$ 365,532	9	$ 316,311	$ 544,068	$ 909,601
House of Representatives						
At large	Bernard Sanders (I)	365,532	50 / 436	316,311	544,068	909,601

Note: Column (1) shows the total amount of Old-Age and Survivors Insurance (OASI) taxes paid during the individual's working life. Column (2) shows the total value of Old-Age and Survivors Insurance benefits collected by the worker and his or her spouse following retirement. Column (3) shows the amount accumulated in a Personal Retirement Account had the worker been able to place his or her OASI taxes in a Personal Retirement Account. The accumulation in this personal account has been reduced by the cost of purchasing life insurance coverage equivalent to the pre-retirement Survivors Insurance portion of Social Security. All amounts exclude both Disability Insurance benefits and taxes. All values include both the portion of the OASI tax paid directly by workers and the portion paid by the employer on a worker's behalf. The losses from not participating in a Personal Retirement Account (columns (3)-(2)) are for illustrative purposes only and do not reflect any specific plan for reforming Social Security. All amounts are expressed in inflation-adjusted dollars for the year 2000. Calculations are based on life expectancies and average earnings for each district.

Inflation-Adjusted Rate of Return from Social Security (OASI) by Birth Year

District	Member of Congress	Single Males			Single Females			Double-Earner Couples		
		1955	1965	1975	1955	1965	1975	1955	1965	1975
Senate										
	Patrick J. Leahy (D)									
	Jim M. Jeffords (R)									
Statewide		1.44%	1.26%	0.99%	2.74%	2.58%	2.42%	2.10%	1.92%	1.69%
House of Representatives										
At large	Bernard Sanders (I)	1.44	1.26	0.99	2.74	2.58	2.42	2.10	1.92	1.69

Note: Rates of return exclude both Disability Insurance benefits and taxes, but include all Old-Age and Survivors Insurance (OASI) benefits and taxes (including pre-retirement Survivors Insurance). All values include both the portion of the OASI tax paid directly by workers and the portion paid by the employer on a worker's behalf. All rates of return are net of inflation. Calculations are based on life expectancies and average earnings for each district.

VIRGINIA

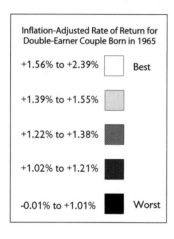

Inflation-Adjusted Rate of Return for
Double-Earner Couple Born in 1965

+1.56% to +2.39% ☐ Best

+1.39% to +1.55% ☐

+1.22% to +1.38% ☐

+1.02% to +1.21% ☐

-0.01% to +1.01% ■ Worst

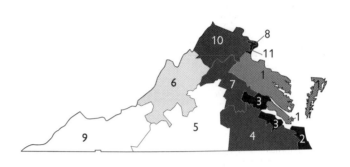

Lifetime Dollar Losses Under Social Security (OASI) Compared with Personal Retirement Accounts for Double-Earner Couples Born in 1965

District	Member of Congress	Loss Under Social Security (3)-(2)	Ranking from Lowest Loss to Highest Loss	Social Security Taxes Paid (1)	Social Security Benefits (2)	Personal Retirement Accounts (3)
Senate						
	John W. Warner (R)					
	Charles S. Robb (D)					
Statewide		$ 560,840	41	$ 370,141	$ 503,389	$ 1,064,230
House of Representatives						
1 *	Herbert H. Bateman (R)	525,439	253 / 436	354,799	494,838	1,020,277
2 *	Owen B. Pickett (D)	501,645	227	315,837	406,592	908,237
3 *	Robert C. Scott (D)	426,816	129	270,287	350,436	777,251
4 *	Norman Sisisky (D)	491,887	215	327,344	449,441	941,327
5	Virgil H. Goode, Jr. (D)	377,538	56	282,020	433,453	810,990
6	Robert W. Goodlatte (R)	409,305	101	303,391	463,141	872,446
7 *	Thomas J. Bliley, Jr. (R)	646,569	353	433,570	600,225	1,246,794
8	James P. Moran (D)	852,981	416	516,657	638,087	1,491,068
9	Rick Boucher (D)	343,148	33	263,766	415,351	758,499
10	Frank R. Wolf (R)	742,369	393	485,342	653,601	1,395,970
11	Thomas M. Davis III (R)	786,451	406	503,899	664,637	1,451,088

Note: Column (1) shows the total amount of Old-Age and Survivors Insurance (OASI) taxes paid during the individual's working life. Column (2) shows the total value of Old-Age and Survivors Insurance benefits collected by the worker and his or her spouse following retirement. Column (3) shows the amount accumulated in a Personal Retirement Account had the worker been able to place his or her OASI taxes in a Personal Retirement Account. The accumulation in this personal account has been reduced by the cost of purchasing life insurance coverage equivalent to the pre-retirement Survivors Insurance portion of Social Security. All amounts exclude both Disability Insurance benefits and taxes. All values include both the portion of the OASI tax paid directly by workers and the portion paid by the employer on a worker's behalf. The losses from not participating in a Personal Retirement Account (columns (3)-(2)) are for illustrative purposes only and do not reflect any specific plan for reforming Social Security. Districts marked * have been subject to boundary changes since publication of data used in this analysis. All amounts are expressed in inflation-adjusted dollars for the year 2000. Calculations are based on life expectancies and average earnings for each district. Because of non-linearity in the benefit function, amounts for each district may not sum to the state average.

Inflation-Adjusted Rate of Return from Social Security (OASI) by Birth Year

District	Member of Congress	Single Males			Single Females			Double-Earner Couples		
		1955	1965	1975	1955	1965	1975	1955	1965	1975
Senate										
	John W. Warner (R)									
	Charles S. Robb (D)									
Statewide		0.34 %	-0.03 %	-0.45 %	2.39 %	2.25 %	2.08 %	1.39 %	1.14 %	0.85 %
House of Representatives										
1 *	Herbert H. Bateman (R)	0.44	0.11	-0.29	2.43	2.30	2.14	1.46	1.23	0.95
2 *	Owen B. Pickett (D)	0.16	-0.77	-1.83	2.53	2.39	2.22	1.40	0.96	0.47
3 *	Robert C. Scott (D)	0.29	-0.42	-1.17	2.47	2.28	2.09	1.42	1.01	0.58
4 *	Norman Sisisky (D)	0.43	0.03	-0.46	2.43	2.28	2.11	1.45	1.19	0.87
5	Virgil H. Goode, Jr. (D)	0.94	0.66	0.31	2.64	2.49	2.32	1.80	1.59	1.32
6	Robert W. Goodlatte (R)	0.89	0.62	0.29	2.61	2.47	2.30	1.76	1.55	1.30
7 *	Thomas J. Bliley, Jr. (R)	0.33	0.15	-0.11	2.33	2.20	2.03	1.35	1.18	0.96
8	James P. Moran (D)	-0.18	-0.65	-1.12	2.21	2.05	1.88	1.07	0.78	0.47
9	Rick Boucher (D)	1.07	0.78	0.44	2.70	2.55	2.39	1.90	1.68	1.42
10	Frank R. Wolf (R)	0.17	0.00	-0.25	2.25	2.13	1.97	1.23	1.08	0.86
11	Thomas M. Davis III (R)	0.07	-0.20	-0.51	2.26	2.14	1.98	1.19	1.01	0.76

Note: Rates of return exclude both Disability Insurance benefits and taxes, but include all Old-Age and Survivors Insurance (OASI) benefits and taxes (including pre-retirement Survivors Insurance). All values include both the portion of the OASI tax paid directly by workers and the portion paid by the employer on a worker's behalf. All rates of return are net of inflation. Districts marked * have been subject to boundary changes since publication of data used in this analysis. Calculations are based on life expectancies and average earnings for each district. Because of non-linearity in the benefit function, amounts for each district may not sum to the state average.

WASHINGTON

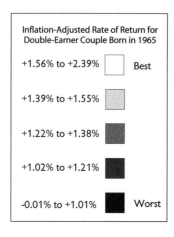

Inflation-Adjusted Rate of Return for
Double-Earner Couple Born in 1965

+1.56% to +2.39%   ☐   Best

+1.39% to +1.55%   ▨

+1.22% to +1.38%   ▨

+1.02% to +1.21%   ▨

-0.01% to +1.01%   ■   Worst

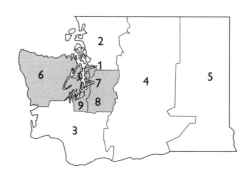

Lifetime Dollar Losses Under Social Security (OASI) Compared with Personal Retirement Accounts for Double-Earner Couples Born in 1965

District	Member of Congress	Loss Under Social Security (3)-(2)	Ranking from Lowest Loss to Highest Loss	Social Security Taxes Paid (1)	Social Security Benefits (2)	Personal Retirement Accounts (3)
Senate						
	Slade Gorton (R)					
	Patty Murray (D)					
Statewide		$ 479,999	29	$ 361,575	$ 559,601	$ 1,039,601
House of Representatives						
1	Jay Inslee (D)	614,036	332 / 436	446,550	670,085	1,284,121
2	Jack Metcalf (R)	455,575	159	351,068	553,974	1,009,549
3	Brian Baird (D)	435,374	137	341,715	547,280	982,653
4	Richard Hastings (R)	363,330	49	299,414	497,681	861,011
5	George R. Nethercutt, Jr. (R)	355,490	42	293,900	489,665	845,154
6	Norman D. Dicks (D)	442,684	143	328,773	502,751	945,435
7	Jim McDermott (D)	525,646	254	375,278	553,522	1,079,169
8	Jennifer Dunn (R)	639,316	349	465,558	699,465	1,338,781
9	Adam Smith (D)	468,518	175	349,211	535,689	1,004,208

Note: Column (1) shows the total amount of Old-Age and Survivors Insurance (OASI) taxes paid during the individual's working life. Column (2) shows the total value of Old-Age and Survivors Insurance benefits collected by the worker and his or her spouse following retirement. Column (3) shows the amount accumulated in a Personal Retirement Account had the worker been able to place his or her OASI taxes in a Personal Retirement Account. The accumulation in this personal account has been reduced by the cost of purchasing life insurance coverage equivalent to the pre-retirement Survivors Insurance portion of Social Security. All amounts exclude both Disability Insurance benefits and taxes. All values include both the portion of the OASI tax paid directly by workers and the portion paid by the employer on a worker's behalf. The losses from not participating in a Personal Retirement Account (columns (3)-(2)) are for illustrative purposes only and do not reflect any specific plan for reforming Social Security. All amounts are expressed in inflation-adjusted dollars for the year 2000. Calculations are based on life expectancies and average earnings for each district. Because of non-linearity in the benefit function, amounts for each district may not sum to the state average.

Inflation-Adjusted Rate of Return from Social Security (OASI) by Birth Year

District	Member of Congress	Single Males			Single Females			Double-Earner Couples		
		1955	1965	1975	1955	1965	1975	1955	1965	1975
Senate										
	Slade Gorton (R)									
	Patty Murray (D)									
Statewide		0.96%	0.71%	0.40%	2.54%	2.42%	2.27%	1.75%	1.57%	1.32%
House of Representatives										
1	Jay Inslee (D)	0.74	0.56	0.30	2.43	2.32	2.17	1.59	1.44	1.22
2	Jack Metcalf (R)	1.04	0.79	0.47	2.59	2.47	2.32	1.82	1.63	1.39
3	Brian Baird (D)	1.09	0.90	0.63	2.58	2.47	2.32	1.84	1.68	1.46
4	Richard Hastings (R)	1.31	1.10	0.80	2.67	2.55	2.40	1.99	1.83	1.59
5	George R. Nethercutt, Jr. (R)	1.32	1.06	0.75	2.72	2.60	2.45	2.03	1.84	1.59
6	Norman D. Dicks (D)	0.96	0.60	0.18	2.59	2.46	2.30	1.78	1.54	1.25
7	Jim McDermott (D)	0.80	0.44	0.07	2.52	2.36	2.19	1.67	1.41	1.13
8	Jennifer Dunn (R)	0.71	0.58	0.35	2.41	2.30	2.15	1.56	1.43	1.23
9	Adam Smith (D)	0.94	0.65	0.26	2.55	2.43	2.27	1.75	1.54	1.27

Note: Rates of return exclude both Disability Insurance benefits and taxes, but include all Old-Age and Survivors Insurance (OASI) benefits and taxes (including pre-retirement Survivors Insurance). All values include both the portion of the OASI tax paid directly by workers and the portion paid by the employer on a worker's behalf. All rates of return are net of inflation. Calculations are based on life expectancies and average earnings for each district. Because of non-linearity in the benefit function, amounts for each district may not sum to the state average.

WEST VIRGINIA

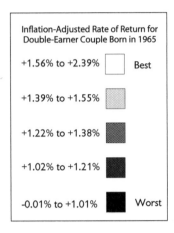

Inflation-Adjusted Rate of Return for
Double-Earner Couple Born in 1965

+1.56% to +2.39% Best

+1.39% to +1.55%

+1.22% to +1.38%

+1.02% to +1.21%

-0.01% to +1.01% Worst

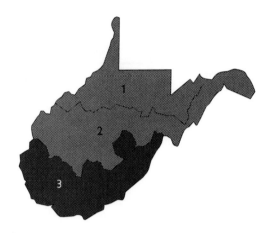

Lifetime Dollar Losses Under Social Security (OASI) Compared with Personal Retirement Accounts for Double-Earner Couples Born in 1965

District	Member of Congress	Loss Under Social Security (3)-(2)	Ranking from Lowest Loss to Highest Loss	Social Security Taxes Paid (1)	Social Security Benefits (2)	Personal Retirement Accounts (3)
Senate						
	Robert C. Byrd (D)					
	John D. Rockefeller IV (D)					
Statewide		$ 451,206	21	$ 300,176	$ 411,859	$ 863,066
House of Representatives						
1	Alan B. Mollohan (D)	434,874	136 / 436	296,680	418,273	853,147
2	Robert E. Wise, Jr. (D)	455,693	160	306,506	425,711	881,404
3	Nick J. Rahall II (D)	461,158	165	296,593	391,738	852,896

Note: Column (1) shows the total amount of Old-Age and Survivors Insurance (OASI) taxes paid during the individual's working life. Column (2) shows the total value of Old-Age and Survivors Insurance benefits collected by the worker and his or her spouse following retirement. Column (3) shows the amount accumulated in a Personal Retirement Account had the worker been able to place his or her OASI taxes in a Personal Retirement Account. The accumulation in this personal account has been reduced by the cost of purchasing life insurance coverage equivalent to the pre-retirement Survivors Insurance portion of Social Security. All amounts exclude both Disability Insurance benefits and taxes. All values include both the portion of the OASI tax paid directly by workers and the portion paid by the employer on a worker's behalf. The losses from not participating in a Personal Retirement Account (columns (3)-(2)) are for illustrative purposes only and do not reflect any specific plan for reforming Social Security. All amounts are expressed in inflation-adjusted dollars for the year 2000. Calculations are based on life expectancies and average earnings for each district. Because of non-linearity in the benefit function, amounts for each district may not sum to the state average.

Inflation-Adjusted Rate of Return from Social Security (OASI) by Birth Year

District	Member of Congress	Single Males 1955	1965	1975	Single Females 1955	1965	1975	Double-Earner Couples 1955	1965	1975
Senate										
	Robert C. Byrd (D)									
	John D. Rockefeller IV (D)									
Statewide		0.47 %	0.10 %	-0.35 %	2.41 %	2.25 %	2.09 %	1.46 %	1.20 %	0.89 %
House of Representatives										
1	Alan B. Mollohan (D)	0.58	0.24	-0.17	2.46	2.31	2.14	1.54	1.29	1.00
2	Robert E. Wise, Jr. (D)	0.49	0.16	-0.25	2.42	2.27	2.10	1.48	1.24	0.94
3	Nick J. Rahall II (D)	0.33	-0.12	-0.64	2.35	2.19	2.01	1.36	1.07	0.73

Note: Rates of return exclude both Disability Insurance benefits and taxes, but include all Old-Age and Survivors Insurance (OASI) benefits and taxes (including pre-retirement Survivors Insurance). All values include both the portion of the OASI tax paid directly by workers and the portion paid by the employer on a worker's behalf. All rates of return are net of inflation. Calculations are based on life expectancies and average earnings for each district. Because of non-linearity in the benefit function, amounts for each district may not sum to the state average.

WISCONSIN

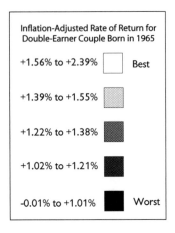

Inflation-Adjusted Rate of Return for
Double-Earner Couple Born in 1965

+1.56% to +2.39% ☐ Best

+1.39% to +1.55% ▧

+1.22% to +1.38% ▨

+1.02% to +1.21% ▦

-0.01% to +1.01% ■ Worst

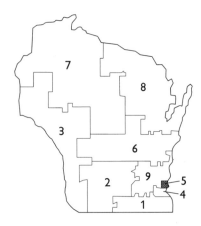

Lifetime Dollar Losses Under Social Security (OASI) Compared with Personal Retirement Accounts for Double-Earner Couples Born in 1965

District	Member of Congress	Loss Under Social Security (3)-(2)	Ranking from Lowest Loss to Highest Loss	Social Security Taxes Paid (1)	Social Security Benefits (2)	Personal Retirement Accounts (3)
Senate						
	Herbert H. Kohl (D)					
	Russ Feingold (D)					
Statewide		$ 405,269	12	$ 325,132	$ 529,550	$ 934,820
House of Representatives						
1	Paul Ryan (R)	424,958	125 / 436	334,729	537,604	962,562
2	Tammy Baldwin (D)	380,733	58	319,476	537,967	918,700
3	Ron Kind (D)	305,490	12	277,485	492,460	797,950
4	Gerald D. Kleczka (D)	444,176	146	346,964	553,571	997,747
5	Thomas M. Barrett (D)	495,978	218	340,187	482,282	978,259
6	Thomas E. Petri (R)	354,564	41	301,940	513,710	868,274
7	David R. Obey (D)	330,604	23	287,637	496,540	827,144
8	Mark Green (R)	387,396	66	317,413	525,374	912,770
9	F. James Sensenbrenner, Jr. (R)	515,997	243	397,921	628,285	1,144,282

Note: Column (1) shows the total amount of Old-Age and Survivors Insurance (OASI) taxes paid during the individual's working life. Column (2) shows the total value of Old-Age and Survivors Insurance benefits collected by the worker and his or her spouse following retirement. Column (3) shows the amount accumulated in a Personal Retirement Account had the worker been able to place his or her OASI taxes in a Personal Retirement Account. The accumulation in this personal account has been reduced by the cost of purchasing life insurance coverage equivalent to the pre-retirement Survivors Insurance portion of Social Security. All amounts exclude both Disability Insurance benefits and taxes. All values include both the portion of the OASI tax paid directly by workers and the portion paid by the employer on a worker's behalf. The losses from not participating in a Personal Retirement Account (columns (3)-(2)) are for illustrative purposes only and do not reflect any specific plan for reforming Social Security. All amounts are expressed in inflation-adjusted dollars for the year 2000. Calculations are based on life expectancies and average earnings for each district. Because of non-linearity in the benefit function, amounts for each district may not sum to the state average.

Inflation-Adjusted Rate of Return from Social Security (OASI) by Birth Year

District	Member of Congress	Single Males			Single Females			Double-Earner Couples		
		1955	1965	1975	1955	1965	1975	1955	1965	1975
Senate										
	Herbert H. Kohl (D)									
	Russ Feingold (D)									
Statewide		1.10%	0.93%	0.68%	2.68%	2.56%	2.41%	1.89%	1.74%	1.53%
House of Representatives										
1	Paul Ryan (R)	1.03	0.87	0.63	2.63	2.51	2.36	1.84	1.70	1.48
2	Tammy Baldwin (D)	1.24	1.06	0.82	2.75	2.63	2.48	2.00	1.85	1.64
3	Ron Kind (D)	1.47	1.32	1.10	2.86	2.75	2.61	2.17	2.04	1.84
4	Gerald D. Kleczka (D)	1.01	0.83	0.58	2.63	2.50	2.34	1.82	1.67	1.45
5	Thomas M. Barrett (D)	0.62	0.23	-0.18	2.48	2.31	2.14	1.57	1.29	1.00
6	Thomas E. Petri (R)	1.28	1.13	0.88	2.76	2.65	2.51	2.03	1.89	1.68
7	David R. Obey (D)	1.35	1.20	0.97	2.80	2.68	2.54	2.08	1.95	1.75
8	Mark Green (R)	1.17	1.01	0.78	2.69	2.58	2.43	1.94	1.80	1.59
9	F. James Sensenbrenner, Jr. (R)	0.85	0.75	0.55	2.58	2.47	2.32	1.72	1.61	1.42

Note: Rates of return exclude both Disability Insurance benefits and taxes, but include all Old-Age and Survivors Insurance (OASI) benefits and taxes (including pre-retirement Survivors Insurance). All values include both the portion of the OASI tax paid directly by workers and the portion paid by the employer on a worker's behalf. All rates of return are net of inflation. Calculations are based on life expectancies and average earnings for each district. Because of non-linearity in the benefit function, amounts for each district may not sum to the state average.

WYOMING

Inflation-Adjusted Rate of Return for
Double-Earner Couple Born in 1965

+1.56% to +2.39% ☐ Best

+1.39% to +1.55% ▨

+1.22% to +1.38% ▨

+1.02% to +1.21% ■

-0.01% to +1.01% ■ Worst

Lifetime Dollar Losses Under Social Security (OASI) Compared with Personal Retirement Accounts for Double-Earner Couples Born in 1965

District	Member of Congress	Loss Under Social Security (3)-(2)	Ranking from Lowest Loss to Highest Loss	Social Security Taxes Paid (1)	Social Security Benefits (2)	Personal Retirement Accounts (3)
Senate						
	Craig Thomas (R)					
	Michael B. Enzi (R)					
Statewide		$ 335,953	7	$ 309,843	$ 555,045	$ 890,998
House of Representatives						
At large	Barbara Cubin (R)	335,953	28 / 436	309,843	555,045	890,998

Note: Column (1) shows the total amount of Old-Age and Survivors Insurance (OASI) taxes paid during the individual's working life. Column (2) shows the total value of Old-Age and Survivors Insurance benefits collected by the worker and his or her spouse following retirement. Column (3) shows the amount accumulated in a Personal Retirement Account had the worker been able to place his or her OASI taxes in a Personal Retirement Account. The accumulation in this personal account has been reduced by the cost of purchasing life insurance coverage equivalent to the pre-retirement Survivors Insurance portion of Social Security. All amounts exclude both Disability Insurance benefits and taxes. All values include both the portion of the OASI tax paid directly by workers and the portion paid by the employer on a worker's behalf. The losses from not participating in a Personal Retirement Account (columns (3)-(2)) are for illustrative purposes only and do not reflect any specific plan for reforming Social Security. All amounts are expressed in inflation-adjusted dollars for the year 2000. Calculations are based on life expectancies and average earnings for each district.

Inflation-Adjusted Rate of Return from Social Security (OASI) by Birth Year

District	Member of Congress	Single Males			Single Females			Double-Earner Couples		
		1955	1965	1975	1955	1965	1975	1955	1965	1975
Senate										
	Craig Thomas (R)									
	Michael B. Enzi (R)									
Statewide		1.64 %	1.44 %	1.14 %	2.82 %	2.64 %	2.47 %	2.23 %	2.04 %	1.79 %
House of Representatives										
At large	Barbara Cubin (R)	1.64	1.44	1.14	2.82	2.64	2.47	2.23	2.04	1.79

Note: Rates of return exclude both Disability Insurance benefits and taxes, but include all Old-Age and Survivors Insurance (OASI) benefits and taxes (including pre-retirement Survivors Insurance). All values include both the portion of the OASI tax paid directly by workers and the portion paid by the employer on a worker's behalf. All rates of return are net of inflation. Calculations are based on life expectancies and average earnings for each district.

3

ANSWERING QUESTIONS ABOUT THE RATE OF RETURN[1]

Experts across a wide spectrum of political opinion now concede that Social Security's retirement program offers a poor return for a lifetime of tax payments. Indeed, President Clinton has argued that Social Security's rate of return needs to be higher.[2] This emphasis on rate of return has reshaped the debate on Social Security reform by focusing attention on matters of higher consequence to America's workers than important, yet arcane concepts such as "trust fund balances" or "dependency ratios." The Heritage Foundation's Center for Data Analysis (CDA) sought to contribute to this debate by offering workers of different ages, income, and ethnicity detailed information about their publicly funded retirement program—information that the Social Security Administration (SSA) has often refused to produce, even when asked by the presidentially appointed Social Security Advisory Council.[3]

Given the current emphasis on Social Security reform and the sometimes contentious nature of the debate, it is necessary to address a few specific points about the methods CDA used to produce this study.

To do this, we will answer specific questions about our methodology that arose after The Heritage Foundation published four papers in 1998 that analyzed Social Security's rate of return.[4]

---

1. This chapter is adapted from William W. Beach and Gareth G. Davis, "Social Security's Rate of Return: A Reply to Our Critics," *Center for Data Analysis Report* No. CDA98-08, November 12, 1998.

2. Remarks by President Bill Clinton before the National Forum on Social Security, Kansas City, April 7, 1998.

3. Members of the 1996 Social Security Advisory Council asked the Office of the Chief Actuary to calculate several rates of return based on several factors, including life expectancy, adjusted for income. The Social Security Administration refused their request. See Sylvester Schieber, *Rates of Return on Social Security Contributions: Good Deal, Bad Deal, or Do We Even Care?* Testimony before the Committee on the Budget, U.S. Senate, January 21, 1998.

MEASURING SOCIAL SECURITY'S EFFECTIVENESS

Question: Is the rate of return a proper measure of the effectiveness of the Social Security program? Rather, shouldn't the system be judged using social criteria, such as its success in reducing the poverty rate among the elderly?

Answer: An effective retirement insurance program must not only protect workers from the threat of falling into poverty after they retire, but also provide an efficient level of income based on the amount of taxes paid. The rate of return measures the difference between the amount that Social Security takes from workers and the amount that Social Security gives back to them or their families as benefits. A low or negative rate of return means that individual families are foregoing higher retirement income because Social Security is returning less to them than they could have accumulated had they been able to invest their payroll taxes in personal accounts. When the rate of return from Social Security for lower-income workers is below the rate available from alternative investments, the program can actually add to the number of retirees in poverty—or, at least, slow the accumulation of wealth.

The founders of Social Security recognized the importance of the program's rate of return. Arthur J. Altameyer, chairman of the Social Security Board from 1937 to 1946 and the Social Security Administration's first commissioner, argued against policies that would lead to the evolution of a social security system that robbed workers of higher lifetime incomes, or a greater safety net, by subjecting them to rates of return below those available from private markets. In 1945, Altameyer noted:

> The indefinite continuation of the current contribution rate will eventually necessitate raising employees' contributions later to a point where future beneficiaries will be obliged to pay more for their benefits than if they had obtained this insurance from a private insurance company.... I say it is inequitable to compel them to pay more under this system than they would have to pay to a private insurance company, and I think that Congress would be confronted with that embarrassing situation.[5]

METHODS OF CALCULATING RATES OF RETURN

Question: Did Heritage use the correct method to calculate Social Security's rate of return?

Answer: Social Security Deputy Chief Actuary Steve Goss criticized our methodology in calculating rate of return, saying:

> [T]he Heritage study erroneously analyzes a single outcome where an individual is assumed to know how long he or she will live.... This approach consistently over-

4. William W. Beach and Gareth G. Davis, "Social Security's Rate of Return," Heritage Foundation *Center for Data Analysis Report* No. CDA98–01, January 15, 1998; "Social Security's Rate of Return for Hispanic Americans," *Center for Data Analysis Report* No. 98–02, March 27, 1998; and "Social Security's Rate of Return for Union Households," *Center for Data Analysis Report* No. 98–06, September 7 1998. See also William W. Beach, Gareth G. Davis, and Sarah E. Youssef, "A State-by-State Analysis of the Returns from Social Security," *Center for Data Analysis Report* No. 98–05, July 30, 1998.

5. Quote from Schieber, *Rates of Return on Social Security Contributions.* Also see I. S. Falk, "Questions and Answers on Financing of Old-Age and Survivors Insurance," Memorandum to O. C. Pogge, Director, Bureau of Old-Age and Survivors Insurance, February 9, 1945, p. 13.

estimates the expected number of years of work and consistently underestimates the expected number of years after reaching retirement age. As a result, it grossly underestimates the expected rates of return from Social Security retirement benefits…. Clearly, computed rates of return for all men will be much higher for all men [*sic*], and, moreover the difference between rates of return for black and white men will be dramatically smaller than if the erroneous Heritage method is used.[6]

This observation is curious at best.Using Goss's own data, Heritage calculates rates of return for 20-year-old white and black male workers to be 0.59 and -0.15 percent, respectively.[7]

CDA analysts carefully considered the advantages and disadvantages of three different approaches for calculating Social Security's rate of return:

1. The **"expected value" method,** which involves summing the expected (or "probability adjusted") value of benefits and taxes on a year-by-year basis,

2. The **"median value" return method,** which calculates the return to the 50th percentile in a population's mortality distribution, and essentially yields the return below which half of a population would receive less, and

3. The **"average life expectancy" method,** which involves first calculating a group's life expectancy and then calculating the return from Social Security for a worker who lives to that life expectancy. This method, which we selected, usually yields results that lie between the expected return and the median return.

Each of these methods includes both strengths and weaknesses. Goss favors the expected value method, and while he characterized the method we selected as "erroneous," he fails to note some of the disadvantages of his method for measuring the average return for members of a particular demographic group. The expected value method is particularly susceptible to distortion from skewed data. This problem can render the expected value method an unsuitable estimator of the likely return from Social Security for a typical member of a population.

A simple analysis of an imaginary lottery with a single prize of $1,000,000 illustrates this point. Say 1,000 contestants each pay $900 for a lottery ticket. According to the method favored by Goss, the expected payout from this lottery would be $1,000 for each ticket holder. This implies that the overall positive (net) return from the $900 investment would be $100. Actually, 99.9 percent of the ticket holders would lose $900. So, to suggest to potential buyers of these lottery tickets that they will receive $100, according to the expected return method, is to, in fact, mislead them.

Although this is an extreme example, there is evidence that the returns from the current Social Security system, particularly for African-Americans, are highly skewed in a similar fashion. Calculations made by Heritage suggest that, while the calculated expected return for a group of recipients may be positive, a large majority of the members of this group (up to 70 percent in the case of African-Americans) may in fact receive negative returns from Social Security.[8]

---

6. Steve Goss, Deputy Chief Actuary, Social Security Administration, Memorandum, "Problems with 'Social Security's Rate of Return: A Report of the Heritage Center for Data Analysis,'" February 4, 1998.

7. *Ibid.*; see also Chart 3.1.

8. See Gareth G. Davis, "Ethnic and Racial Differentials from Social Security Old-Age and Survivors Insurance," presented at the Annual Meeting of the Western Economic Association, July 9, 1999. Available from the author upon request.

Thus, while the expected rate of return may be useful to the actuary who is responsible for administering an entire program (such as the administrator of the imaginary lottery) and who must account for all participants (including those like the single winner of the lottery), it often is a less useful tool for those charged with advising individual participants on how they likely will fare in the program. Many actuaries, especially in the private sector, recognize the weaknesses associated with the expected value method. In offering investment advice to their clients, they routinely use the average life expectancy method that is employed in Heritage's study. Since Heritage's objective is to enable ordinary Americans to compare the probable consequences of remaining in today's Social Security system with their likely returns from personal investments, it was also logical to adopt the average life expectancy method.

Critics have also mischaracterized or misunderstood the data Heritage used to determine rates of return. For example, Robert Myers, former Chief Actuary of the SSA, mistakenly claimed that Heritage used a life expectancy of exactly 69 years for a 21-year-old African-American male.[9] In fact, we use a life expectancy of 73.81 years, which was based on projections made by the U.S. Bureau of the Census and the Social Security Administration, which take into account future improvements in longevity.[10]

Perhaps the most flagrant mischaracterization of our approach was a table of life expectancies for 20-year-old white and black males created by Steve Goss and featured prominently in a 1997 paper by the Center on Budget and Policy Priorities (CBPP).[11] The use of this table was misleading on a number of levels:

- The table refers to examples that were not computed in the 1998 Heritage rate of return studies. For example, Heritage analysts did not calculate the rates of return for any white or African-American males born after 1975.

- The data presented in the Goss table were drawn from a different source (the *1992 Life Tables of the United States*[12]), which were inappropriate for calculating rates of return from Social Security. In particular, the *Life Tables* figures are based solely on demographic conditions prevailing in 1992 and, unlike the data used by CDA, do not take into account likely future improvements in life expectancy.

Ironically, despite these shortcomings, the data presented by Goss in this table and prominently featured in the CBPP study can be used to illustrate both the shortcomings of the expected value method favored by Goss and the robustness of the general results calculated in the Heritage study.

According to the data in the *1992 Life Tables*, half of all 20-year-old black males who enter the labor force will die before they reach the age of 69.7. Half of all white 20-year-old males will die

---

9. Kilolo Kijakazi, *African Americans, Hispanic Americans and Social Security: The Shortcomings of the Heritage Report* (Washington, D.C.: Center on Budget and Policy Priorities, October 5, 1998).

10. William W. Beach and Gareth G. Davis, "Social Security's Rate of Return," Heritage Foundation *CDA Report* No. CDA98-01, January 15, 1998, pp. 21–22.

11. *Ibid.*

12. National Center for Health Statistics, *Vital Statistics of the United States, 1992 LifeTables,* Vol. II, Section 6, April 1998. It should be noted that this life table is based only on conditions prevailing in 1992. It does not reflect changes in life expectancy that may occur in subsequent years. The original Heritage analysis uses a life table that was adjusted to take into account changes in longevity. The *1992 Life Table* cited here is also the one quoted by Steve Goss in his "Problems" memorandum and is used for the purpose of allowing direct comparison with his examples.

before age 77. If the retirement age is 65, this means that half of all black male workers will die before receiving Old-Age and Survivors Insurance (OASI) benefits for 4.7 years, and half of all white male workers will die before receiving OASI benefits for 12 years. According to the expected value method used by Goss, however, "average" black and white males would receive, respectively, 8.1 years and 12.1 years of benefits. In reality, over 60 percent of black males and 50 percent of white males will die before collecting benefits for this length of time.

■ Table 3.1

The Goss Expected Value Method vs. The Experience of Median Worker

	Years of Paying Taxes	Years of Receiving Benefits	Number of Tax Years Per Year of Benefits
Goss "Average"			
Black Male	39.1	8.1	4.8
White Male	42.2	12.1	3.5
Experience of 50th Person From a Population of 100, *1992 Life Tables*			
Black Male	45	4.7	9.6
White Male	45	12.0	3.8

Sources: Steve Goss, Social Security Administration, "Problems with 'Social Security's Rate of Return: A Report of the Heritage Center for Data Analysis,'" Memorandum dated February 4, 1998; Heritage calculations, based on National Center for Health Statistics, *Vital Statistics of the United States, 1992 Life Tables,* 1998.

The expected value method produces results that do not represent the experiences of African-American males. As Table 3.1 shows, the Goss method suggests that an "average" black male worker fares much better from Social Security (paying taxes for only 4.8 years for each year of benefits) than the median black worker (paying taxes for 9.6 years for each year of benefits). In statistical terms, this difference is due to the concentration of very high rates of return among a very few individuals. But, as noted above, far fewer than half of all black males will receive a rate of return as favorable as the average rate of return predicted by Goss's method. The racial disparity between the return received by the 50th white worker and the return received by the 50th black worker is also much greater than the disparity revealed in Goss's "expected value" method.

Even if the expected value methodology and data cited by Goss are used to evaluate the rate of return from Social Security, the major conclusions of the Heritage study remain unrefuted. To demonstrate this, the expected rate of return from Social Security for the two men described in the Goss memorandum was calculated using the expected value method. Consistent with U.S. Department of Labor data, CDA assumed that the white worker would earn 118 percent of the national average wage and the black earner would earn 89 percent of the average wage.[13] The results are shown in Chart 3.1.[14] The chart shows that a black worker who was 20 years old in 1998 can look forward to an inflation-adjusted rate of return of -0.15 percent. His white counterpart, however, will "enjoy" a return of 0.59 percent. This is a better rate, but it still does not compare with what he would get from a personal retirement account.

These calculations show that the real rate of return from Social Security remains well below the measures of the opportunity rate of return, even when the expected value method is used (this is

---

13. These are the ratios of median-wage, full-time employed white and black male workers in the final quarter of 1997. See U.S. Department of Labor, Bureau of Labor Statistics Release, "Usual Weekly Earnings of Wage and Salary Workers, Fourth Quarter, 1997," January 22, 1998.

the case whether one uses the 2 percent discount rate used by SSA analysts, the 2.5 to 3 percent available from long-term government securities, or the 7 percent real rate of return that the Social Security Advisory Council estimates to be available from equities). In short, regardless of the method used to measure rates of return, Social Security remains a poor retirement investment for American's minority as well as majority populations.

Finally, a number of critics of Heritage's rate of return analysis refer to a series of U.S. Treasury Department studies conducted by researchers James Duggan, Robert Gillingham, and John Greenlees.[15] Steve Goss, for instance, claimed:

■ Chart 3.1 ▬▬▬▬▬▬▬▬▬▬▬▬▬▬▬▬▬

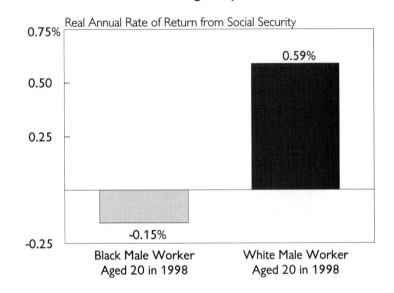

Real Rate of Return from Social Security for 20-Year-Old Males Using "Expected Value" Method

Real Annual Rate of Return from Social Security

0.59%

-0.15%

Black Male Worker Aged 20 in 1998

White Male Worker Aged 20 in 1998

Note: Based on National Center for Health Statistics, *Vital Statistics of the United States, 1992 Life Tables,* 1998 and data based on 1997 Social Security *Trustees' Report.* This analysis assumes current law benefits and taxes.
Source: Heritage calculations based on data from Social Security Administration and National Center for Health Statistics.

> [I]n fact more careful research reflecting actual work histories for workers by race indicates that the non-white population actually enjoys the same or better expected rates of return from Social Security than for the white population. (See Duggan et al., "The Returns Paid to Early Social Security Cohorts," *Contemporary Policy Issues* (October, pp. 1–13)).[16]

The evidence from that valuable study, however, has been distorted. For one thing, studies carried out by Duggan, Gillingham, and Greenlees refer only to workers born *before* the period cov-

---

14. In calculating this rate of return, Heritage analysts made a number of assumptions in order to keep the calculation as close as possible to the example contained in the Goss memorandum. It is assumed that current law taxes and benefits continue in effect, even though the Social Security Trustees project that trust fund outgo will exceed income from 2013 onwards. The calculations were based entirely on the mortality conditions contained in the National Center for Health Statistics' *1992 Life Tables of the United States* the source used by Steve Goss in his analysis of the life expectancies of the two workers contained in his memorandum. Because mortality rates for 1992 are available only up to age 85, post-85 mortality rates in 1992 are assumed to be the same ratio of the death rate at age 85 as they were reported to be in the National Center for Health Statistics' *1989–91 Life Tables of the United States.* Only Old-Age and Survivors Insurance and tax benefits are contained in these calculations.

15. See James Duggan, Robert Gillingham, and John S. Greenlees, "Returns Paid to Early Social Security Cohorts," *Contemporary Policy Issues,* Vol. 11, No. 4 (October, 1993), pp. 1–13.

16. Goss, "Problems with 'Social Security's Rate of Return.'" The authors are puzzled by Goss's criticism that they did not use these data in their rate of return studies, because the Duggan et al. study is based on data that are not available to nonfederal researchers.

■ Chart 3.2 ■■

For Workers Born in 1918, Treasury Department Data Show That Social Security Offers African-American Workers the Lowest Rate of Return

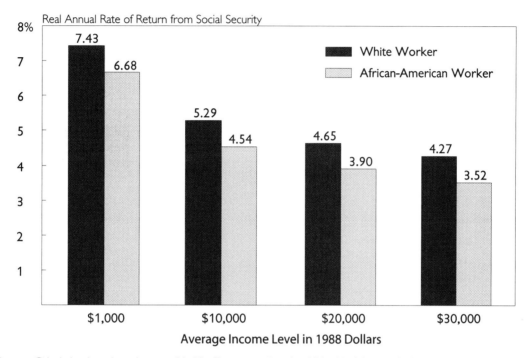

Source: Calculation based on data provided by Duggan et al. and published in Sylvester Schieber, *Rates of Return on Social Security Contributions: Good Deal, Bad Deal, or Do We Even Care?* Testimony before the Senate Budget Committee, January 21, 1998.

ered in the Heritage study. In particular, the report cited by Goss is based on workers who were born between 1895 and 1922 and who retired between the early 1950s and the mid-1980s. By contrast, the Heritage study calculates returns for workers born after 1932 and retiring from 1997 until 2042. The people in these two periods will have vastly different experiences, both in the structure of their Social Security taxes and benefits and in socioeconomic differentials in life expectancy. For example, recent trends and projections suggest that the longevity gap between African-Americans and whites, as well as rich and poor, is growing.[17]

Goss also implies that the Duggan et al. study calculated a general weighted average annual rate of return for all African-Americans and all whites. This is not the case. Such an average is almost impossible to calculate and in practice is meaningless, requiring as it does an amalgamation of workers of all income levels, marital status, ages, etc. Rather, the aim of the analysis is to compare workers of similar age, income level, and family structure.[18] In this respect, the result of the U.S.

---

17. For information on the widening socioeconomic differentials in mortality, see G. S. Popper, W. Hadden, and G. Fisher, "Increasing Disparity in Mortality Between Socioeconomic Groups in the U.S.," *New England Journal of Medicine,* July 8, 1998.

18. Duggan et al. did estimate an average for all of the observations in their data. However, because of the lack of data on spouses and family members, these calculations cannot be viewed as unbiased estimates of returns received by the entire white and black populations. For a more extensive discussion, see Daniel Garrett, "The Effects of Differential Mortality Rates on the Progressivity of Social Security," *Economic Inquiry,* July 1995.

Treasury Department studies is unequivocal: *For the African-American worker, Social Security offers a worse deal than it does for a white worker with an identical income and family structure.*

Chart 3.2, which is based on data from the most recent study by Duggan, Gillingham, and Greenlees, shows that black workers born in 1918 can expect a real rate of return from Social Security that is 0.75 percent below that which a white worker with an identical income will receive.[19]

COMPUTING RETURNS ON PERSONAL ACCOUNTS

Question: Are the rates of return on personal investments assumed in the Heritage study too high? If so, wouldn't this exaggerate the benefits of a personally held individual account?

Answer: CDA analysts used very cautious assumptions regarding the rates of return on personal investments. For the years up to 1998, the actual annual historical rates of return on bonds and equities were used. For 1999 and future years, the real rate of return on equities was estimated to be 7 percent, and the real rate of return on bonds was projected to be 2.8 percent (See Chapter 1).

The 7 percent real rate of return on equities lies well within the long-term rates found in the professional literature. For example, the Social Security Administration's 1994–1996 Advisory Council used a projected return of 7 percent on equities after considering a wide range of expert testimony.[20] During the 1926 to 1998 period, the return on large company stocks averaged 7.9 percent after inflation, while small company stocks yielded an average post-inflation return of 9.1 percent.[21]

The 2.8 percent return on U.S. government bonds is the same as the long-term rate used by the Social Security Administration in the *1998 Report of the Trustees of the Federal Old-Age and Survivors Insurance and Disability Insurance Trust Funds.*

In the original Heritage rate of return study, CDA analysts assumed that individuals were extremely risk-averse in their investment strategies and would concentrate their investments among low-yield, ultra-secure investments. The riskiest portfolio we used was one in which half of all investments were made in long-term government bonds and the remainder in a broad-market equity index. The projected future rate of return on this portfolio is 4.9 percent before taking into account administrative costs, with the bond component returning only 2.8 percent annually.[22]

EXCLUDING DISABILITY INSURANCE

Question: Why does the Heritage study ignore Disability Insurance (DI) benefits, when it appears Disability Insurance taxes are included? To put matters differently, wouldn't the inclusion

---

19. See Schieber, *Rates of Return on Social Security Contributions.*

20. Social Security Advisory Council, "Findings and Recommendations," *Report of the 1994–1996 Social Security Advisory Council*, Vol. 1, January 1997, p. 35.

21. Ibbotson Associates, *Stocks, Bonds, Bills and Inflation, 1999 Yearbook* (Chicago, Ill.: Ibbotson Associates, 1998).

22. A 0.7 percent administrative cost was assumed in all computations. Thus, all the figures presented in this report are ultimately based on *net* returns of 4.2 percent. The new 30-year Series I Savings Bonds currently pay a guaranteed return of 3.3 percent above inflation.

■ Chart 3.3 ▬▬▬▬▬▬▬▬▬▬▬▬▬▬▬▬▬▬▬▬▬▬▬▬▬▬▬▬▬▬▬▬▬▬▬▬▬▬

Annual Health Expenses per Person by Age

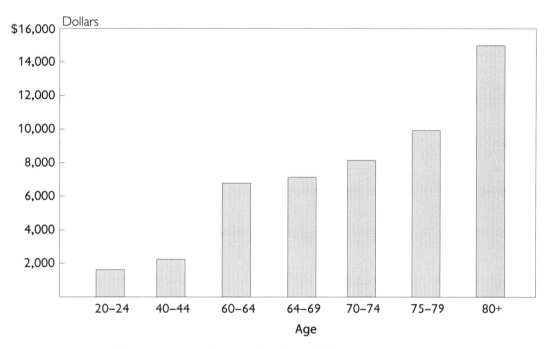

Source: Sylvester J. Schieber, *From Baby Boom to Elder Boom,* 1996.

of both DI taxes and benefits reverse many of the findings? And wouldn't ths reversal be particularly true for African-Americans, who have very low rates of return from Social Security?

Answer: Heritage's study explicitly examines only the Old-Age and Survivors Insurance (OASI) program within Social Security. Disability Insurance (DI) is a separate program within the Social Security system with its own tax rate and its own trust fund. All Heritage studies exclude Disability Insurance from rate of return computations, and *neither the DI taxes nor the DI benefits are included in the flow of payments examined in this study.*

The first 1998 Heritage study on rate of return constitutes a complete and consistent analysis of the Old-Age and Survivors Insurance portion—and *only* this portion—of Social Security. In effect, it assumes that, in a hypothetical, partly privatized system, Disability Insurance and pre-retirement Survivors Insurance are retained exactly as they exist under current law.

No empirical study exists to support the criticism that including the DI program in rate of return calculations will offset the racial differentials embedded in the OASI program, a criticism offered by defenders of the status quo.[23] They cite higher than average DI payments to black workers as a defense against any analysis that Social Security yields a lower than average retirement rate of return for African-Americans. Besides the fact that DI payments are made to workers and not retirees,[24] the argument that Disability Insurance is the principal means by which Social Security makes up for poor retirement rates of return is a particularly tortured defense of the

23. See Schieber, *Rates of Return on Social Security Contributions,* p. 30.

24. Disabled retirees may receive an Old-Age benefit that equals their previous DI payment.

current system. It is like telling people whose bank gives a poor return on their savings accounts that they should not worry because their homes are insured.

Even if a study of the combined OASI and DI programs were conducted and led to a narrowing of racial differentials in rates of return, such a study would itself be vulnerable to the criticism that it failed to include the effects of Hospital Insurance (HI)—more commonly known as the Medicare program. Chart 3.3 shows that medical expenditures are highly concentrated among the very old.

The inclusion of both DI and HI is likely to increase racial differentials in Social Security's rates of return rather than reduce them. Compared with the general population, African-Americans have a much lower probability of reaching the very old ages at which medical costs tend to escalate. For example, according to the *1992 Life Tables* cited by Goss, a white male has a 40.1 percent chance of living to the age of 80, while a black male has only a 24.3 percent chance.[25]

RISK OF PERSONAL RATES OF RETURN

Question: Given that most people are risk-averse and that personal investments are highly risky, compared with Social Security, if the returns from a personal system are adjusted for uncertainty, wouldn't they compare much less favorably with those from Social Security?

Answer: It is important to recognize that Social Security is *not* inherently less risky than personal investments. There are at least two major risks associated with Social Security: a (1) *demographic risk* and a (2) *political risk*.

Demographic Risk. Every participant in the Social Security retirement program faces the risk of dying before reaching retirement age. In the event of a worker's death, Social Security pays a monthly benefit to the worker's children who are under the age of 18 and to the spouse who cares for them (if they are under the age of 16). However, if a deceased worker has no surviving children or has children over the age of 18, the family receives no pre-retirement Survivors Insurance benefits other than a one-time death benefit of $255.

Widowed retirees sometimes collect Old-Age benefits based on the taxes paid by their spouse. But if they do, they receive nothing in return for the taxes they themselves have paid. Thus, when one partner of a married couple dies without leaving children under the age of 18, at least one spouse ultimately loses all of the taxes he or she has paid into the system.

Most families of workers who die between ages 50 and 70 face a high risk of receiving little or nothing in return for a lifetime of paying Social Security taxes. In most cases, their children, if any, are older than age 18 when they die and are ineligible for pre-retirement Survivors Insurance benefits. The families of those who die in a slightly narrower age range (50 to 65) are not eligible to collect full retirement benefits, and the families of those who die at age 70 can only collect less than five years' worth of full Old-Age benefits.

Chart 3.4, which is based on the National Center for Health Statistics data cited by Goss, shows that 13 percent of white males and 22 percent of African-American males will die between the ages of 50 and 65.[26] Another 8 percent of all white males and 11 percent of all African-American

---

25. National Center for Health Statistics, *1992 Life Tables of the United States.*

26. Goss, "Problems with 'Social Security's Rate of Return.'"

■ Chart 3.4 ■■■■■■■■■■

African-American Males' Higher Mortality Rates Lead to Lower Rates of Return for Social Security-type Investments

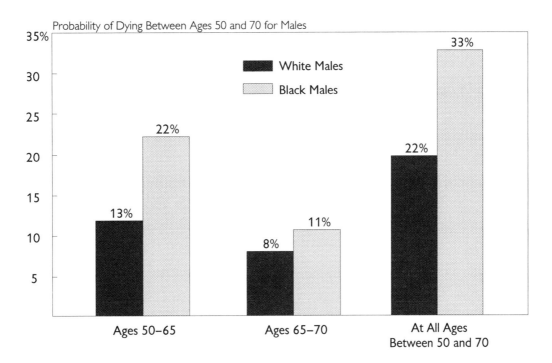

Probability of Dying Between Ages 50 and 70 for Males

Legend:
- White Males
- Black Males

Ages 50–65: White Males 13%, Black Males 22%
Ages 65–70: White Males 8%, Black Males 11%
At All Ages Between 50 and 70: White Males 22%, Black Males 33%

Source: National Center for Health Statistics, *Vital Statistics of the United States, 1992 Life Tables*, 1998.

males will die between the ages of 65 and 70. Thus, one in three African-American males and one in five white males will die between ages 50 and 70.

Stanford University economist Daniel Garrett drew on such data and calculated the variation in returns from Social Security for a single cohort of individuals with the same average life expectancy and income. These variations are shown in Chart 3.5. For this set of workers, the lifetime net present value of participation in Social Security ranges from -$92,259 for the worst-performing percentile to $85,993 for the best-performing percentile (in terms of 1988 dollars using 1990 present values).[27]

Indeed an even more recent study also shows that the returns received by workers will vary widely based on their longevity. For single white males, the net present value of participation in Social Security ranges from -$161,872 for the 150th male in a population of 1,000 to die, up to a positive $41,508 for the 95th longest-lived percentile. For black males, these values range from -$103,946 (for the 35th percentile to die) up to $64,882 (for the 95th longest-lived percentile).[28]

Political Risk. The political risk in Social Security arises because workers and families do not enjoy secure property rights—enforceable in court—over their future Social Security benefits. In

---

27. Daniel Garrett, "The Effects of Differential Mortality Rates on the Progressivity of Social Security."

28. See Gareth G. Davis, "Ethnic and Racial Differentials from Social Security Old-Age and Survivors Insurance." Estimates are expressed in 1997 dollars.

Percentile Distribution of Returns to OASI Program in 1990 For Average-Earners Born in 1925

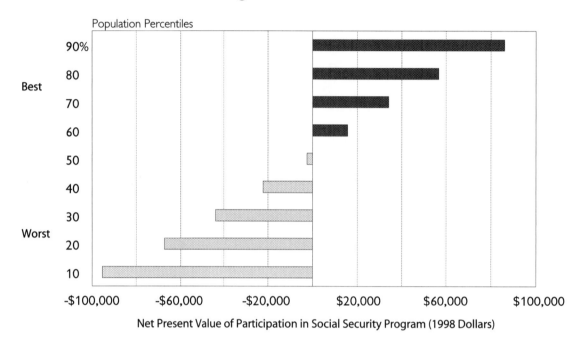

Source: Daniel Garrett, "The Effects of Differential Mortality Rates on the Progressivity of Social Security," *Economic Enquiry,* July 1995.

1960, the U.S. Supreme Court ruled in *Fleming* v. *Nestor* that a worker's claim to Social Security benefits is

> non-contractual and cannot be soundly analogized to that of a holder of an annuity, whose right to benefits are [*sic*] bottomed [based] on his contractual premium payments…. To engraft upon the Social Security system a concept of accrued property rights would deprive it of the flexibility and boldness in adjustment to ever-changing conditions which it demands.[29]

In other words, the future benefits to retirees are dependent upon voters and politicians. Given the tax burden needed to fund promised benefits under the current system, it seems appropriate to assign a considerable degree of political risk to future Social Security benefits.

EMPLOYER'S SHARE OF PAYROLL TAXES

Question: The Heritage study included not only the employee's share of taxes, but also those paid by the employer. Consequently, won't the study overestimate the costs of the program to workers?

Answer: Glen Lane, district manager of the Social Security Field Office in Cedar Rapids, Iowa, was among those who has criticized the inclusion of the employer's share of the Social Security tax burden.[30] However, the "employer's share" of Social Security taxes is part of the total amount an

---

29. *Fleming* v. *Nestor*, 363 U.S. 603 (1960).

employer spends on employee compensation, which includes the worker's wages and employer-provided benefits. The term "employer's share" is an accounting label, rather than a meaningful distinction. In the absence of Social Security taxes, this money from the employee's paycheck would be available for the worker to invest in a personal account or available as additional take-home pay. As Dean Leimer, chief author of the Social Security Administration's own calculations of its rate of return, has observed:

> [I]gnoring the employer share of the tax is clearly inappropriate, because it results in the comparison of benefits with taxes that are insufficient to fund those benefits; as a consequence, Social Security appears to be a much better deal than it actually is when all taxes required to fund the program are considered.[31]

ADMINISTRATIVE COSTS AND PERSONAL RATES OF RETURN

Question: Why does the Heritage analysis exclude administrative costs? Would including these remove much or all of the gains from privatization for most workers?

Answer: The Heritage analysis assumes that each year administrative and management fees for each account equal 0.7 percent of the total account value. This assumption lies well within the range of the expected administrative costs of a private system.

A close benchmark of how a system of personal accounts would work exists in the defined contribution retirement plans currently operated by private employers across the United States. A study based on 1996 U.S. Department of Labor data suggests that the expenses associated with administering defined contribution plans are very low. In 1992, total annual costs for these plans amounted to $34.99 per participant, or just over 0.17 percent of the value of total assets held in these accounts.[32]

A study by the Actuary's Office for the 1994–1996 Social Security Advisory Council estimated that administrative costs for its proposed Personal Security Accounts (PSA) plan, which would privatize a substantial part of Social Security, would be only 1.0 percent of fund assets.[33] The mean administrative cost for mutual funds indexed on the Standard & Poor's 500 was lower still—0.39 percent, according to Lipper Analytical Services.[34] And the Thrift Savings Plan, a privatized retirement plan run by the federal government for its employees, has administrative costs for its three funds that range from 0.08 percent to 0.10 percent.

These lower estimates are supported by data from Australia's privatized social security system. According to government statistics, annual administrative costs for Australia's system of private accounts totaled 0.85 percent of fund assets in the first quarter of 1998—the equivalent of an annual average cost per participant of $70 in Australian dollars (or US $45). A number of funds in Australia offer participants total fixed annual costs of $52 in Australian dollars (or US $33).[35]

---

30. Glen Lane, "Don't Distort Benefits Offered by Social Security," *Cedar Rapids Gazette,* February 5, 1998.

31. Dean Leimer, "A Guide to Social Security Money's Worth Issues," Social Security Administration, Office of Research and Statistics, Working Paper Series No. 67, April 1995.

32. See Olivia S. Mitchell, "Administrative Costs in Public and Private Retirement Systems," in Martin Feldstein, ed., *Privatizing Social Security* (Chicago, Ill.: University of Chicago Press, 1998), p. 433.

33. See David C. John and Gareth G. Davis, "The Costs of Managing Individual Social Security Accounts," Heritage Foundation *Backgrounder* No. 1238, December 3, 1998.

34. Lipper Analytical Services, unpublished data, October 1998, available from the authors upon request.

The structure of the plan is also important. Limiting investment options and creating larger investment pools will hold costs down. These are features of most privatization plans. Also, costs decline rapidly after the plan starts. For instance, administrative costs for the Thrift Savings Plan for federal employees are 76 percent lower than they were when the plan began operations in 1988.[36]

One low-cost option would be to allow individuals to invest their Social Security taxes in the new 30-year Series I Savings Bonds, which currently pay a guaranteed return of 3.3 percent above inflation. These bonds can be obtained at virtually no cost, and they pay a substantially higher rate of return than the current Social Security system.

TRANSITION COSTS

Question: Is it true that Heritage's analysis not only fails to take into account the cost of the transition to a system of personal Social Security accounts, but the rates of return cited also fail to acknowledge that workers entering a personal system would have to pay for their own retirement as well as support the benefits paid to those who are currently retired or close to retirement?

Answer: The purpose of pursuing an in-depth analysis of Social Security's rate of return for different American workers is to develop a yardstick for measuring the performance of the current system, not to propose or cost out alternative plans. To that end, a comparison of outcomes under Social Security today with outcomes under a hypothetical system that allows American workers to invest their Social Security retirement tax dollars into personal accounts can illustrate the opportunity costs under the current program. *In other words, Heritage's studies provide a benchmark for anyone who wishes to compare alternative reforms.*

Rate of return outcomes will vary enormously, of course, depending on the transition rules that are adopted. Interim financing could be raised through tax increases, benefit cuts, and the issuance of debt, which pose widely different implications for the rates of return for different groups. To impose an arbitrary transition rule on the model would undermine the validity of the analysis as an examination of the "pure" opportunity cost of the current system. For example, one study conducted in early 1999 by opponents of Social Security reform skewed its analysis of the returns under a private system by imposing all of the burden of the transition to the system on a single generation.[37]

It is far from certain that including transition costs would significantly alter the differences in rates of return between the current system and a personal system, since maintaining the current system as a viable long-term program also involves huge costs. Nevertheless, Mark Weisbrot of the Institute for America's Future has claimed that "as soon as we take into account the real world costs of moving from Social Security to a system of personal accounts, the superior return that the [Heritage] authors calculate for personal savings vanishes, and in fact becomes negative."[38] In

---

35. Australian Government Publishing Service, *Insurance and Superannuation Commissions Statistical Bulletin*, various issues. U.S. dollar valuations based on exchange rate of 1.57 (quoted on *http://www.cnnfn.com* on November 8, 1999).

36. See Thrift Savings Plan at *http://www.tsp.gov/features/tspcx.html#sub3*.

37. Gareth G. Davis and David C. John, "The Mueller Social Security Report Is Flawed" Heritage Foundation *Executive Memorandum* No.583, March 25, 1999

38. Mark Weisbrot, *Flawed Assumptions, Fatal Errors: An Analysis of the Recent Heritage Foundation Report on Social Security's Rate of Return* (Washington, D.C.: Institute for America's Future, undated), p. 2.

■ Table 3.2 ■

SSA-Calculated Return for Low-Income Single Males Under Current System and Under PSA Plan

Birth Year	Current Law Social Security System	"Personal Savings Account" Plan	Increase in Return Under Private Account
1920	4.37%	4.37%	0.00%
1930	3.06	3.06	0.00
1937	2.66	2.66	0.00
1943	2.36	2.46	0.10
1949	2.43	2.40	-0.03
1955	2.45	2.46	0.01
1964	2.37	2.63	0.26
1973	2.32	2.95	0.63
1985	2.16	3.01	0.85
1997	1.95	3.00	1.05
2004	1.83	2.99	1.16

Source: 1994–1996 Social Security Advisory Council. Private Savings Account return scenario is based on a Social Security Administration analysis of projected returns from 401(k)-type investments and includes all transition costs. Current law scenario assumes payroll taxes are increased to fund promised benefits.

support of his criticism, he cites the increased taxes contained in the 1994–1996 Social Security Advisory Council's Personal Security Account (PSA) proposal to fund the transition to a partially privatized Social Security system. However, Weisbrot failed to note that Social Security's Office of the Chief Actuary analyzed the PSA proposal and found that, *even when transition costs are included*, it actually offers a higher rate of return to virtually all participants than the current Social Security system does.[39]

Table 3.2 shows the returns calculated by the SSA for a low-income single male worker who made $11,000 in 1995, under both the current system (fully funded, using the SSA's own assumptions) and the PSA proposal of Carolyn L. Weaver, Sylvester J. Schieber, and several other members of the Social Security Advisory Council.

PAYROLL TAX ASSUMPTIONS

Question: Is it true that Heritage inappropriately assumes that if Social Security is not partially privatized, it will be restored to balance entirely by raising payroll taxes and that this tax increase will begin in 2015, a decade earlier than the Social Security actuaries project would be necessary?[40]

Answer: Beginning early in the next century, the Social Security system's own actuaries project that it will begin to take in less money than it needs to pay benefits that are promised in current law. Congress does have several ways to balance the Social Security system within the current framework. In addition to increasing payroll taxes, Congress could cut benefits, increase the retirement age, or require all state and local government workers to participate. Each of these pro-

---

39. Social Security Advisory Council, "Findings and Recommendations," p. 51.

40. Kijakazi, *African Americans, Hispanic Americans and Social Security.*

posals would have a different impact on workers of different ages and income levels. For example, extending Social Security coverage to all state and local government workers would create a massive unfunded liability among existing state and local employee retirement funds that would have to be corrected either by cuts in payments to retired state and local employees or by increased taxes.[41]

For Social Security's calculations of the rate of return in the current system, its actuaries used two assumptions to reflect the system's financial imbalance. The first assumes that the system is balanced through across-the-board cuts in Social Security benefits. The second assumes that balance is achieved by increases in payroll tax rates. Dean Leimer, who authored SSA's rate of return calculations, found that the rate of return from Social Security for workers born between 1932 and 1975 is higher under a regime of payroll tax increases than in a scenario where benefit cuts are used to balance the system.[42] This higher return occurs because current workers bear the full costs of benefit cuts while bearing only a partial share of future tax increases.

This analysis assumes that the benefits promised in current law are paid in full and that, beginning in 2013, payroll tax rates are increased annually to the level where they are sufficient to meet these benefits. Had the assumption of reduced future benefits been chosen, the rate of return reported in this study would have been even lower.

The Social Security trust funds are composed entirely of non-negotiable U.S. Treasury bonds, which means they are a set of IOUs that one part of the federal government (the U.S. Treasury Department) has written to another branch of the federal government (the Social Security Administration). When the Social Security system starts taking in less money than it needs to pay its promised benefits (as it is scheduled to do in 2013),[43] then the federal government as a whole will have to meet the shortfall. It can do this by redeeming the IOUs in the Social Security trust fund (which would mean raising non-Social Security taxes or cutting non-Social Security spending), by cutting promised Social Security benefits, or by raising payroll taxes. For example, President Bill Clinton's Fiscal Year 1999 Budget states that:

> These balances are available to finance future benefit payments...only in a bookkeeping sense. They do not consist of real economic assets that can be drawn down in the future to fund benefits. Instead, they are claims on the Treasury that, when redeemed, will have to be financed by raising taxes, borrowing from the public, or reducing benefits, or other expenditures.[44]

In each case, Social Security participants will have to bear the burden of this shortfall through increased federal non-Social Security taxes, reduced federal non-Social Security spending, Social Security benefit cuts, or Social Security tax hikes. In making their projections, Social Security's actuaries merely assume that the IOUs in the trust fund are redeemed, and they do not take into account the non-Social Security tax hikes and spending cuts that the rest of the federal government will have to implement to repay these IOUs.

---

41. See Robert J. Scott, Testimony Before the Social Security Subcommittee, House Ways and Means Committee on Mandatory Social Security Coverage of Public Employees, March 21, 1998.

42. Leimer, "A Guide to Social Security Money's Worth Issues."

43. Social Security Administration, *1998 Report of the Trustees of the Federal Old-Age and Survivors Insurance and Disability Insurance Trust Funds*.

44. The White House, *Analytical Perspectives, Budget of the United States Government, Fiscal Year 2000* (Washington, D.C.: U.S. Government Printing Office, 1999), p. 337.

APPENDIX

METHODOLOGY

To calculate a worker's rate of return for Social Security, researchers must have access to three key pieces of information about that worker: annual gross income, benefits (calculated on the basis of earnings), and life expectancy (to determine how long the worker will pay taxes and/or collect benefits).

For this study of rates of return by congressional district, we estimated the average life expectancy for males and females born in 1945, 1955, 1965, and 1975 in each congressional district. We also estimated average earnings for workers in each age group. Two sources of data were used to calculate these values. The 1990 U.S. Decennial Census provided the socioeconomic data, and the mortality data came from the Centers for Disease Control.

USING SOCIOECONOMIC DATA TO ESTIMATE MORTALITY

Researchers have long noted large differences in life expectancies across socioeconomic groups. Marital status, income, residence, and ethnicity have all been shown to have a profound impact on life expectancy.[1] A recent study by Harvard University researchers has shown that these socioeconomic differences are also reflected in very large geographic differentials in life expectancy. For example, the Harvard study revealed that male life expectancy at birth in 1990 ranged from 77.54 in Cache and Riche Counties in Utah to a mere 61.04 years in Bennett County, South Dakota.[2]

---

1. Both Harriet Orcutt Duleep and Robert Waldmann have conducted detailed studies on the interactions between socioeconomic factors and death rates. See Harriet Orcutt Duleep, "Measuring Socioeconomic Mortality Differentials Over Time," *Demography*, Vol. 26, No. 2 (May 1989), pp. 345–351. See also Robert Waldmann, "Income Distribution and Infant Mortality," *Quarterly Journal of Economics*, Vol. 107, No. 4 (November 1992), pp. 1283–1302. On the differences in life expectancies among racial groups in the United States, see Verna Keith and David Smith, "The Current Differential in Black and White Life Expectancy," *Demography*, Vol. 25, No. 4 (November 1988), pp. 625–632; Lloyd Potter, "Socio-Economic Determinants of White and Black Males' Life Expectancy Differentials–1980," *Demography*, Vol. 28, No. 2 (May 1991), pp. 303–321; Eui Hang Shin, "Black-White Differentials in Infant Mortality in the South 1940–1970," *Demography*, Vol. 12, No. 1 (February 1975), pp. 1–19; Paul Menchik, "Economic Status as a Determinant of Mortality Among Black and White Older Men: Does Poverty Kill?" *Population Studies*, Vol. 47, No. 3 (November 1993), pp. 427–436.

2. C. L. Murray, C. M. Michaud, M. T. McKenna, and J. S. Marks, *US Patterns of Mortality by County and Race:1965–1994* (Cambridge, Mass.: Harvard Center for Population and Development Studies, 1998).

Unfortunately, data on longevity are currently not available for congressional districts. Indeed, it is only recently that nationwide mortality data on a sub-state level has been made available to nongovernmental researchers in the form of the Centers for Disease Control's Compressed Mortality File (CMF). These data include annual mortality rates for each county for 13 age groups, ranging from less than a year old to 85 and above. These mortality rates are also available by gender and race. Data from the CMF were extracted for every county and averaged for the years 1987 to 1993. Using this range of years enabled us to expand the sample size of deaths for many of the smaller counties, but because the years were centered on 1990, it allowed for the calculation of death rates that are similar to those prevailing in 1990.

Our next step was to estimate the relationships between mortality and a set of socioeconomic variables in the 3,146 counties for which both death-rate and socioeconomic data were available. Because socioeconomic variables (such as ethnicity, income, marital status, and education) are important determinants of age-adjusted mortality, it is possible to use a multivariate regression analysis to estimate life expectancy for non-county geographical entities such as congressional districts. The only source of socioeconomic data that is available for both congressional districts and counties is the U.S. Census Bureau's 1990 Decennial Census STF3A tape. Given this constraint, a set of socioeconomic variables that are available for both counties and congressional districts was created from the STF3A tape.

MODEL SPECIFICATION AND GOODNESS-OF-FIT TEST

The Heritage model for this analysis contains 16 equations, one for each of the seven age groups for both genders. Table A.1 contains the list of groups for which equations were estimated. Each equation estimates the differences between a county's mortality rate for a specific gender and age group and the state's corresponding average mortality rate for the same group. The use of equations incorporating state-indicator variables allows researchers to capture not just the general effects of socioeconomic differences in mortality, but also the impact of specific regional and state factors (such as different health-care policies and different climates).

Due to the presence of large disparities in the size of county populations (ranging from 60 persons to 7 million persons), the relationship between counties and states was estimated using a weighted least squares method, which weighted the observations according to the absolute number of deaths. The equations were estimated in an iterative process, excluding variables that were insignificant at the 10 percent level. The independent variables ultimately used in the equations were determined by choosing the set that maximized the adjusted R^2. Table A.2 shows the set of independent variables used in at least one of the regressions. Several diagnostic procedures were carried out to verify the suitability of the equations estimated. In

■ Table A.1 ■

Groups for Which Equations Were Calculated

1	Males Aged 20–24
2	Males Aged 25–34
3	Males Aged 35–44
4	Males Aged 45–54
5	Males Aged 55–64
6	Males Aged 65–74
7	Males Aged 75–84
8	Males Aged 85 and Above
9	Females Aged 20–24
10	Females Aged 25–34
11	Females Aged 35–44
12	Females Aged 45–54
13	Females Aged 55–64
14	Females Aged 65–74
15	Females Aged 75–84
16	Females Aged 85 and Above

Complete List of Variables Used in Regressions

asi	Proportion of Relevant Age and Gender Who are Non-Hispanic Asian
bla	Proportion of Relevant Age and Gender Who are Non-Hispanic Black
brnforei	Proportion of Population Foreign Born
colldorm	Proportion of Population Residing in College Dormitories
farm	Proportion of Population defined as "Rural: Farm"
feunem	Female Unemployment Rate
grade12	Proportion of Population Aged 25 and Over with Education 12th Grade or Below
his	Proportion of Relevant Age and Gender Who are Hispanic
ind	Proportion of Relevant Age and Gender Who are Non-Hispanic American Indian, Eskimo or Aleut
insurban	Proportion of Population Aged 16 to 64 and Over with no Disabilities
kidsin25	Average Number of Children Ever-Born per Woman Aged 25 to 34
kidsin35	Average Number of Children Ever-Born per Woman Aged 35 to 44
kidsin45	Average Number of Children Ever-Born per Woman Aged 45 and Above
marr25	Proportion of Women aged 25 to 34 and Over Ever Married
marr35	Proportion of Women aged 35 to 44 and Over Ever Married
marr45	Proportion of Women aged 45 and Over Ever Married
maunem	Percentage of Male Labor Forced Unemployed
milquart	Proportion of Population Resident in Military Quarters
mnodis16	Proportion of Relevant Gender Aged 16 to 64 and Over with No Disabilities
nodis65	Proportion of Relevant Gender Aged 65 to 74 and Over with No Disabilities
nodis75	Proportion of Relevant Gender Aged 75 and Over with No Disabilities
nursing	Proportion of Total Population Residing in Nursing Homes
outurban	Proportion of Population Defined as "Urban: Outside Urbanized Area"
p080a001	Median Family Income in 1989
pov	Proportion of Population in Relevant Age Group with 1989 Income Below Poverty Line
selfemp	Proportion of Workers Classed as Self-Employed
totcoll	Proportion of Population Aged 25 and Over with Education Above High School Graduation Level

Note: Not all of these variables were used in each regression. From the *Census of Population and Housing, 1990*, STF3A tape, U.S. Census Bureau, 1992.

each case, only independent variables that were statistically significant at the 5 percent level were retained in the regressions.

Table A.3 shows one of the 16 equations that were estimated. The dependent variable in this equation is the difference between state and county death rates for males aged between 25 and 34. The results in the table indicate that there is a negative relationship between death rates for males aged 25 through 34 and the following five independent variables: the proportion of that population that is Asian or Hispanic, the percentage of women aged 25 though 34 ever married, the proportion of the population aged 16 though 65 who have no disabilities, median family income, and the proportion of the population aged 25 and above with education beyond the high school level. Higher death rates are associated with larger percentages of the population being foreign born, African-American, and Native American, and with a higher proportion of the age group living in poverty. All of the variables included are statistically significant at the 1.0 percent level. The goodness-of-fit tests show a high level of correlation for an equation that estimates the deviation of a variable from a mean. The adjusted R^2 for this particular equation is 0.62, which means that our regression explains over 60 percent of the deviation of the county death rates from the state average death rate. The F-statistic at 453.1 is also highly significant.

In addition to checking the goodness-of-fit tests for each equation, a number of diagnostic procedures were carried out to test the validity of the general approach. The equations were used to calculate death rates by age and gender in each county in the United States. Death rates from these equations were then combined to produce estimates of period life expectancy at age 25 for each

■ Table A.3

Estimated Equation for Difference Between County and State Death Rates for Males Aged 25 to 34

Dependent variable =
(State Death Rate for Males Aged 25 to 34)
– (County Death Rate for Males Aged 25 to 34)

	Estimated Coefficients	T-Statistic
(Constant)	-0.01458	-15.098
brnforei	-0.00223	-10.954
maasi25	0.00169	5.561
mabla25	-0.00053	-3.743
mahis25	0.00073	5.707
maind25	-0.00175	-5.789
marr25	0.00240	14.615
mnodis16	0.01277	12.496
p080a001	1.988×10^{-8}	6.763
pov25	-0.00219	-5.633
totcoll	0.00059	3.568
F-Stat	453.1	
Significance	0.000	
R^2	0.622	
Adjusted R^2	0.620	

gender in every county in the United States. Because the estimated life expectancies are based on combining information from all of the regressions completed for each gender, they offer a good test of the overall reliability of the estimation method.

In general, the period life tables estimated for each county using our model closely matches the period life expectancies observed in our data. Table A.4 shows the correlation between period life expectancy as estimated by the mortality rates predicted by our estimated model and actual life expectancy as observed in the Compressed Mortality File.

■ Table A.4

Unweighted Correlation Between Predicted and Actual 1990 Period Life Expectancy at Age 25

	Male	Female
All Counties	80.3%	70.5%
Counties with 50,000+ Populations	84.2	78.2
Counties with 500,000+ Populations	86.7	86.6

One of the problems in analyzing mortality is that death can be an uncommon event for younger populations. For example, in 1994 there was only one death per 1,721 females aged 25 in the United States.[3] Many counties have small populations, which means that just a few deaths occurring in a single year can greatly skew the death rate (and life expectancy) for that year. In

Predicted vs. Actual Life Expectancies for Females in 100 Most Populous Counties, by Actual Life Expectancy

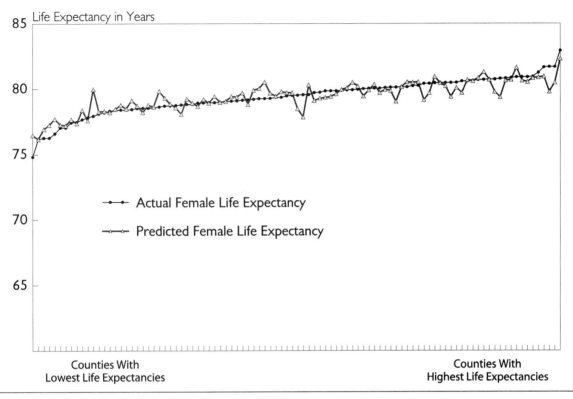

fact, over 38 percent of all U.S. counties have populations of 15,000 or less. When such populations are sub-divided by age and gender groups, the sample size of the population within each group drops even lower. In some cases, a random variation of just three or fewer deaths in an age group can have a very large effect on the death rate recorded for that county. This means that the observed life expectancy in many, if not most, counties will be subject to a high degree of fluctuation. While large-scale regressions based on data from the 3,146 counties in the United States will average out these random fluctuations and give a valid picture of the underlying socioeconomic determinants of mortality, comparing the values projected by the model with the actual observed life expectancies (which are subject to large-scale random fluctuation) will result in a less than 100 percent correlation.

Nevertheless, if we analyze the results for all counties (including those with populations of 100 or less), the model explains over 70 percent of the variation in female life expectancies and over 86 percent of the variation in observed male life expectancies. The accuracy of the model improves even more as we examine counties with larger populations that are less susceptible to random fluctuations in death rates. For counties with populations of 500,000 or more, roughly equal to the population of a typical congressional district, our model explains 86 percent of the variation in both male and female life expectancies.

---

3. Social Security Administration, *Annual Statistical Supplement to the Social Security Bulletin,* December 1997, Table 4.C6.

Predicted vs. Actual Life Expectancies for Males in 100 Most Populous Counties, by Actual Life Expectancy

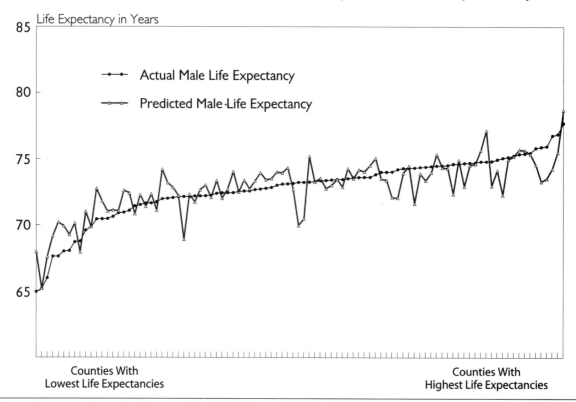

Counties With
Lowest Life Expectancies

Counties With
Highest Life Expectancies

A sense of the degree of accuracy of our model can be seen in Charts A.1 and A.2. These charts show observed life expectancy and the life expectancy predicted by our model for females and males in the 98 U.S. counties that are at least as large as a typical congressional district (a population of 500,000 or greater). As can be seen from the data, our model's predictions closely match the large variations present in this diverse group of counties.

ESTIMATING CONGRESSIONAL DISTRICT LIFE EXPECTANCIES

Because the county-based model uses socioeconomic data that are also available by congressional district, these coefficients can be used to compute differences between the mortality rates prevailing in a congressional district and the state's average mortality rates. This is done by applying county-based coefficients to socioeconomic data for each congressional district as reported in the U.S. Census Bureau's 1990 Decennial Census STF3A tape.

Cohort life expectancies beginning in 2000 were calculated for four age groups (those born in 1945, 1955, 1965, and 1975) for both genders. Mortality rates at each age and for each gender in a district were assumed to fall over the period 1990 to 2075 at the same rate as projected in the intermediate assumptions of the *1998 Report of the Board of Trustees of the Federal Old-Age and Survivors Insurance and Disability Insurance Trust Funds*. Chart A.3 shows the distribution of cohort life expectancies at age 25 for 435 congressional districts and the District of Columbia for males born in 1975.

■ Chart A.3 ▮▮▮

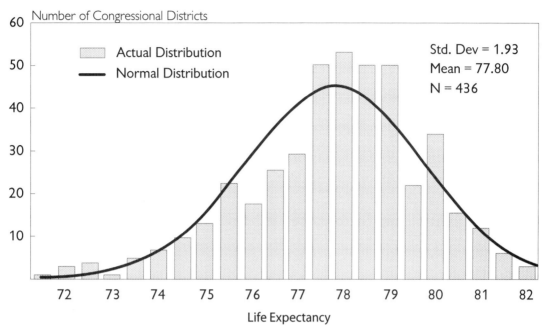

Distribution of Cohort Life Expectancies at Age 25 for Males Born in 1975 for 435 Congressional Districts and District of Columbia

For the purposes of analyzing Social Security's rate of return, the relevant life expectancy is not the period life expectancy, which is usually based on mortality experience in a population over a single calendar year, but rather it is the cohort life expectancy, which accurately captures the mortality experiences of an age group over an entire lifetime (and so includes future reductions in mortality that are driven by such factors as improved medical technology). For this reason, cohort life expectancies shown in Chart A.3 exceed the period life expectancies shown in Chart A.2.

ESTIMATING EARNINGS BY CONGRESSIONAL DISTRICT

This study builds upon earlier CDA analyses of the rate of return for Social Security by utilizing separate earnings amounts for males and females and by adjusting earnings for age. (Like the standard methodology used by the Social Security Administration, previous Heritage studies assume that workers earn a fixed percentage of the average wage during their entire careers.) For consistency with earlier data, earnings in each congressional district were estimated using data from the U.S. Census Bureau's 1990 Decennial Census. An age-earnings profile for both an average female and male worker was created for each congressional district in three steps, based on two sets of data taken from the 1990 Census.

The first stage in developing an earnings profile was to calculate the mean value of total earnings per employed worker for each congressional district using the U.S. Census Bureau's STF3A tape. This number was divided by the national average to estimate average wages for all workers in each congressional district in 1990 as a percentage of the national average wage.

Worker Age-Earnings Profile by Gender

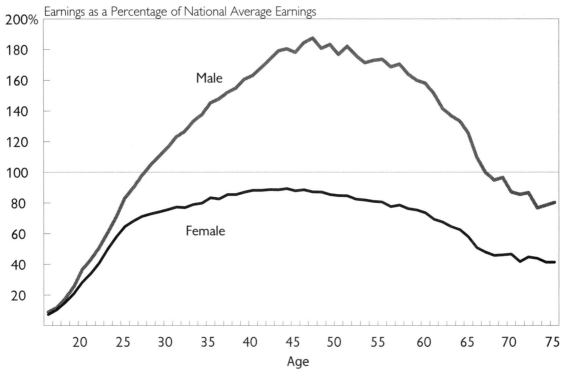

Source: U.S. Census, 1990 PUMS database.

The second stage involved calculating earnings per worker at each age and for each gender in 1990 as a percentage of the total average wage for all workers. More than 2.5 million observations in the 1990 Decennial Census Public Use Micro-Sample (PUMS) file were used in this calculation.[4] As can be seen in Chart A.4, average earnings varied widely by gender as well as across the age spectrum. Earnings peak in middle age, and male earnings typically lie above those received by females.

In the final stage, earnings for workers of a certain age in a congressional district were calculated by multiplying the average wage rate prevailing in a congressional district by the proportion of the average wage earned by a worker of that age and gender in 1990. To calculate a worker's actual dollar earnings for a specific calendar year, the percentage of the national average earnings a worker of that gender and age makes was multiplied by the percentage of the average wage earned in that particular congressional district and then by the total national average wage for that year as predicted by the *1998 Report of the Board of Trustees of the Federal Old-Age and Survivors Insurance and Disability Insurance Trust Funds.*

The three-step procedure described above produced estimates of the dollar earnings of males and females born in 1945, 1955, 1965, and 1975 from age 16 to retirement. The procedure also

---

4. Both the U.S. Census Bureau's STF3A and Public Use Micro-File Sample (PUMS) are based on returns filed during the 1990 Decennial Census.

produced estimates of earnings amounts that are specific to the worker's age, congressional district, and gender, and the national wage rate for the year in question.

CALCULATING BENEFITS AND TAXES

Calculations of Social Security benefits and taxes were made by processing data from earnings histories and life expectancies through The Heritage Foundation's Social Security Rate of Return Model. This model applies the payroll tax and benefit formula in current Social Security law (and, where applicable, previous legislation) to each worker's earnings record. This enables annual tax and benefit entitlements to be calculated for each worker. When the tax and benefit information is linked to the worker's life expectancy, the model can calculate a rate of return from the Social Security Old-Age and Survivors Insurance program and analyze how the worker would fare under Social Security compared with placing their payroll taxes in a retirement account composed of personal investments.

In calculating a worker's rate of return from Social Security, a number of assumptions must be made. First, it is assumed that all of the workers begin working at age 21. This essentially excludes the taxes paid by workers between the ages of 16 and 21.[5] Second, the worker works until the age at which he or she is entitled to full Social Security retirement benefits before retiring (equivalent to the National Retirement Age).[6] Third, according to the *1998 Report of the Board of Trustees of the Federal Old-Age and Survivors Insurance and Disability Insurance Trust Funds,* the Social Security Old-Age and Survivors Insurance (OASI) program will no longer collect enough revenues to fund current benefits in 2014. Beginning that year, either the U.S. government must raise payroll taxes, increase non-payroll taxes, or cut Social Security benefits.[7]

In this analysis, it is assumed that increasing the Social Security payroll tax rate to the level necessary to fund benefits in a given year covers the shortfall. Finally, the returns calculated here apply only to the Old-Age and Survivors Insurance program. Only OASI taxes and benefits are included. The value of pre-retirement Survivors Insurance included in these calculations is priced at the actuarial cost of a private term life insurance policy offering similar coverage.

COMPARING SOCIAL SECURITY WITH PERSONAL INVESTMENTS

To better evaluate Social Security's performance, we also considered how workers and their families would have fared under a system in which they were allowed to invest their Social Secu-

---

5. Because this excludes five years of taxes paid by an average worker without reducing benefits (which are based on a worker's 35 best years of earnings), adopting this assumption will increase the estimated rate of return from Social Security.

6. Under current law a worker is not eligible to collect full Social Security retirement benefits until he or she reaches age 65. Beginning with workers born in 1940, this age of eligibility is scheduled to increase gradually. Workers born in 1960 or later will only be eligible to collect full Social Security benefits upon reaching the age of 67.

7. Although there are Social Security trust funds, the term "trust fund" has a different meaning than it does in normal financial dealings. While private-sector trust funds contain stocks, bonds, or other assets that can be sold for cash, Social Security's trust funds contain only IOUs that will have to be paid with future taxes. President Bill Clinton's budget submission for Fiscal Year 2000 notes that, "These balances are available to finance future benefit payments...only in a bookkeeping sense. They do not consist of real economic assets that can be drawn down in the future to fund benefits. Instead, they are claims on the Treasury that, when redeemed, will have to be financed by raising taxes, borrowing from the public, or reducing benefits, or other expenditures." *Analytical Perspectives, Budget of the United States Government, Fiscal Year 2000*, p. 337.

rity OASI taxes in a personal retirement account (after having purchased private life insurance equivalent to the value of pre-retirement Survivors Insurance). It is important to note that in this study we are not comparing Social Security with any specific privatization or partial privatization plan (each of which differs significantly in their rate of return implications for different workers and in the amount of payroll tax they allow workers to invest). Rather, we are comparing Social Security with a hypothetical system so that we can benchmark the performance of the current system in a meaningful way.

Social Security's current investment performance is compared with a portfolio made up of 50 percent long-term U.S. Treasury bonds and 50 percent large company equities. For the years prior to 1999, the actual historical yields on their assets are used.[8] For 1999 and beyond, a return of 7 percent on equities and 2.8 percent on Treasury bonds is used. These projections are consistent with the Social Security Administration's estimates of asset returns that are published in the *1998 Annual Report of the Board of Trustees of the Federal Old-Age and Survivors Insurance and Disability Insurance Trust Funds* and in the *1994-1996 Social Security Advisory Council Report*.[9] An annual administrative cost equal to 0.7 percent of the value of assets in the account is also assumed.[10]

Two measures of the relative performance of Social Security and personal alternatives are reported. The first is the internal rate of return for each investment. The internal rate of return measures the annual percentage rate at which the dollars the worker invests in Social Security (or a personal portfolio) grows or shrinks. It takes into account both the time-profile and the amount of any payments made or benefits received. A second measure of performance is the dollar value (in year 2000 dollars) of lifetime Social Security retirement benefits. This value is compared with the amount accumulated in a personal account at retirement.[11] These amounts can be used to estimate the absolute dollar value of the loss or gain that a family experiences by participating in the Social Security system.

---

8. Ibbotson Associates, *Stocks, Bonds, Bills and Inflation 1999 Yearbook* (Chicago: Ibbotson Associates, 1999), p. 123.

9. Social Security Administration, *Report of the 1994–1996 Advisory Council on Social Security*, 1997.

10. This estimate of 0.7 percent lies at the upper end of what it would cost to administer a set of personal retirement accounts. See David C. John and Gareth G. Davis, "The Costs of Managing Individual Social Security Accounts," Heritage Foundation *Backgrounder* No. 1238, December 3, 1998.

11. Unlike other analyses, we do not apply a discount rate to the Social Security retirement benefits received by a family so as to express them in terms of net present value at the date of retirement. Applying such a discount rate would reduce the value of Social Security benefits below the amounts shown in this study.

GLOSSARY OF SOCIAL SECURITY TERMS

Administrative cost. The expenses incurred in managing investments, generally paid by an investor to a financial service provider, such as a bank or brokerage firm. Usually expressed as a percentage of the total funds under management, these fees reflect the costs of processing financial transactions; preparing and printing documentation; and accounting, legal, and management services.

Advisory Council on Social Security. Thirteen-member committee appointed every four years pursuant to Title VII, Section 706, of the Social Security Act to examine the Social Security program and its trust funds. Members are supposed to represent American workers and employers. Their mission is to examine the financial status of the trust funds as well as general issues affecting Social Security. The most recent Advisory Council (1994–1996) was unable to agree on a common recommendation and submitted three different plans for Social Security's future.

AIME. See Average Indexed Monthly Earnings.

Annual Report. See Trustees' Report.

Average Indexed Monthly Earnings. A worker's highest total annual wages (adjusted by the growth rate of average national wages) over a 35-year period divided by 420 (the number of months in 35 years). The amount is used to calculate Social Security benefits.

Bend point. Part of the formula that determines Social Security benefits. After Average Indexed Monthly Earnings (see above) have been determined, Social Security pays a retirement benefit that is roughly equal to 90 percent of the first $500, 32 percent of the amount between $500 and $2,900, and 15 percent of the amount above $2,900. Each of these income steps is referred to as a bend point. The exact amount of each bend point varies with the year the worker is born. For a worker born in 1936, Social Security will pay a benefit equal to 90 percent of the first $477 of AIME, 32 percent of the amount over $477 and below $2,876, and 15 percent of the amount over $2,875. Benefits are paid only on income subject to Social Security retirement taxes. In 1999, income above $72,600 would not be included in calculating retirement benefits.

Bond. An interest-bearing security issued by private companies or governmental units. The issuer promises to periodically pay a fixed or inflation-indexed amount of interest for the life of the bond or to pay a stated interest plus the principle on a specified date, called the date of maturity.

CPI. See Consumer Price Index.

Consumer Price Index. Measurement of the change in the prices of certain goods and services during a specified period of time. The index is prepared by the Bureau of Labor Statistics at the U.S. Department of Labor and is used as a measurement of inflation.

Continuous Work History Sample. A random sample of the earnings and benefit histories of about 1 percent of all Social Security participants. The Social Security Administration uses this sample to develop estimates of Social Security's future financial health. The sample is also used to project the financial consequences of proposals that would reform Social Security.

CWHS. See Continuous Work History Sample.

Disability benefit. A monthly amount paid by Social Security after a worker has become disabled and is unable to work. Social Security's disability benefit is financed by a tax of 0.9 percent of payroll taxes paid by both the employer and the worker, for a total of 1.8 percent of payroll. The benefit is equal to the amount of retirement benefits the worker has earned at the time of the disability. Additional amounts can be paid to a spouse or minor children.

Equities. Another term for stocks. Represents shares of ownership in a company.

Federal Insurance Contribution Act. The federal law that requires employers to deduct the employee share of Social Security and Medicare taxes from their wages and send them (together with the employer share) to the federal Treasury. Instead of listing each payroll tax separately on the employee's paycheck, employers often will group the deductions together under the term "FICA."

FICA. See Federal Insurance Contribution Act.

Health Insurance Trust Fund. The trust fund used to support Medicare. It is financed by a tax separate from those that finance Social Security's retirement and disability programs.

HI. See Health Insurance Trust Fund.

Index fund. An investment fund that attempts to match the performance of another portfolio by investing in the same securities and in the same proportions as those in the other portfolio.

Life expectancy. A statistical measurement of the number of years an individual is expected to live given that person's date of birth or the number of years that person has remaining after reaching a certain age.

Normal retirement age. The age of eligibility under current law for full retirement benefits, currently age 65. Eligible workers born between 1938 and 1942 have a normal retirement age between 65 and 66; those born between 1943 and 1954 have a normal retirement age of 66. For workers born between 1955 and 1959, the normal retirement age ranges between 66 and 67; those born after 1960 have a normal retirement age of 67.

NRA. See Normal retirement age.

OASI. See Old-Age and Survivors Insurance.

OASDI. See Old-Age, Survivors and Disability Insurance.

Office of the Chief Actuary. The Social Security Administration office responsible for collecting and analyzing financial, economic, and demographic information in order to forecast the program's future financial health. The office also examines how proposals to change Social Security would affect the system's finances.

Old-Age Dependency Ratio. A ratio equal to the number of people over 65 divided by the number of people aged 20 through 64.

Old-Age and Survivors Insurance. The name of the Social Security trust fund that finances the program's retirement and survivors programs. Technically, this is a sub-trust fund along with the Disability Insurance (DI) trust fund that finances disability benefits. The overall trust fund that includes both of the sub-trust funds together is known as the Old-Age, Survivors and Disability Insurance (OASDI) trust fund. See Trust Fund and Old-Age, Survivors and Disability Insurance.

Old-Age, Survivors and Disability Insurance. The trust fund responsible for ensuring the long-term viability of Social Security's retirement, disability, and survivors program. It consists of two sub-trust funds: Old-Age and Survivors Insurance (OASI) and Disability Insurance (DI).

Pay-as-you-go financing. A financial scheme in which benefits paid to current retirees are financed by taxes collected from current workers.

Payroll tax. A tax schedule based on a percentage of earnings and income. In Social Security's case, both employer *and* employee pay a tax equal to 5.3 percent of payroll for retirement and survivors benefits, and a tax equal to 0.9 percent of payroll for disability benefits.

Personal retirement account. An investment account that is financed with a portion of the worker's existing Social Security taxes and used to provide all or some of the worker's retirement benefits.

Present value. The worth, at the present time, of a stream of future income or expenditures.

Rate of return. The percentage increase, usually on an annual basis, in the value of an asset, plus any net income the asset produces. Rate-of-return calculations frequently are expressed in real terms (that is, adjusted for inflation). Rates of return are important in the Social Security reform debate because workers would receive much higher returns if they had the freedom to take the money now consumed by Social Security payroll taxes and put it into personal savings.

Retirement age. See Normal Retirement Age.

Retirement benefit. Social Security provides lifetime monthly income to retired workers and their spouses. The amount is based on their earnings and how long they were employed. The program works like an annuity in that the retiree receives a fixed monthly payment and the total received depends on how long he or she lives. Every January, payments are adjusted for inflation through a cost-of-living adjustment (COLA). Workers can either claim full benefits when they retire at age 65 or qualify for a reduced monthly benefit level at any time after they reach the age of 62. Retired individuals under 70 years of age who earn wages may be subject to a reduction in their Social Security benefits.

Series I U.S. Savings Bonds. A form of United States Savings Bond that is designed for retirement savings. Series I bonds pay an inflation-adjusted rate of return that is guaranteed for their 30-

year life. They can be purchased for no cost from almost any local bank branch in denominations as low as $50.

Social Security Administration. Independent federal agency, based in Baltimore, Maryland, that operated until 1993 as part of the U.S. Department of Health and Human Services.

Social Security Advisory Council. See Advisory Council on Social Security.

Spousal benefit. Benefit received by a worker who retires and whose spouse has no work history. The worker receives the full retirement benefit for which he or she is eligible, and the spouse receives a benefit equal to 50 percent of that amount.

SSA. See Social Security Administration.

Stock index fund. An index mutual fund that attempts to duplicate the performance of the overall stock market by investing only in stocks listed in a specific market index such as the Standard and Poor's 500. Stocks are purchased in the same proportion as they are included in the index. As a result, the risks associated with these mutual funds are much lower than the risks associated with those that attempt to generate higher returns by picking specific stocks. Since they do not require extensive research into individual companies, and since the stocks are purchased with computers, index funds have lower administrative costs than other types of mutual funds.

Survivors benefit. Benefits received by surviving children under the age of 18 if a worker dies before he or she reaches retirement age. The widowed spouse also can receive benefits if any of the surviving children are under the age of 16, or if the spouse has reached retirement age. The monthly amount depends on the worker's income history. A widowed spouse is eligible for up to 100 percent of the worker's benefits when he or she reaches full retirement age. This benefit is paid regardless of whether the worker died before or after retiring. However, the widowed spouse cannot receive both his or her own retirement benefit and that of the worker; only the higher of the two will be paid. In addition, a $255 lump-sum death benefit is paid to members of the family.

Taxable wages. Employee compensation, including salary, tips, and benefits, subject to taxation. Payroll taxes that finance Social Security's retirement, survivors, and disability programs are assessed only on the first $72,600 (in 1999) of a worker's income.

Thrift savings plan. The defined contribution portion of the pension plan for federal government employees.

Transition costs. The net extra costs incurred by workers when moving from a pay-as-you-go system (see above) to a funded retirement system. These transition "costs" may actually be lower than the future costs associated with retaining the current system.

Trust fund. When used in relation to Social Security (as opposed to its regular financial sense), a collection of government bonds that will have to be redeemed to pay for Social Security benefits once the system's cash flow is unable to make all benefit payments. In the words of the Office of Management and Budget, "*They do not consist of real economic assets* that can be drawn down in the future to fund benefits. Instead, *they are claims on the Treasury*, that, when redeemed, *will have to be financed by raising taxes*, borrowing from the public, or reducing benefits or other expenditures. The existence of large trust fund balances, therefore, does not, by itself, make it easier for the government to pay benefits." (Emphasis added.)

Trustees' Report. An annual report by the trustees of the Social Security trust funds about the trust funds' financial condition. Issued each spring, the report for the Old-Age and Survivors Insurance trust fund, which includes the Social Security retirement program, includes over 200 pages of charts, tables, and other very detailed information.

TSP. See Thrift savings plan.

Wage base. See taxable wages.

Wage cap. See taxable wages.

ABOUT THE AUTHORS

Gareth G. Davis, a Policy Analyst in the Center for Data Analysis, concentrates on analyzing Social Security's rates of return, and on developing statistical models to project the economic and fiscal effects of Social Security reform. The *New York Times*, *Wall Street Journal*, *Los Angeles Times*, and *Washington Post* as well as CNN Headline News have either featured or referenced his work. Davis has worked on international trade, economic history, tax reform, and global economic freedom. He also serves on the Board of Directors of the Edmund Burke Institute, Ireland's first free-market think tank. Davis holds a B.A. (with honors) in Economics from Trinity College in Dublin, Ireland, where he was a Foundation Scholar. He also holds an M.A. in Economics from George Mason University, where he is currently a Ph.D. candidate in economics.

Philippe J. Lacoude, the Senior Database Programmer, supports the statistical work of the Center's analysts and develops databases to help measure the impact of changes in taxation as well as entitlement and spending policy on families, businesses, and the economy. Lacoude has written extensively on French economic policy. Prior to joining The Heritage Foundation, he was a lecturer at the University of Paris-Dauphine. A native of France, Lacoude earned his B.A. in both Applied Mathematics and Economics, M.SC. in Applied Mathematics, M.A. in Economics, and Ph.D. in Economics from the University of Paris-Dauphine.